LOUIS G. REDSTONE

From Israeli Pioneer
to American Architect

LOUIS G. REDSTONE

From Israeli Pioneer
to American Architect

Louis G. Redstone
FAIA

IOWA STATE UNIVERSITY PRESS
Ames, Iowa

First edition, 1989

Library of Congress Cataloging-in-Publication Data

Redstone, Louis G.
    Louis G. Redstone : from Israeli pioneer to American architect /
Louis G. Redstone. — 1st ed.
      p.   cm.
    ISBN 0-8138-0186-9
    1. Redstone, Louis G. 2. Architects—United States—
Biography. I. Title.
    NA737.R42A2 1989
    720′.92—dc20
    [B]

                        89–11119
                            CIP

Book design by Joanne Elkin Kinney

To my parents, Aaron and Anna; my brothers, Wolf, Jacob, and Solomon; my sisters, Riva, Rosa, and Elsa; to my wife Ruth; to my sons Daniel and wife Barbara, Eliel and wife Linda; and grandchildren, Adam, Carly, and Ariel.

To my nephew Samuel and wife Beatrice; sons David, Allan, and Michael.

To my sister Rosa's family, the Harudi's in Kibbutz Ein Shemer and to my co-workers and friends of the pioneering years in Israel.

To the Klar families of Detroit—Irving and Gladys, Ben and Blanche, Edward and Shirley who included us in every religious holiday and family celebration over the past fifty years.

To the Rosenbaum families, my wife's brothers and sisters: Dr. Myron Rosenbaum and Florence, Betty Bloom and Harold, Edith Eisenberg and Phillip, Dr. Maurice Rosenbaum and Kitty who initiated the bi-annual family reunion and compiled the family history.

To the officers and staff members of the Redstone firm who made invaluable contributions to the success of the firm.

To the many loyal clients and friends who stood by me over the years through the low as well as the high peaks of the economic cycles.

To my fellow architects and artists, here and in the many countries around the world, who strive for more beauty in the everyday living environment.

CONTENTS

FOREWORD

by James A. Kelly
President, National Board for
Professional Teaching Standards

When Louis Redstone asked me to write the Foreword for his autobiography, I was both flattered and surprised. I was flattered that a person of his experience and distinction would think that my comments could help the reader appreciate the rich chronicle that is Lou Redstone's life. My surprise was attributable to how different Lou Redstone and I are in many respects—he an architect and I an educator—and thus how strange that I, having known Lou for only a few years, would be entrusted with this assignment.

But as I thought about it, my surprise faded. How like Lou Redstone in his mid-eighties to reach out and find a new friend—and a close friend—and in doing so to ignore differences of age, religion, and profession. For Lou Redstone is a person who has never lost interest in people—mentors, disciples; brothers, sisters; wife, children; colleagues, clients; architects, artists; old friends, new friends.

Lou Redstone's story is not simple. It is multifaceted, reflecting a life of diverse interests, fascinating experiences, and enormous talent.

Lou Redstone, this is your life: honored architect; urban planner; painter; author; lecturer, and art critic/judge; bricklayer; advocate of art in public places; world traveler; Israeli Pioneer; American immigrant; senior statesman of the Jewish community; successful businessman; active citizen; loving husband; proud father; family leader; good friend. I can only imagine the sequel, ten years hence, on Lou's tenth decade!

A man whose distinguished professional achievements are clear for all to see, the paramount image emerging from these pages is that of Redstone the person. Redstone the author is himself at least as interested in Redstone the person as in Redstone the architect. But the author makes a deeper point: it is foolish to draw semantic lines between parts of a person's life. This story is not only about a long and productive life, but is about the way that all the phases and facets of that life fit together in the integrated persona that is Lou Redstone.

More than a personal saga, however, Louis Redstone's life is a tribute to American democracy. While Redstone himself is a remarkable man with unusual talents, the store of his achievements in this country is happily unremarkable because so many others can tell the same tale: he arrived at these shores possessing only intelligence, ideas, energy, an insatiable desire to learn, and a willingness to work hard. Upon that foundation he built a good life. In no other nation is such a remarkable story commonplace.

As one who has spent his professional years in the field of education, I am struck by the role that America's educational system has played in the lives of immigrants. It has been the key to the American dream, unlocking doors of opportunity for countless millions.

Louis Redstone, hungry for education, enrolled in evening classes at Detroit Institute of Technology while, by day, he laid bricks at construction sites. Later, he studied architecture at the University of Michigan and developed his budding interest in sculpture and drawing at the School of the Society of Arts and Crafts, later to become the Center for Creative Studies. The Oxbow School of Art, a summer project of the Chicago Art Institute, drew him to Saugatuck where he took great pleasure in painting with fellow artists. And some twenty years after obtaining his bachelor's degree and by now an accomplished architect, Redstone again spent his evenings in school. This time it was at the Cranbrook Academy of Art where, under the guidance of the world famous architect Eliel Saarinen, Redstone obtained a master's degree in urban design. Translating architectural theory and artistic sensitivity into practical application, he designed a unique three-house compound in Detroit for his extended family, utilizing the design motif of Saarinen's architectural treasure, Cranbook.

Throughout Louis Redstone's life, he never stopped learning—from educational institutions, from others he encountered, from the experiences of life. My wife Mariam Noland and I recall the first time he saw our house. Designed by his mentor Eliel Saarinen and Eliel's son Eero (a distinguished architect in his own right), the house fascinated him. He poked and explored and marvelled, learning yet again a thing or two from work the Saarinens had done many years before. While we had been cordial acquaintances earlier, the house and the pleasures it brought to him solidified our friendship.

It is easy to like this man. His optimism is infectious. He is gentle and self-effacing in a profession populated by people with notable egos. Again and again, as we read the story of his life, we see him confronting the scowl of prejudice. He expresses his disappointment, perhaps even anger, at this injustice—after all, as a teenager he fled for his life from anti-Semitism in Russia—but he quickly moves on to find the good in people. It is like him to seek the silver lining, however muted its glow. He is appreciated, too, for his sense of humor—even whimsy—shared with family, friends, and colleagues.

As I read this book, I thought it an elegant testament to the nonlinearity of life. Louis Redstone zigged and zagged across occupations, cultures, continents, and decades, meeting fresh challenges eagerly. We can all learn from this book about seizing opportunity from the surprises of life; about the value of tenacity, dedication, and simple hard work; about stretching one's talents to explore every interest.

My advice to the reader is to sit back, relax, and prepare to enjoy the story that follows. It is not a novel, but it is a *great* story. It deserves to be read and remembered.

What a life this man has lived. How good it is that he has put it all down so that we, and others in the future, can take lessons in living from it.

PREFACE

It is the depth of winter in a midwestern American city. My studio window faces a large backyard covered with freshly fallen snow. The drifting winds have created unusual shapes, with the afternoon shadows of large tree trunks superimposed on these constantly changing, smoothly rounded valleys and ridges. Fascinated, I seem mesmerized by these white volatile images. Nearly blinded by the reflecting light snow, I squint. Suddenly the pure white snow surfaces become a gigantic white screen on which in rapid kaleidoscopic succession—as from an unseen projector—emerge images of childhood and adulthood happenings. The first impressions are followed by graphic memories of life dreams, struggles, and frustrations. That all of these images, worlds apart, could occur within the short span of one's normal lifetime seem unreal.

My memories take me back to a one-room *Heder* (religious school) where a small group of six-year-old boys are learning the Hebrew alphabet. From this beginning the images run incomprehensively to the prestigious Cranbrook Academy of Art thirty-five years later and the moment I received a master's degree in architecture and urban design.

The images run through my early youth at home, the escape to Palestine, and the pioneering work and the upbuilding of the country. My training in the building trades was to become the basis for an architectural career. Then there are the crowded recollections of frustrations and struggles as well as of joys of a young immigrant man adjusting to an overwhelming new culture in America in the 1920s. Recalling the celebrations of fifty years of office practice in 1987 and of the many honors awarded over the past years by professional and academic peers, I felt compelled to record this "stranger than life" story.

ACKNOWLEDGMENTS

T his story of my experiences lay dormant in early diaries, correspondence, newspaper articles, architectural talks and slide presentations of travels, watercolor exhibitions, architectural book publications. The encouragement to publish this book came from a number of longtime friends: from Rabbi Sherwin Wine of the Birmingham Temple (Farmington Hills, Michigan); James A. Kelly, president and chief executive officer of the National Board for Professional Teaching Standards; Susan Jackson Keig, a fellow and past president of the Society of Typographic Arts; Dr. Bernard Goldman, now retired Wayne State University Art History professor and director of the Wayne State University Press; Dudley Randall, poet laureate of Detroit, and Jean Owen of the Wayne State University Press staff who worked with us in the initial stages of the writing. Sarah Bell, the librarian of the United Hebrew Schools of Metropolitan Detroit and Jean Levy, her assistant, gave invaluable help in finding background information. I called on Rabbi Joseph Gutmann and Phillip Slomovitz, editor emeritus of the Detroit *Jewish News*, from time to time.

All of the incidents described are true, and with a few exceptions the real name of the person involved is used. Only where identity needed to be protected was a fictitious name used, mainly in personal relationships.

A special thanks goes to my secretaries, Gloria Barnabo Tonelli and Barbara Quigley. And above all, I am indebted to my wife, Ruth, who was by my side throughout the entire writing process and helped me to unravel the memories of my early life.

LOUIS G. REDSTONE

From Israeli Pioneer
to American Architect

1

RUSSIAN BEGINNINGS
Grodno, 1903–1914

Grodno, the city where I was born in 1903, was the capital of the state of Grodno, Russia, which had passed from Polish to Russian rule in 1795. The city of sixty thousand was centered around the tree-lined Batorega Square. Facing the square were two large churches, the Kosciol Farny Catholic church and the Greek-Orthodox church, from which the cobblestone streets radiated outward. There were several monasteries in the city and a number of ancient brick castles fallen into disrepair. Although these were historical landmarks, they were in the poorer section of the town on the north side of the river Niemen, which flowed along the edge of the city.

An important Jewish landmark, the largest and oldest "Great Synagogue," was located several blocks away from the square. There my brothers and I shared many satisfying hours of close association with our father. The white stucco building had replaced a famous and historic eighteenth century wooden structure that had been destroyed by fire long before I was born. The exterior presented a modest image devoid of any ornamentation. The only element suggesting a house of prayer was a small cupola projecting out above the center of the building. In contrast to the stark and windowless exterior, the interior was indeed imposing with its high ceiling. On the east wall, symbolically facing Jerusalem as in all synagogues, was the gilded, carved wooden ark for keeping the six or seven Torah scrolls. A gold thread–embroidered blue velvet curtain depicting the lion of Judah covered the ark doors when closed. In the center of the synagogue, directly under the cupola on a raised platform or "bimah" there was a large wooden lectern covered by an embroidered white cloth with long fringes. A large ornate bronze candelabra hung over the bimah to provide the light for reading the Torah and prayers. The rest of the synagogue was lit with smaller, simpler designed fixtures. As was customary, the women's section was separate, located at one side several steps above the main floor behind a transparent cloth curtain.

Our family went to this synagogue only on the main religious holidays. For weekly sabbath prayers and minor holidays we used the small neighborhood house of prayer, Beth Midrash, conveniently situated near us. There were a number of these

3

in different neighborhoods, usually located in one large room off the court of an apartment complex.

Most of my happy childhood memories are linked to the Niemen river—swimming and boating in the summer and skating in the winter. Because of its fast currents, swimming in the river was dangerous. Special wooden enclosures, separate for men and women, were erected above the water close to the river bank and connected to it by narrow wooden walkways. Inside these enclosures was a large open swimming area. Along the sides were cubicles for dressing. In the summer boats from the city plied their way downriver ten miles to the resort of Lososno and on to the famous spa Druskeniki, about twenty miles away.

The city's main source of income was a huge tobacco factory owned by the Shereshevsky family. It employed nearly two thousand men and women and its products were shipped all over Europe. Logging down the Niemen river to Grodno from the forest miles away, was another important source of employment. Logs were floated downriver as rafts. Built on these rafts were small wooden huts to protect the loggers from the weather and to provide space for sleeping and cooking. On the industrial side of the river the logs were pulled ashore with chains and carted to the sawmills nearby, where they were sawed into planks or sold for firewood to the local merchants. Wood was the only available fuel, so the arrival of the yearly supply of timber was marked by a burst of activity, and there were jobs for many at the sawmills and in the city. The logging season began in the late spring after the ice melted and ended in the late fall.

Merchants and artisans benefited from the presence of a large Russian garrison located nearby. The officers and their families had apartments in the city, while the enlisted men were billeted in barracks at the base. This garrison was important to many Grodno merchants and supplied our livelihood for my father, who was a military outfitter.

The educational, cultural, religious, and philosophical influences of the Jewish community were strong in my town. The population of the city was a mixed one: Poles, Jews, and Russians. Over 60 percent were Jews who had been forced to move to this and other areas on the peripheries of Russia, the so-called "Pale for Jewish settlements" in the nineteenth century. The Jews who had been living outside the designated Pale area were compelled to live within its restricted boundaries. Transplanted to new surroundings with only what they could carry with them, Jews in the Pale survived only by creating supportive organizations.[1] Such was the case in Grodno. The *Gmilas Hesed* (the Hebrew Free Loan Association) made modest loans without interest charges to help start new businesses and to help individuals during times of economic stress. Families supported each other informally as well. In time, the Jewish community established a hospital, an orphanage, and a home for the aged, as well as a trade school. There was also a society for the care of the sick (*Bikkur Holim*). On Thursdays the very poor went around to all the shopkeepers to collect alms so that everyone would have food for the Sabbath.

---

[1] The tradition of helping the needy, as well as the neighbor in distress, is based on the biblical teachings which say, "If you have a poor man among you . . . you shall open wide your hand to him and freely lend him enough for his needs." (Deut. 15:7–11).

The apparently cordial relations between the Jewish majority and the Christian minority contributed to what seemed to me a tranquil atmosphere in my town. Though ethnic groups tended to live in separate neighborhoods near each other, their businesses were side by side on the same streets.

One large building in our area housed the four elementary grades and the eight-year high school, the gymnasium. Further away, near the outskirts, was a six-year, technically oriented high school. Both were government sponsored, for boys only, and a small fee was charged that even then very few families could afford. No more than 10 percent of the students could be Jewish. Jewish boys who did not get in under the quota were tutored privately if their parents could afford it. Many of the parents of the tutored students hoped that when the time came their sons would eventually be accepted by special examination in a university outside the Pale. For girls, there was a government-sponsored school attended mostly by Christians. Nearby was a private school, the Waldman Gymnasium, for Jewish girls, where my older sister Riva studied. (During the German occupation, 1915 through 1918, the coeducational Reali Gymnasium, including grades one through six and stressing mechanical and technical subjects, was opened to all).

Despite the limitations and restrictive quotas in Grodno, the cultural life of the Jewish community was a flourishing one when I was a boy. There were teachers' seminaries for Jewish studies, and poets and writers were published in the daily Yiddish newspaper. The first Hebrew book published in Russia had appeared in the late eighteenth century in Grodno, indicative of the city's role as a center of Jewish studies. There were always cultural activities going on that everyone could afford. We had a small but well-designed opera house that was the center for concerts, plays, readings, and lectures by outstanding visiting artists with offerings as diverse as Yiddish plays by Sholem Aleichem and Russian plays by Chekhov. The Poles were very proud of their own famous Polish woman writer, Orzeskova, who lived in Grodno, and they honored her by naming one of the main streets after her.

The wooden building in which the Routenstein (our name Routenstein was translated to Redstone by my brother Solomon when he came to Detroit in 1916) family lived was on one of the two main cobblestoned business streets. Four shops on the ground floor faced the street with apartments above. Other apartments were clustered around the cobblestoned courtyard, a place of many uses. The entrance to the apartments was through two large wooden gates leading into the courtyard. There was a narrow walk alongside our apartment building; the brick wall of the adjoining building was on the opposite side. Nestled against this wall was a small, pear-shaped, fenced grassy area. Here an apple tree struggled to survive, closely guarded by the janitor-caretaker of the building when the apples began to ripen.

The court served as the children's playground year round. In the summer our favorite pastime was the "Devil's Game," played by teams of three or four boys, each with a long stick. Each side took turns in throwing the sticks at the other team. Points were scored when the team warded off the oncoming sticks. Most of us were about ten years old. Our families could not afford to buy us the regulation smooth sticks from the lumber yard, so we had to be content with discarded pieces of wood, some of which still had protruding nails. One play left me with a lifelong scar when the aim of one of the opposing players was off and I was hit on the left temple with a nail-studded stick. As a result of this mishap I was made an "honorary" member of the team.

In September all the families in the building used the court as the setting for the tabernacle holidays, called Sukkoth, the traditional celebration of the gathering of the harvest in ancient Israel. A temporary wooden enclosure, called the sukkah, was erected. The roof was lightly covered with pine branches so the sky could be seen through the tracery of pine needles. Wooden benches and tables were brought in and for seven days all the families in our building had their main meals there. The meal started with the blessing of the challah, a specially baked, long-braided white bread. Then followed the delectable chicken soup, chopped eggplant, baked chicken, cabbage rolls, sweet potato–carrot casserole, ending with stewed fruit compote, strudel (apple-raisin cake), honeycake, and tea with lemon. As children it was always exciting to eat at the tables outdoors with the adults, singing and enjoying the festivities.

As the weather changed the courtyard became a storehouse for fuel for heating and cooking during the winter months. Each family was allotted a small area of the court in which to pile its wood. The logs were bought at the sawmill down by the river, and families hired a team of woodcutters to cut the long logs into useable lengths. Two men would saw or chop; the third man's function was to encourage the other two, calling out "One, Two" when they were sawing, or uttering a loud "Ha" when they swung their axes, an arrangement enjoyed by the third man on the team.

In the wintertime the space in the middle of the woodpiles was used as an irregular-shaped skating area. Since most families could not afford a pair of skates for each child, most children had only one skate and pushed themselves along the ice with the other foot. When skating season ended with the beginning of the winter thaw, our nemesis, Vladek the caretaker, appeared. He opposed all games, which he considered mischievous. One day, when all the roof downspouts and gutters were solidly frozen, he used a portable propane burner at the bottom of each waterspout to melt the ice. He was squatting down low using the burner when my brother Sol skated by, screeched into a flashy turn, and skidded into the caretaker's large behind—skate first. A torrent of abuse and fist-swinging ensued, and courtyard skating was eliminated for several seasons to placate Vladek.

Our apartment was upstairs in a two-story wooden structure at the end of the courtyard. We entered by a covered wooden stairway that led to the second-floor hallway. Facing the stairs was the apartment of the chief rabbi of Grodno who lived there with his wife and two teenage daughters. People were always coming to ask the rabbi's opinions on religious or civil matters. On the other side of the hall was a bookbinder, a hardworking family with three boys and five girls who were teenagers. Although the bookbinder was an alcoholic, in his sober moments he did artistic work that was much in demand. As I recall, the girls sometimes worked as seamstresses, and one of the boys was apprenticed to a shoemaker. With their meager income they could afford to send only the two younger boys to school.

We entered our apartment through a kitchen, really a multipurpose room where cooking, canning, and baking were done in a wood-burning stove, and a weekly bath was taken in a round tub. The kitchen opened into a room with two beds and an oilcloth-covered table with chairs, used for weekday meals. Beyond this room was the main living-dining room. There was a child's bed in one corner and two couches for sleeping, with one against the wall of the tiled oven that heated all the rooms; a large dinner table with chairs; and a cabinet for dishes, silverware, and glassware. We used this room for dinners on Friday nights, Saturdays, and holidays. The dining room opened directly to two bedrooms, a large one for my parents and a small windowless room for our maid. There was a large dark wood wardrobe and bureau in my parents' room. Common toilets serving the three apartments (both men and women) were located on an open, back balcony, which also led to storage rooms allotted to each tenant. The service balcony was the view seen from our dining room and my parents' bedroom. The apartment was kept spotlessly clean; the red wooden plank floor was always repainted during the summer while the family vacationed at a nearby farm. Framed photos of my grandparents were hung on the wall, as well as photos of important events in the family such as high school graduations and wedding pictures.

My mother was an attractive, delicate woman of medium height, with blond hair and deep blue eyes. In her wedding pictures she appears to be a beautiful bride. She was busy from morning till night—shopping, cooking, and mending. In addition she managed to help my father in his military outfitting store, located across the street. In later years her health showed this strain, and in the summer of 1914 she traveled to Germany for treatment of pleurisy. Fortunately she returned just a few days before the outbreak of World War I. My father was short, with dark hair, brown eyes, and an ample growth of sideburns, beard, and moustache. His approach to reprimanding us, which seldom happened, was to look at us in a special penetrating and disapproving way without saying a word. And it worked. I cannot recall my parents ever raising their voices to each other or to us. We were seldom reprimanded, though on one occasion when my mother found out that my brother Jacob, then age fourteen, was playing cards in the firewood storehouse, she became furious and slapped his face. This was the only physical punishment I ever saw.

I was the fifth of seven children, four boys and three girls. My oldest brother Wolf studied to be a bookkeeper, and he was the first to leave home for the big city of Warsaw. He always came home on Passover, Purim, Rosh Hashana, and Yom Kippur. These visits were festive and exciting events as he always brought gifts and candies for everyone. At Purim he purchased the noise makers and cap guns to celebrate the historic downfall of Haman, the chief minister of the Persian King Ahasuerus. (Haman was the enemy of the Jews and had planned their total destruction on the fourteenth day of the Jewish month of Adar, which corresponds to our month of March.) Next in age was Yakov, who wanted to be a merchant and helped my father in the store. As a young man he was interested in a local amateur theater group, played small parts, and was usually on the lookout for new members. On one occasion, when I was ten, he even persuaded me to play the part of a girl. This turned out to be a complete fiasco; I was so self-conscious on stage that I had to be replaced by a real girl. When he married he moved to nearby Suwalki and established a store to supply insignia, decorations, and swords to the army, very much like my father's store. My sister Riva was the next youngest. She was a gentle, attractive girl and a brilliant student. She graduated with honors from the girls' gymnasium and spent most of her time thereafter reading books on philosophy, history, and psychology, as well as tutoring students in mathematics and languages. My own knowledge of German and French is still good, thanks to her teaching.

Next came Sol. He was the "firebrand" of the family, uninterested in studies, always unprepared, and ashamed to bring his report card home for my parents' signature. Because of his natural intelligence, however, he always managed to cram for examinations and pass them. The educational system was very strict: one had to pass all the exams before being allowed to enter the next class. If a student failed an exam, he was given one more chance. A second failure meant staying in the same class another year. Failure to pass the exams after the second year in the same class meant expulsion from school. Sol was especially alert to take advantage of various happenings in the courtyard. Often a horse and buggy would be driven into the courtyard of our apartment with a load of supplies. The driver would usually have his lunch in a nearby lunchroom, providing my horse-loving brother the opportunity to remove the horse's harness, mount, and go for a long ride. When the driver returned to find his horse gone, the search for Sol would be a lengthy one, much to the dismay of my parents and to the fury of the driver. Next youngest were my sisters Elsa and Rosa, born two years apart. Both graduated from the girls' gymnasium. Elsa was more sophisticated and the coquettish type, while Rosa was a serious student and belonged to a group of teenagers who were preparing themselves to go to Palestine to live on an agricultural kibbutz.

Our family life was greatly affected by my paternal grandfather, Chaim Shmuel, who lived with us until his death at the age of eighty. He plays a part in my earliest memories (I do not remember my grandmother). My grandfather established the military suppliers business my father subsequently took over. His daily routine in retirement was completely separate from that of the rest of the family. He was served his meals by himself at a different hour, eating only his special foods. He especially liked noodles and potato kugel (casserole). He spent most of his waking hours at a small synagogue located in the next courtyard, where he went three times daily to pray. As a very old man he became careless and sloppy in appearance. All these eccentricities created a disruptive problem for the family and became a great burden to my mother who took care of him.

When I was ten years old my grandfather got up as usual, walked around the apartment as if in a daze, and kept saying, "Why are so many candles lit? What holiday is it?" After a while he went back to his bed and died in his sleep a few hours later. It was my first experience with death and the traditional funeral ceremonies: the body lying on a straw pallet on the floor of the dining room, the group of professional mourners praying all night by the light of the candles around the corpse. The next day the family and friends followed the horse-drawn black hearse to the cemetery about half a mile away, I suddenly felt myself threatened by the thought that the same thing would happen to my own parents and I was filled with dread. I recall, as through a haze, the seven day "shiva" period of mourning. The traditional noon and evening services were held in the living room by the rabbi and the synagogue members, about fifteen to twenty men. Not until this week of prayer was over did I feel something vital was gone in the home. The following nights when the house was quiet, I found myself in tears as I lay awake on my bed near the comforting warm tiled oven. With the daily routines soon reestablished, the traumatic experience with death receded into the background of family memories.

At the age of five, Jewish boys in our town were sent to a teacher (*melamed*) to learn the Hebrew alphabet and to read some of the prayers. It was an old joke that any man who could not make a living, or was a misfit in the marketplace, could be a teacher. This characterization applied as well to my teacher, who had a limited knowledge of Hebrew and even less of cultural background. The pay was minimal, barely enough for the teacher and his family to survive. Each family paid weekly a prearranged fee, generally based on its financial means. My teacher Reb Haim lived on the fourth floor of a run-down, four-story apartment building. His apartment consisted of a kitchenette, a living-dining room, and one bedroom. The ten or twelve students, aged five to eight, were taught in the living room, so that the teacher's wife and his two small children were crowded into the bedroom during the two-hour class period. Reb Haim's left arm had been paralyzed early in life by a stroke, but he was able to swing it to punish a child for misbehavior, lack of attention, or lateness in paying the weekly tuition. On that occasion the pants came down and a number of strokes with a straight-edge ruler were administered. Latecomers were punished in a variety of ways. At times Reb Haim's paralyzed left arm would swing like a club on whatever was nearest his hand; at other times a ruler would come down hard on a child's arm. One of the teacher's favorite punishments was the "fidele" or "little violin." He would squeeze a child's little finger slowly but firmly until the victim shrieked with pain. Very seldom were these punishments administered to children of the well to do, and I was fortunate to be among those spared.

The next phase of my education was handled by a more modern and younger teacher in his thirties. The religious school, or *cheder*, located several blocks away, was a large neat room with a dozen benches and stools and long narrow tables. The lighting, when needed, was by candles. The red-bearded Reb Mendel was our teacher. His knowledge of Hebrew and ability to teach were only slightly superior to Reb Haim's. Because of the limited knowledge he had to impart, he took only a short time each day to transmit it. We children went home for lunch. On occasion, in midafternoon, the teacher would fall asleep with his head on the desk. In the wintertime when it grew dark early the candles would be lit. Then a prankster would pour melted candle wax over the teacher's beard and, when it hardened, make a noise to startle him. When he jerked his head up, tearing at his beard, he would be in pain and very angry. The class would be dismissed, and we happy children would be sent home. How pleasant it was to walk through the snow-covered darkened streets with a lantern in hand, in company with the other students. How eagerly I looked forward to the warmth of my home, where my mother always had ready for me hot tea and fresh fragrant-smelling onion rolls. Other schools serving the poorer Jewish children provided lunches. Since the tuition fee was very low, the teachers saved on the food. Bread and potatoes were served every day, but each day at mealtime the teacher and pupils would chant aloud together, "Today we have meat" or "Today we have fish." The power of this suggestion over empty stomachs was doubtful.

In the following years during the German occupation, 1915 to 1918, the government allowed semiprivate, eight-year schools, which combined intermediate and high school curriculum. Although German was the new official language, most of the instruction continued to be in Russian. In addition to the regular gymnasium curriculum—algebra and trigonometry, Latin, German and French languages, Russian literature—technical subjects were offered such as mechanical and architectural drafting.

These schools were called Reali gymnasiums. It was here that my interest in architecture was first aroused. Little did I think then that this was to be the start of my life's career. There was no quota system in this school, and the Jewish students were in the majority. However, many students were unable to enroll because of the high tuition fee.

One of the most interesting approaches in this school was the method of studying the Russian classics. For example, the actions of the characters in *The Brothers Karamazov* were "judged" before a judge and jury of students and by members of our class. The prosecuting and defense attorneys presented their cases, and the students became deeply involved in the story and the character portrayal and in the process sharpened their analytical capabilities. During the lunch and recess periods there was lively discussion among the students, Jewish and gentile, on the controversial aspects of the literature we read. The most popular classics were *Anna Karenina* and *War and Peace* by Leo Tolstoy and *Crime and Punishment* by Feodor Dostoevski. However, this social atmosphere was not carried over after school. I cannot recall ever visiting the home of a Polish friend, or inviting one to mine. Each of us accepted our separate way of life without question.

With the approach of my thirteenth birthday, my parents hired a tutor to prepare me for the bar mitzvah, the celebration when a boy is accepted by the congregation of the family synagogue as an adult member. The tutor came to our home in the evening three times a week. We sat at the kitchen table repeating in a singsong manner the Hebrew readings and prayers from memory until they were word perfect. What stands out in my memory is the tutor's insistence on the perfect pronunciation of the guttural "ch" sound (as in "chutzpah"). His method was to make me blow my nose hard to clear it. I ended with the proper sound and a nosebleed after every lesson. When my parents finally dismissed him, it wasn't too soon for me.

I cannot explain why one seemingly unimportant incident has remained all these years in my memory. The gymnasium in Grodno conducted a yearly Flower Day at the end of the spring term to raise funds for books for needy students. As a boy with good marks, I was appointed chairman of the committee. With my two assistants I was to go to the fields on the outskirts of town, pick armfuls of wild flowers, pin a flower or two to a bit of cardboard, and have these "badges" ready to sell to our fellow students at school the following day. We arrived at school the next morning and started our sale. We went from student to student and pinned a flower on each lapel, receiving a *grosh* (penny) or two from each one. I pinned a flower to the lapel of one little boy and waited for his donation. He looked embarrassed, reached into his pockets, and with lowered eyes whispered that he hadn't any money. Without giving it a thought, I simply pulled off the flower and moved on to a more likely prospect. An instant later I realized how mortified the little fellow must have been and I ran back to find him but he had disappeared. More than seventy years later, the image of that child with the sad eyes is still with me.

My father's military store had swords, medals, insignias, and epaulettes; he made overcoats and dress coats for all ranks from corporal to general. The design and embroidery of the decorations were the task of my father and two assistants, an older man who had learned embroidery from my father and who remained with him until the outbreak of World War I, and a young girl. Dozens of tiny silver and gold cylindrical beads of different sizes were threaded on the needle to make these complex patterns, a craft requiring the utmost patience as well as precision. Our excellent craftsmanship came to the attention of the Czar himself when my father sent him an embroidered pillow bearing the emblem of a wild boar, the symbol of the state of Grodno. In response my father was designated "Craftsman to his Imperial Majesty the Czar."

My mother assisted in the store almost daily, and the relationship between the Russian customers and my parents was generally friendly enough. However, on the slightest provocation or misunderstanding, this polite atmosphere could vanish. Delay of a delivery, shortage of some item, or some other circumstance beyond my father's control could create a crisis. Many times some officer, slightly displeased, would shower insults on my mother in crude street language. My mother would be stiff with fear and shock, as I watched helplessly.

Mother: Anna Routenstein.   Father: Abraham Aaron Routenstein.

(*Left to right*) Riva, Mother, Wolf, Yakov, Father.

Louis at eight years old, 1911.

(*Left to right*) Riva, Louis, Wolf, Solomon, Yakov.

(Standing, *left to right*) Yakov, Wolf's wife Pola, Wolf,
Riva. (*Front row*) Mother, Rosa, Father, Elsa, Solomon.
(*Inset*) Louis, 1921.

German occupation of Grodno, 1915–1918. Author, age sixteen, with Otto Schreier, a German soldier and next-door neighbor.

Author's watercolor depicting Grodno at the Niemen River.

The Great Synagogue, Grodno.

Street scene, Grodno.

2

THE GUNS OF WAR
1914–1920

Apart from entering the gymnasium, the high point of my ninth year was the great centennial celebration of the Russian victory over Napoleon at Borodino in 1812. It was a thrilling spectacle as the army represented by infantry, cavalry, and some old artillery pieces paraded by the reviewing stand near the governor's palace in a seemingly endless procession of pomp and ceremony. Two years later I saw this mighty army "melt away" at the first encounter with the Germans in the summer of 1914.

When World War I broke out, all young men from the city and surrounding farm areas were called up and mobilized in town. Grodno was the largest city close to the Russian border and was in the direct line of the German advance. Our assembly point was Batorega Square. There we boys watched the recruits change into their ill-fitting new uniforms and boots. There were rifles and munitions for only a small number; the remainder practiced with wooden rifles. After only a few days of training these raw recruits were sent to the Prussian front. The townspeople were panicky at the sight of these slapdash military preparations and many families, ours included, began packing their trunks with the idea of fleeing farther east into Russia for safety. Rumors of the German advance were rampant and fear of a German occupation fed our determination to flee. After much soul-searching, the family decided my parents and older brother Jacob (aged 22) would stay in Grodno; my three sisters, my brother Sol, and I would go to Minsk in the charge of my sister Riva, who was twenty-one. Minsk was chosen because it was the farthest city to the east from the Prussian border and seemed to be a safe distance away. Our two trunks were loaded onto a horse-drawn dray, which we followed to the railroad station. There, hundreds of families with their trunks waited their turn to buy tickets for the limited train space. We waited the entire day and night before we heard the terse announcement that there would be no more trains available for the civilian population. With mixed feelings we realized that we would have to stay with the rest of the family. When we prepared to go home, however, we learned that our trunks had already been put on an outgoing freight train to Minsk where we were to be relocated. Naturally we were upset over the loss of household and personal belongings— everything of value we owned. Riva was heartbroken over the loss of her gymnasium diploma that was in her trunk. Without this document she could not get a job or continue her education. (We finally retrieved our trunks after the war, four years later and after tremendous efforts.) For me, at eleven, this disturbing incident was just one more adventure in a time of strange happenings.

To bolster the morale of the troops, Czar Nicholas II was persuaded to visit the Grodno garrison. Schoolchildren waving flags, I among them, waited at the railroad station to welcome the military entourage. The Czar's ashen face finally peered through the window of his automobile as he drove through the town. Yet his presence was apparently not enough to revitalize the Russian army, and a hasty retreat from Prussia began about a month later. The German strategy had been to let this ill-equipped and untrained Russian army advance well into Prussia, far into a swamp area. There the German troops could cut them down easily with their new and deadly machine guns. The strategy worked. Bedraggled, dazed, and wounded, the Russians were chased back across the Niemen River into Grodno—some walking but many wounded, carried on peasant carts. This defeat marked the beginning of the collapse of the entire Eastern Front.

By the spring of 1915 the noise of the German artillery bombardment grew louder. The big gates of the apartment courtyards, which had always stood open, were now shut tight and locked while Russian and German soldiers fought in the streets outside. One group of Russian soldiers managed to break into our courtyard and lined up the people they found hidden in the surrounding apartments. One of the soldiers announced he had been cheated by a merchant whose store was located in our building. When he could not recognize the merchant among the people there, he decided to fire his rifle at random into the group, his head turned away as he fired. Fortunately only one man was slightly wounded. The soldiers then departed. An hour or so later, when the bombardment had subsided, the more curious residents ventured into the street and found the vengeful soldier sprawled dead at the entrance of another courtyard. We found dead soldiers and horses all over the streets of the town. Russian and German soldiers were dead in the alleys, the parks, and at the railroad station. Many, taken by surprise, were found in strange postures—some on their knees, some partly supported against a wall, some squatting to defecate. The next day the advance troops of the main body of the German army arrived. Hordes of Russian prisoners were assembled in the central plaza, guarded by a few German soldiers who wouldn't allow the civilians to throw food either to the hungry or wounded.

The daily routines of life in our family continued despite the war and the arrival of the German occupation troops. My mother, as usual, baked the sabbath challah for our family and for relatives living several streets away. I was the one who delivered it. Stray shots were still being exchanged. We did not realize the danger of these deserted streets, in which any moving and, even more, any running person was a possible target. I came running back to the house safely, much to everyone's relief.

I had another "close shave" at this time. Many families from our courtyard used to gather in the landlord's apartment, which faced the street. Driven by curiosity, one or two of us would peer out to see what was happening. On one of these occasions, as I was sitting near an open window one day drinking tea, a rifle bullet came through the window into the apartment, bounded off the ceiling right above my head, and fell down into my cup of tea with a big splash. Everyone fled to the rear of the apartment, away from the street, dragging me along with them. Later in the evening all of us celebrated my good luck.

After several days the fighting was over and the streets returned to normal. With German efficiency and arrogance, civil order was restored quickly. Even during the period of bombardment and street fighting the Germans insisted on enforcing one-way pedestrian traffic on the sidewalks. Now male inhabitants, young and old, had to get off the sidewalk into the street and tip their hats at the sight of a German officer. This humiliating order, however, was rescinded after a period of several months.

As soon as the occupation stabilized, we moved to a newer apartment building several blocks away. It was a walk-up on the third floor, overlooking the main jail. One improved feature was an inside toilet, which was off the kitchen. There were still no flush toilets in use, and the slop pail had to be carried down regularly to a special underground septic tank in the courtyard. Some of the apartments were occupied by German officers. The military personnel in large cities such as ours generally behaved fairly well, and the officers who were quartered in an apartment in our building were friendly. We even took group photographs of all of us as a memento. One officer quartered next door to our apartment had an orderly who supplied him with everything from culinary delicacies to women. We never found out what his duties were, as he seldom left his apartment. He was a man in his fifties, and we assumed that he must have been called up from the reserves. In another apartment in our building there were two middle-aged officers, former professors of philosophy at the University of Berlin. My sister Riva and her girlfriend became acquainted with them and invited them to come to our apartment to discuss philosophy, which they did. None of us could have imagined that thirty years later a German army would be in our town again with the prime purpose of annihilating the entire Jewish population. Another memory of the occupation stands out, the visit of Kaiser Wilhelm and Field Marshal Von Hindenburg to our city. Unlike Czar Nicholas, who had sat frightened and pale in an enclosed car, the Germans rode triumphantly in an open car, their helmets towering over their heads. They nodded to the crowds and to us schoolchildren, who had been ordered to appear on the sidewalks waving German flags supplied by the occupation authorities.

As I explained earlier, the Reali Gymnasium offered more technical subjects and drafting classes than the regular high school. The drawings I submitted in the drafting classes caught the attention of the instructors. They encouraged my interest in perfecting these skills and hoped that I would eventually be able to study architecture.

Under the occupation the German language became the language of the institution, but Russian textbooks were also used, although stuffed into the desk whenever the school inspector visited. At the end of the occupation, during the transition period in 1918 when the city switched from German to Lithuanian hands and then to Polish rule, the process of displaying the textbooks of the occupying power on top of the desk and putting the other books inside became a routine matter.

By the time I was fourteen I was generally considered a good student in math and geometry, and some students in the class ahead of me asked me to tutor them. One afternoon just before the summer holiday began I opened the door in response to a timid knock. Before me stood a husky six-foot young fellow about sixteen years old. He introduced himself as Nicholai. He appeared to be from a farm, with his sunburned face and hands and his rough work clothes. (I was to learn later that he did live with his family on a farm some distance from Grodno.) "I would like to see your brother," he said. I asked "What for?" He replied that he wanted a tutor during the summer months so he could transfer to the Grodno gymnasium in a higher class. The only subject preventing him from doing this was math. He was shocked that I was the tutor he wanted, and he could not imagine how a small boy, two heads shorter than he and in a grade lower, would be able to help him. We started on an intensive and accelerated course, working every day from three in the afternoon until midnight. Nicholai, beneath his rough appearance, possessed a brilliant and retentive mind. In three months he learned two terms of math and passed the exams in the fall, to our delight.

For relaxation I played chess with my best friend Moses Lubitch. We became so proficient that we decided to enter a statewide chess tournament taking place in our city. After much effort we persuaded the organizers to let us participate. Even then the older players were reluctant to play with fourteen year olds. They were stunned at the first game when I succeeded in checkmating one of the prominent players. I still recall how, at my exclamation "checkmate!" the man leaped up from his seat as though he had been shot.

The years of the occupation were a struggle for survival. The food shortage posed a real challenge to the homemakers. Bread was baked with a half-potato mixture replacing hard-to-get flour. Strange substances were mixed with cooking oil that was in extremely short supply. Sugar was unobtainable on the market, and black marketers smuggled it out of military storage sheds under the very noses of the guards. A sense of humor helped. In our family we tied a lump of sugar to a string hanging from the ceiling above the small dining table next to the kitchen. As we sat there drinking our unsweetened tea, our eyes were focused on that swinging lump of sugar. The tale was well remembered and retold over the years. The food distribution center set up by the occupying forces employed many townspeople. A careful search of all packages was made when these employees left the premises, so the workers used their ingenuity. They fashioned a tin container about an inch wide and eight inches high that fastened around the waist like a corset under the clothing. Sugar could be furtively poured into it and the opening was then plugged with a cork. Under the clothing, the tin was not visible. A neighbor who worked at the center told us about this device, a well-kept secret throughout the German occupation.

Food had to be obtained by any means possible. Many small meat-packing operations sprang up in different locations as a source of livelihood. Food distribution and pricing were strictly controlled by Germans. As a consequence there was an active black market, especially in meat processing. Pork was the easiest to obtain and distribute. My oldest brother Wolf became a partner in one of these clandestine shops that happened to be located near a German police station. The main problem was getting the hams to the various customers. Most of them were non-Jewish, but even Jews bought these hams for gifts and bribes. To avoid suspicion, young boys were used to deliver the meat, and I was one of the recruits.

My first assignment ended up in a near catastrophe. It was about ten o'clock in the evening when I started out on my "mission." I was to take the bundle of meat home—a distance of six blocks—for temporary storage. I started out with the ten-pound bundle under my arm. The dimly lit streets were deserted. As I hurried across one intersection a German soldier appeared out of the darkness yelling "Halt! What's in the package?" Before I could say a word, the appetizing odor wafting from the bundle was answer enough. I was pushed along the street to the police station nearby. Inside a soldier took me to a large room on the second floor where about a dozen other soldiers were playing cards and drinking beer. The arresting officer talked to one of them and then motioned me to follow him. He took me to a small windowless room furnished only with a wooden bench. I already saw myself being tortured to reveal the source of my bundle. Then I heard the man's command, "Lay it down." I lay myself on the bench expecting the worst. He shouted again, "No, not you, you fool, put the package down and get out of here!" This frightening experience ended my brief career in the black market.

My brother Sol had a different experience. He and another young fellow were trying to earn some money by delivering slaughtered hogs to the butcher shops. They had borrowed a horse and wagon from a nearby farmer to make the deliveries. One Friday late in the afternoon they were hurrying the horse so they could make their last delivery and get home before sundown. The route took them past a synagogue facing a circular plaza and by sheer luck the plaza was empty of people. As they whipped the horse round the curve, the carcass slipped out of the back of the cart onto the pavement. The two boys shoved and hauled their pig back onto the cart in frantic haste with superhuman strength and made their getaway from the synagogue in great embarrassment. Later, when the family recalled this incident, the boys had a good laugh.

The worst part of the occupation years for young people in Grodno, however, was not so much the food shortages. Travel outside the city was not allowed except with a special permit issued by the occupation authorities. So we were confined to our own resources to create sports training and cultural and social club programs that made our life more tolerable. One of these activities was centered around the popular Maccabi sport club named for the heroic Jewish fighters against the Hellenistic Seleucid Kingdom of Syria (167 B.C.E.) in biblical times. The club had facilities for gymnastic exercises, parallel and horizontal bar training, and instruction in rowboat racing. Our instructor, Lev Jaffee, a man in his thirties and a former officer in the Russian army, was a strong muscular individual and a strict disciplinarian, but we liked him and our spirits were always high after our workout at the club. I became very adept with the parallel bars and enjoyed showing off my somersaults and other complex figure exercises, especially for the girls. I wanted to impress one girl in particular, whose name was Sonja. Whether it was the parallel bars or not, we did become longtime friends. In addition to the Maccabi club, boys and girls organized educational and recreational clubs and rented basement rooms or small storefronts where they could meet. Records were played, discussions were held, and romances began.

All these activities, as helpful as they were in making our life more satisfying, did not remove the underlying feeling of oppression by the occupying armies. I, as a sixteen-year-old student, did not feel any antagonism toward the German soldiers or the occasional civilian administrator with whom I came in contact. Even then, my family reflected the general hope that the Germans would eventually lose the war and withdraw from our city.

In 1919 when the German army retreated there was a brief occupation for a few months by Lithuania, followed by a two-year period when the Poles took over. The new Polish government was attempting to regain their former territories in Russia. After the initial success of the Polish army, the Red Army forces regrouped, stopped the Polish advance, and started a counterattack. The Russian cavalry, although poorly armed and in "uniforms" running the gamut from pajamas to top hats, began pushing the Poles back toward Grodno with Warsaw its ultimate objective. The apprehensive Polish garrison in Grodno prepared for evacuation. The atmosphere became more and more strained and ominous. There would be another official language, Polish, to be learned, and new rules and restrictions on businesses to be dealt with. Everyone in the Jewish community feared the resurgence of Polish nationalist sentiment with, as always, its strong anti-Semitic element.

For young Jews, the outlook for continuing our education or gaining employment was grim. It would take years for the city's commercial life to recover from the war and postwar depredations, white-collar civil service jobs were open only to Poles; Jewish gymnasium graduates, especially seemed doomed. Even at best, if there was a chance for some to continue their education in the university, there still would be no openings in the professions in the depressed postwar economy, especially for Jewish graduates.

My own thoughts were in complete disarray. Deep in the back of my mind was the hope that I would somehow realize my goal of studying architecture. This was certainly a remote dream under the present conditions. To go to Palestine as a Pioneer seemed like an excellent opportunity for a seventeen year old to channel his energies in a constructive way. There was an element of idealism in rebuilding a Jewish homeland that reinforced my decision to volunteer as a Pioneer. Although the work would emphasize the restoration of land for farming and reforestation, I knew they would need to provide housing for the new immigrants. Here I hoped that I could learn the building trades—a good start for my goal.

In the climate of hopelessness and economic uncertainty, the ever-dormant yearning for a more fulfilled and productive life in a Jewish homeland in Palestine was aroused. The Balfour Declaration of 1919 establishing a homeland for the Jewish people under British Mandate, with the proviso that the rights of the existing Arab population would not be jeopardized, was responsible for fanning these Zionist "flames into a blaze."

As far back as 1890 there had been a Zionist movement in Grodno, and in 1918 the town became headquarters for recruitment and training of a Zionist youth corps called *Chalutzim,* or "Pioneers." The Polish authorities approved of these activities and unofficially looked with favor on the emigration of the Jews. Adolescent Jews were being taught the fundamentals of farming on small tracts of farmland outside the city. This was a totally new experience for them since farming had been an occupation forbidden to Jews for centuries under the Polish and Russian regimes. The ultimate goal of this pioneering Zionist movement was to transform the desert and wastelands of Palestine into a flourishing and self-sustaining oasis for all Jews who wished to start a new life there. Grodno's youthful pioneers were among the first to join the 1920 exodus, called the third *aliyah* or "the third ascent."[1]

For my parents Palestine was only a symbol invoked in the familiar prayer, "May we be next year in Jerusalem." To permit two of their children—me at the age of seventeen and nine years later my young sister Rosa—to embark on this risky trip to the unknown must have been an agonizing decision. Only the realization that the economic and political crisis in Grodno could only worsen, persuaded them to go along with our plans. The one source of support in the family from the beginning was my brother Wolf, who helped me with advice and money for this trip. Wolf, who was twenty-seven and who had been living in Warsaw for several years, had a broader understanding and a more realistic appraisal of the future the Jewish youth faced than did my parents and their friends.

My Pioneer group's plan was to leave for Palestine in June 1920 at the end of our last year at the gymnasium. The rapidity of the Russian advance forced us to hasten the day of our departure. Under a Russian occupation the route to Palestine would be cut off. The Pioneer organization had planned for us to go first to Warsaw; from there to Vienna, Austria; then to Trieste, Italy, where a cargo boat would take us to Jaffa, Palestine; with a stopover in Port Said, Egypt. It soon became clear that the Russians would be in Grodno within a short time. Chaos gripped the city. In the middle of this confusion, the head of the gymnasium hurriedly called all thirty graduates together in his office to distribute the graduation diplomas. No parents were invited. It was a sad and unnerving affair and close friends parted with reunions doubtfully planned for the future.

I rushed home from school clutching my precious paper to find my parents and the rest of the family in tears. As much as they wanted a better life for me, as the moment of parting neared, they had grave doubts. Mother even called our plan a "feverish dream." Still, she kept on preparing special food for the trip—toasted black bread dipped in beer, which was said to preserve it for many months; big rounds of cheeses and dried fruits; her special cookies; cans of condensed milk; a huge salami; bars of chocolate; a tin dish, cup, fork, knife, spoon, and water jug. There was also a blanket roll; a small pillow; a flashlight, and extra batteries. The last thing she put in my knapsack was a packet of writing paper: "Be sure to write every week!"

Our Pioneer group—two girls and eight boys, aged seventeen to twenty-two, from Grodno and the surrounding towns—met several days before departure at the end of June for final briefings by the leaders. There was a good rapport between the group members, and I became friendly with everyone except one girl whom I disliked right away because of her domineering, bossy personality. One of my closest friends David, a fellow graduate who was to go with the group, reneged at the last moment. I regarded his defection as a personal betrayal, and it took me a long time to get over it.

Our speeded-up departure was now slowed down another few days while final arrangements were made. The period of waiting was painful for all of us, though I longed to stay another day with my family, especially for the last Sabbath. That was to be my last day in the city. I went down to the river and spent much of the

---

[1] The first aliyah, which began in 1890, was made up mainly of Ukrainian Jews, who had suffered most from the government sponsored anti-Semitic persecutions, the second aliyah in 1904 by the Russian Jews in the aftermath of bloody pogroms.

afternoon recalling all of the happy moments I had spent there with my friends—boating, swimming, and playing. I returned home saddened for what turned out to be my last meal there. It would be the first time that I had ever been away from home and family and the first time I would ride on a train.

Grodno was already nearly completely evacuated. Only the rearguard of the Polish army remained. The last passenger trains had left and one freight train was still at the station to take us. It was a sad Sunday. Our group, accompanied by our parents and friends, arrived at the station an hour before departure. We had to bribe our way onto one of the freight cars. Only many years later when I had children of my own could I imagine what my parents must have suffered in that hour—their youngest son leaving, on a filthy freight train, a protected and secure life for a destination that might never be reached. At the station we were shocked to see hundreds of panicky townspeople trying to climb into the freight cars, desperate to get away from the Russians. Our group, with knapsacks, finally managed to force our way into a car that would accommodate all of us. Sixty minutes seemed like sixty hours, and finally the train started to roll, slowly. In my mind this momentous parting had always been thought about in a haze of uncertainty. This moment of actually being torn away from my roots left me fearful and numb, unable to express the overwhelming feelings within me. I knew I was causing my family pain. I also knew I had to leave. As much as I felt like crying, no tears would come. My tearful family on the platform soon faded into the distance and new impressions started to crowd out my unhappy feelings. Before long the train started to roll across the ill-fated wooden bridge over the Niemen River. This bridge had been rebuilt by the Germans in 1915 after the retreating Russians blew it up. Two hours after we crossed, it was blown up again by the retreating Polish army in their effort to delay the Russian advance.

Our immediate destination was Warsaw via Bialystok. There we would obtain exit visas. The train rattled slowly along toward Bialystok where my mother's family had a successful wine-making business. This large family was closely knit and devoted to one another. They corresponded occasionally and there were rare visits between the Bialystok and Grodno families. My mother must have written to them about the train stop in Bialystok, for when we arrived my name was called. I jumped down from the freight car and found myself surrounded by a large group of relatives, many of whom I was meeting for the first time. They stuffed my pockets with packages of food for the trip and little gifts. As anxious as we were to keep moving for fear of being intercepted by the oncoming Russian army, this surprise farewell did much to raise our spirits. As the train started to move, goodbyes were intermixed with expressions of envy—"How we wish we could go with you."

After four hours, which seemed like an eternity on the slow-moving train, we finally reached Warsaw. Tired, exhausted, and dirty, we climbed down from the freight car as we were met by several organizers of the Pioneers who had been waiting for us for hours. A dilapidated truck was our transportation to a training farm near the village of Grochow, about fifteen miles from Warsaw. The barracklike camp was in complete disorder. No one seemed to know what was going on. The fatigue of the train trip and the emotional strain made us irritable. Worst of all, there were no regular meals provided and our group had to subsist on the food we were carrying for the journey. We were given a large space in one of the barracks for sleeping.

Straw mattresses covered the entire floor where we slept, crowded together. Despite the discomfort, I had my first sound sleep in three nights since leaving home.

The sound sleep did not prevent a painful headache when I arose the next morning. To be thrown into these harsh new surroundings was very difficult, even though we thought we were ready for any adverse situation. After a hurried breakfast of bitter coffee and black bread with marmalade, I started to plan with some members of my group our next step, which was to get visas from the English consulate. The group of volunteer farm workers already there, approximately fifty boys and girls, still had some training to go through before leaving for Palestine. Because our group had already completed its training, we were scheduled to go first. The whole process of moving out was accelerated because of the critical military situation. The strategic location of Warsaw, with its central railroad network, made it a vital last stand against the rapidly advancing Red Army.

The major task of the Pioneer leaders was to assist us in obtaining visas. In my case I decided to contact my paternal uncles, Ephraim and Lazar Routenstein, who lived in Warsaw. They had not heard of my plans to go to Palestine but received me with open arms. After a warm bath and a good meal, I felt revived. The next day I started for the British consulate to apply for the necessary visa for Palestine. Because the city was already in a stage of siege, all able-bodied men had been rounded up and taken to the outskirts to dig trenches. To leave my uncle's house and walk through the deserted streets to the consulate was a dangerous journey. My identification papers had been issued by the short-lived Lithuanian occupation forces in Grodno after the German retreat. Although I was not legally a Polish citizen, the raiding military parties on the streets did not make such fine distinctions. In many cases they tore up non-Polish passports. One member of our group was caught in one of the roundups and was sent to dig trenches. During the dragnet, all courtyard gates to apartment buildings were closed and locked by the caretakers so that whoever was caught on the street had nowhere to hide. I had to go back to the British consulate seven or eight times; there was always a long line of people, questions that I was unable to answer immediately, or additional documents required. I was terrified of being caught in one of the military sweeps. What probably saved me was my youthful appearance; with my slight build I could pass for a fifteen year old. Still, my virtual imprisonment in my relatives' apartment was a real punishment. I spent much of the time writing letters home to my family and friends. The nervous tension of waiting almost overwhelmed me.

It was September when the glorious moment arrived. The visas were finally issued and our group was told to come to the main railroad station the next morning to board a passenger train to Vienna. All around us people were taken off the train for additional inspection of documents or for lack of necessary papers. At the last moment the military police forced us out again for final inspection of the baggage and passports. Although all was in order, they took one of our group back with them. He had a Lithuanian passport, which the soldiers tore up on the spot. This incident stunned and horrified us. Once again we experienced another example of our helplessness in this situation. A year later this fellow managed to get away and eventually made his way to Palestine.

How quickly our mood changed when the wheels of the train started to roll. As we crossed the Polish border we immediately felt the joy of freedom. No longer would we be hunted down. Our hearts began to beat faster when we realized a new life was now possible. We greeted the Czech border with cheers and songs. At a small border town while we were transferring to another train for Austria, two boys from our group, David and Chaim, decided to look around. They did not return on time to the train and we had to leave without them. We thought that we would never see them again. However, to our great joy and relief they joined the group in Vienna two days later. They told us how the friendly station master gave them food and let them sleep in the station overnight until the arrival of the next train to Vienna.

After the fearful experiences at the Warsaw station, Vienna seemed a new and happier world. We were met at the station by several organizers of the Pioneers who were ready to take us to their shabby headquarters where food and lodgings were ready for us. But the authorities had other ideas. Instead, we were taken to a municipal "delousing station." There we undressed and went through hot showers while our clothes were put through a disinfecting oven, which shrunk anything in our pockets made of leather—gloves, wallets, belts—to a quarter of their original size. These articles were gifts from our friends and family and had great sentimental value. On the plus side, we really felt clean! After the delousing process we had to spend the night in the municipal lodging quarters for transients. Cots were placed so close together we barely had enough room to get through, but this did not disturb our deep sleep. The next morning our representatives were waiting to take us to their headquarters where we were given a light snack of bread and salami. For most of us the snack only whetted our appetites and we again had to supplement it with our own reserves of hard biscuits and cheese. To make tea we had to beg for hot water from the people in the adjoining buildings. Regardless of the meager food rations, our group spent two glorious days absorbing the sights of the beautiful city—the Danube River with its numerous bridges, the tree-lined boulevards, fountains and parks, coffee houses with the famous pastries we could not afford, and the older section with its narrow streets and picturesque houses.

Vienna was the assembly center for the Pioneer groups from Poland, Lithuania, Romania, and Hungary. It took nearly a week before the Pioneer organizers completed arrangements for all the groups to travel by train to the port of Trieste in northern Italy. There we would board an Italian freighter that would take us to Port Said, Egypt; a coal freighter would take us to Jaffa. This long and difficult route was the only possible way to reach Palestine at that time because of the postwar tranquillity prevailing along this route. We boarded the train to Trieste with our meager belongings, pleasant memories of Vienna, and empty stomachs. It was a slow train giving us an opportunity to see the picturesque Alpine villages and small towns, one of which remains vivid after all these years—the village of Udine in the mountain pass from Austria to Italy. It was midnight when we pulled in, and the moonlit whitewashed houses and church steeples formed a picture as though from a fairy tale. As much as we needed to sleep, excitement and anticipation kept us awake all night. Finally we reached Trieste with a screeching of brakes.

If there had been at least a semblance of organization in Vienna, in Trieste there was none. No definite date had been set for our departure from Trieste. Boat arrangements were uncertain and haphazard, and because the Pioneer organization depended mainly on contributions, the cheapest travel arrangements were made. Thus the scheduling arrangements and dates had to be made to fit the convenience of the shipping company. Neither our leader nor we had the money to go to even the cheapest hotel to wait for our ship's arrival. Several other groups were to join us on the ship to Port Said, which meant a three- to six-day wait. Someone had a brainstorm—we would build our own "hotel"! We walked down to the docks, chose a quiet spot, and dragged some large empty packing crates (*Kastens*) together to form a small hut (or shanty), a prefab approach to housing. We called our lodgings "Hotel de la Kastens." Once we were protected from the weather by our makeshift hotel, we turned our attention to food. We pooled our meager funds, bought some liverwurst and bread, and took our teakettles to the seamen's nearby bars to get some hot water for tea. As the days went by with no ship in sight, we roamed the streets by day, discouraged and wondering whether we would ever escape from this city. Trieste had a large German population and our high school German helped us to communicate with the people. We discovered a bakery that gave us its unsold bread at the end of the day and this became our main staple. As discouraged as I was with the delay, I knew that it was only a matter of time before our boat would arrive, and I wrote my mother, "Nothing will stop us from reaching Palestine, unless the Adriatic freezes over!" I am not sure whether this humor alleviated her worry about my trip. The food situation improved as other Pioneer groups arrived at the docks with their leaders. It was like greeting old friends since nearly everyone spoke Yiddish. These new arrivals were better organized and had money to buy necessities they shared with us. We still remained in our makeshift quarters at the docks while they were able to afford inexpensive lodgings nearby.

The ship finally arrived! It was an Italian freighter, which took on a full cargo, leaving the upper deck relatively free and this was to be our open air accommodation. The time of year was in our favor (it was now August) and so was the warm relationship that was established between the crew and our group. The generous helpings of spaghetti, served twice a day, were as manna from heaven to us. So began a glorious journey, without a care. We ate, we danced the Israeli "hora" at the slightest pretext, and sang.[2] In our serious moments we talked about the direction our new life would take. Would we be part of a kibbutz where living, working, and worldly goods were shared? Would we be assisted in establishing our own kibbutz?[3] Or would we be assigned to special projects: road building, housing construction, or planting of forests for land restoration? Most reacted favorably to a life in the kibbutz in a communal venture. Some preferred the "Moshav" plan where each family had its

[2]The hora is a circle dance originating in Roumania. It became the most popular folk dance among immigrants during this period. The dancers interlock arms behind their backs or on their shoulders, starting the movements slowly and gradually increasing the tempo with strong stamps and kicks.

[3]A kibbutz is a communal settlement, for the most part agricultural. There is no individual ownership and all income from labor and sale of products is distributed to each member according to need. Dagania was the first, founded in 1909 near Lake Kinneret. By 1918 the number of kibbutzim grew to twenty-nine. Many others were established with the increased immigration from Russia and Poland at the time of the third aliyah, 1919. The land on which the kibbutzim were established was purchased from the Arab owners at current prices by the Jewish National Fund through contributions from American and European Jews. Each kibbutz elected its own executive committee, which made the work assignments and was responsible to the central kibbutz federation.

own house and plot of land but shared all the necessary equipment to operate successfully—tractors, seeds, fertilizer, irrigation, utilities, and land improvements. Very few wanted to be individual farmers and there were no votes for city life. The ideals of the Pioneers were in essence "back to the land."

The boat docked in Venice for a short stopover. All were anxious to see the city of our dreams. Because we had only a few hours, we rushed off and started to explore the canals, palaces, bridges, and the famous piazzas. Our outfits must have been something to behold, judging from the increasing number of youngsters who started to follow us. We began to feel self-conscious about our wrinkled clothes, worn out shoes, and disheveled hair. Because of our travel conditions and the delousing in Vienna, our clothing was in a bad state of disrepair, almost in tatters. The unfriendly shouts gave us the idea that we were not welcome here. However, we were determined to enjoy being tourists. When we heard our ship's whistle blow we ran back to the dock, arriving just in time before the gangplank was taken up. Here, as in the stopover at the Czech border, we lost two of our group for whom the captain would not wait. The deck accommodations continued to be excellent (when compared to all our previous experiences), with sunshine, food, dancing, and singing.

This carefree paradise lasted for seven days until we arrived in Port Said. The coal freighter, manned by a Russian crew, which was to take us to Jaffa, was already in port and ready to sail the following day. We spent the day in the port area, swimming in the harbor and getting ready for our last leg of the journey to the "Promised Land." The trip was to take only thirty hours, but the sea between Port Said and Jaffa at this time of the year was exceptionally stormy and treacherous. In contrast to the crew of the Italian ship, the Russians were hostile and unaccommodating. We were forbidden to stay on deck and were forced to stay in the hold on top of mountains of black coal.

As soon as we were out in the open sea, the Mediterranean became a mass of high pounding waves. The winds tossed the waves with such impact that we rolled from side to side like jelly beans in a boy's pocket. This was my first experience with being seasick. The storm lasted all night and we were too sick even to be scared or worried about the ship capsizing. Down in the hold of the ship where we crouched, the coal rolled from side to side filling the air with a thick black dust that made us choke, cough, and gasp for air. Toward early morning the storm subsided and shortly thereafter we heard the thud of the anchor as it dropped offshore in sight of Jaffa, the ancient city. Only then were we allowed to come on deck to disembark. Our depressed spirits were soon restored by the fresh air, the sight of the shoreline, the buildings, and the dim hilly silhouette in the distance. As we crowded on the deck and watched, we could see Arabs rowing small boats toward our barge to take us and our baggage ashore.

In 1920 there were no docking facilities in Jaffa. To add to the difficulties, the Jaffa bay was filled with many huge rocks and the submerged ruins of an ancient fortress. It was a dangerous trip even for the small boats to reach the shore. The Arab boatmen feared their boats might be smashed against the rocks by the waves and prayed loudly to Allah throughout the entire trip. We were truly frightened, and it seemed to us that getting into Palestine was as hard as the proverbial entrance into Heaven. And so we reached the Promised Land—weary but excited.

Map (1920) showing escape route from Grodno, through
Warsaw, Vienna, Trieste, Venice, Port Said to Jaffa in
Palestine.

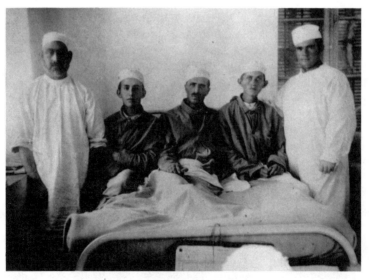

Author, hospitalized with typhoid fever, at the English
Hospital on the outskirts of Jaffa, November 22 to
December 20, 1921.

Author, seated with friends, 1922. (*Left to right*) Kulik,
Yanovski, Furman, Stoliarski, and Gershowitz.

Haifa, 1922. The first organizational meeting of the
establishment of the "Histadrut," the Workers Federation of
Labor. Four of our group were represented here.

The Ramleh Construction Group,
author seated (*center*), 1922.

Louis Routenstein at a reforestation project,
Carmel, Palestine.

Start of construction of the Levant Fair along the Tel Aviv
shoreline, 1933. Construction materials are carried by
camels.

Architectural staff on site of Levant Fair.

World's Fair, Paris, 1937, Architects and designers for the
Palestine Pavilion (author, *middle left*).

Defenders of a settlement.

Port of Jaffa, closed by Arab riots, 1936. A jetty was
erected overnight by volunteers in Tel Aviv to receive
supplies from the boats offshore.

3

ISRAELI PIONEER
1920–1923

Physical exhaustion disappeared as if by magic as we scrambled, one after another, to be the first ashore and to feel firm ground under our feet. The fresh air, bright sunshine, and blue skies cleared our coal dust-filled lungs. We had no idea of what to expect when we reached shore. To our surprise and joy a large group was there to welcome us and we were warmly received by the representatives of the Pioneer movement. Some of the crowd first thought that we were Africans, because of our layers of black soot! We were taken to the Pioneer House, a small reception building, where the first thing we did was to take hot showers and receive new clothing. The feeling of exhilaration mounted by leaps and bounds—it felt like being reborn. We were served fresh challah (Sabbath white bread), jam, cheese, and tea. I cannot recall ever enjoying a meal more. A pleasant surprise added to the happiness of the day. Hannah, an aunt by marriage, learned of my arrival and came to meet me. She had settled in Palestine in 1912 before the outbreak of the war in Europe. Hannah was a nurse who lived with an older sister in Tel Aviv and I was her guest for several days. While the plans for our group work assignments were being made, she hired a horse and carriage to drive me and my friends through the old city of Jaffa and to the nearby agricultural school, Mikveh- Israel. The entry to the school was through a beautiful palm-lined road to a complex of buildings where young people were taught the science of agriculture. Here experiments were conducted to test which kinds of crops were best suited for the variety of soils in the country. Because of the scarcity of water, the tropical climate, and the centuries-old neglect of the soil that had been denuded of trees, new strains of plants had to be developed. These trainees later became the cadre of teachers for the development of a network of Jewish agricultural settlements through-out the country. On the drive back to Tel Aviv we passed by areas of newly laid out streets in the sand dunes. Small whitewashed houses were beginning to appear here and there. Who could imagine this would become a metropolis of three-quarters of a million people sixty years later?

These glorious days spent with Hannah left a warm feeling of belonging that was to remain with me and play a significant role in my years ahead in Palestine. For this seventeen year old, away from family for the first time, Hannah symbolized home. In the next three years her home was mine whenever I had free time to visit her. She shared with me her extensive knowledge of the country. She also related her personal experiences during World War I when Palestine was ruled by the Turks. She and many other Jews were expelled and interned in Egypt until the allies defeated Turkey. This gave me a valuable perspective on the recent history of the Palestine Jewish community, called the *Yishuv*. Her parting words were "When in need, count on my help."

Our "tourist" days came to an end when our group of fourteen was notified of our work assignment—a reforestation project on the barren rocky slope of Mount Carmel overlooking the Bay of Haifa and the Mediterranean. A slow and noisy train took us—eleven boys and three girls—to Haifa. We gazed with awe at the formidable height of the mountain, and after a short rest and snack that we carried with us, we started to climb up along a narrow path, carrying our gear on our backs. We stopped often, as we were not accustomed to mountain climbing. We finally reached a high flat plateau where wooden barracks were to have been erected and ready for us. Instead, the lumber was stacked on the site, and that was it. There was one consolation—the view from the area was beautiful with a vista opening onto the Mediterranean. We spent the night in the open air, exhausted and disappointed, wondering what the next day would bring.

The next morning we had a pleasant surprise. Two carpenters arrived with their tools and equipment to start the erection of the barracks. With them came one of the administrators of the Pioneers who brought tents and an assortment of cooking utensils, tin dishes, several charcoal stoves, and a variety of foods such as bread, eggs, eggplant, olives, and large metal containers of drinking water. Importing our drinking water in containers was to be temporary. For an adequate supply of drinking water in Palestine it was customary to cut deep into the solid rock to prepare a cistern to hold the rainwater. The rough shaping was done with dynamite and finished off by hand chiseling. A large area around the opening of the cistern was cemented over so that the flow of the rainwater would be directed into the opening. A team of Arab diggers was hired and the work was started immediately, not far from the barracks.

Meanwhile the carpenters mobilized both girls and boys to assist in erecting the main assembly room, combining dining and kitchen facilities. We carried the planks to the site, anchoring planks to the rocky ground; then we erected the vertical studs to which the exterior wall planking was nailed. Larger roof beams spanned between the outer walls and were covered with roof planks. Because there was no waterproofing material, this roof would protect us merely from the heavy night dew, not from the rains that would be coming in the winter months. The barrack was sufficiently completed in a week to be put to use. This was my first experience at physical work, and the process of creating a shelter with my own hands was exhilarating. Somehow I suspected that this was to be the direction I would be taking.

Benches and tables were soon fashioned from the rough lumber boards and we finally sat down to our first meal in our new quarters. The term "meal" is really a misnomer. No thought had been given by anyone, including the Pioneer advisors, to training us in the rudiments of basic food preparation. Even our girls, who came from middle-class homes where most of the food was prepared by a housemaid, knew little or nothing about cooking. In theory all work assignments were to be shared equally between the sexes. In our case the hard labor to which the boys were assigned, such as clearing rocks on the mountain slopes to create terraces, would have been too difficult physically for the girls. The shortage of essential ingredients and water along with the girls' inexperience meant that we were served less than appetizing meals. In the beginning we were always so hungry that we paid little attention to the sameness of the menu—fried eggs, olives, bread, and tea. One morning the boys rebelled. After the food was served, the boys lifted the far end of the long dining table so that the plates slid off. The noise of the flying metal dishes was accompanied by the rhythmic stomping of feet imitating the wheels of a train— with a slow start coming to a crescendo of cha-cha-cha-cha, cha! This rejection of their culinary efforts so shocked the girls that they ran out of the dining hall in tears. It took us the entire next day to persuade them to come back to the kitchen and in addition a sincere promise not to repeat the "train act" again.

Three more barracks for living quarters were erected. Meanwhile we slept in small tents, each accommodating three cots. After a week we began our reforestation project. We were fortunate to have as our instructor Dr. David Ashbel, a former science teacher who had practical experience with Palestine's flora and fauna. From him we not only learned the biblical history of the area, but also the geological rock formations. He described the poisonous insects and snakes that were ever present in the craggy and rocky slopes; his main warning to us, as we prepared the terrace for the plantings, was to watch out for scorpions. These deadly insects were usually concealed under the numerous loose rocks we had to move, fill in the holes they left with soil, and plant pine seedlings in the crevices. We were constantly on the lookout for these creatures, but on several occasions the scorpions got a victim. The scorpion carries a deadly poison in its conical tail and delivers a hammer blow with its sharp point. A sting from a male scorpion, however painful, is seldom deadly. However, a sting from a female scorpion is fatal unless treatment is administered immediately. We resorted to an age-old remedy practiced by the Arabs when one of our group was stung by a female scorpion. A strike from a female induces an imme- diate fainting spell. The Arab remedy was to apply hot salt to the bite and simply burn out the accumulated poison. This remedy was indescribably painful and the victim had to be forcibly held down by several people, no anesthesia being avail- able. However, with the exception of a few scorpion bites, the clear and dry moun- tain air kept us generally healthy and free from serious illnesses. (Visiting the area forty years later, I viewed with pride a mature, thick, and fragrant pine forest with scenic roadways and housing developments nearby.) There was great satisfaction in the feeling that we were resurrecting long neglected areas of natural beauty.

Reforestation work went on for about six months. November to March was the rainy season when clay ground was nearly impassable. We had planks laid out between the barracks, but it usually took two to three days after the rainfall before the soil was dried out sufficiently for us to reach the work areas.

The rainy days and cold nights of the Palestinian winter had a depressing effect on us. As a consequence of the enforced leisure, coupled with our close quarters, cliques were formed. As a seventeen year old, I was the youngest in the group and did not compete for the affections of the older girls. These girls were different from the companions I knew so well in high school. I probably lacked the confidence that an aggressive approach on my part would succeed. With only three girls in the group, competition soon developed. One of the biggest surprises was the romance of Eli and Rachel. Eli, who considered himself a "Don Juan" and constantly ridiculed the walk and mannerisms of Rachel, married her within the year.

Two incidents especially stand out in my memory from this Carmel period. One had serious political implications, the other purely human and somewhat comical, although it could have had tragic consequences. In 1920 relations between the Jewish settlers and Arab farmers and traders were, in general, friendly and cordial. Most Arabs accepted the young idealists' intent on resurrecting the countryside. Jobs became more plentiful for them as orange groves and vineyards were developed by the already established and enterprising Jews. In essence, we were living witnesses to the effects of the British colonial policy of discouraging close and friendly relations between Jews and Arabs. "Divide and rule" facilitated English colonial governance. The rich Arab *effendis* (landowners) saw in the growing Jewish immigration a threat to their own domination and a loss of their financial and political influence. The *effendis* reacted by starting and planning anti-Zionist propaganda among the Arabs living near the Jewish settlements charging "the new immigrants would take their land away, would destroy their mosques, and would take away their jobs." The result of this hate campaign was felt immediately. Jewish settlements in upper Galilee in the north were attacked. Tel-Hai and other settlements were destroyed despite heroic defense efforts of a few settlers under Joseph Trumpeldor against organized and well-armed marauding groups. In April 1920 anti-Jewish riots broke out also in the cities of Jaffa and Jerusalem. The Jewish population suspected, rightly or wrongly that the British local authorities, both civil and military, were not in sympathy with the aims of the Balfour Declaration for a Jewish homeland and sided openly with the aspirations of Arab nationalists. As a consequence, the authorities "looked the other way" when Arabs attacked. At the same time, they arrested the Jewish defenders and sentenced the leader, Vladimir Jabotinsky, to fifteen years at hard labor.[1] Encouraged by this attitude, Arabs singly, or in groups, began attacking the isolated farm settlements, killing people and stealing livestock. These riots caused the Jewish settlements to develop their own defensive measures—the *Shomrim* or guards who patrolled the settlement on horseback and on foot and the underground defense unit—the *Haganah* or voluntary quasi-military group whose purpose was to defend the settlements against Arab attackers. The British considered the *Haganah* an illegal and dangerous organization. Possession of arms was punishable by long prison terms and heavy fines. Frequent raids and searches for arms were carried out in the Jewish settlements, often brutally. Arrests were frequent and in some instances, resistors were shot on the spot.

These restrictions made it hard to acquire firearms. Smuggling was the only way to get arms to the fledgling settlements. I recall one incident in which I was involved. Immigrant boats were arriving daily in Haifa, and many of the arrivals had small arms hidden away in water flasks, glass jars, and in other innocent-looking utility items. Still the newcomers couldn't take any chances because the search of personal belongings was very thorough and it was difficult to get by the British

[1]Following an outburst of public indignation that erupted in Palestine, England, and the United States, Jabotinsky was given amnesty by the Palestine High Commissioner, Sir Herbert Samuel, on 8 July 1920 and the verdict was quashed in 1921.

authorities. A way had to be found to transfer these items through the fence around the immigration area undetected by the police. A Haganah officer came to our group on the Carmel and asked for volunteers to be in the Haifa port area when an immigrant ship was due to arrive. We, as well as most of the Jewish settlers, considered the Haganah our protective shield and were anxious to cooperate with them in any way we could. Five of us, four boys and a girl, were assigned to go down to the port area and pick up unobtrusively the innocent looking items that would be passed to us through the wire fence. We dressed in shorts, sport shirts, and sandals just like the other young people who came to the dock to meet newcomers and relatives. One of us carried a blanket roll on his shoulders, others had knapsacks on their backs or arms full of bundles while we exchanged greetings across the fence. We managed to get a number of small objects from the immigrants without being noticed. The one I received was a water flask I was told contained a pistol. These flasks were made in two parts so that a small pistol could be inserted and the parts sealed. I attached the flask loosely to my belt on the left side. In spite of our precautions and confidence in the success of our mission, it took a tremendous effort to control our jitters. Evening was approaching and it was getting dark. As we left the port, we scarcely spoke a word, although everything was going smoothly. On the last leg of our return trip we heard the heavy tramp of a British police patrol. Almost immediately they appeared in front of us. The captain at the head of the column pointed his flashlight on us—the beam fell on my flask. Thoughts kept racing through my mind. How had they spotted us? Who could have betrayed us? The blade of the steel bayonets glinted, and there seemed to be no alternative but to give up. We could take a chance and run for it, but that would endanger the other plans of the underground. The eyes of my comrades were focused on the flask spotlighted in the rays of the flashlight. My right hand moved toward the flask and in a daze I heard myself saying to the captain "If it's water you want, the flask is empty." The captain's voice bellowed "I don't want your damned water. I want to know the time!" Suddenly it dawned on me that the rays of the flashlight were shining on my wristwatch! "It's 8:30, sir." In spite of my fright, my voice rang out, sharp and relieved. This was my first dramatic encounter in Palestine.

Another incident that could have ended in tragedy occurred during my stay on the Carmel. Bathing in the Mediterranean was one of our main pleasures. Once we got used to climbing up and down the mountain, we made it a habit of going down to the sea after work, generally in a group, boys and girls. Between our work camp and the sea, midway in the mountain area, was another camp occupied by "Gippos," as the British called the Egyptian servants or orderlies who did the chores for a British military camp located nearby. Usually the Gippos were conscripted from the poorest class of the Egyptian population. The British army provided only the minimum shelter and food, although they did give them a bonus by providing prostitutes once a week. This "activity" took place outdoors, where cots were placed, partitioned by straw mats. A long line of Gippos would be lined up to await their turn impatiently. One evening we returned from the beach and were climbing up the mountain path towards our camp. Our group became separated, some walking fast, and some strolling along. Suddenly we heard an ear-piercing scream coming from the group ahead of us. We ran in the direction of the noise and found a Gippo struggling with one of the girls in our group. The Egyptian fled, leaving the girl in hysterics and the rest of the group shaken by this unexpected incident, so far from our unsophisticated minds. The next day at the breakfast table, with the incident still on our minds, we expressed regret to the poor victim that we had fallen so far behind the previous evening. Although still upset, she thanked her rescuers and told us the horror she experienced when the man tried to rape her. Twenty-five years later I was invited to spend a weekend with friends in Chicago. One of the guests was a middle-aged woman from Israel. At dinner we began to reminisce about our youthful experiences in Israel, and I told about my life on Carmel, then recalled this incident. The Israeli woman showed extraordinary interest, then half-closed her eyes and exclaimed, "I was that girl!" I had not recognized her after all these years.

Our daily life was guided by three senior advisors whom we nicknamed the "Old Workers." Their age was about thirty-five, which to us seemed ancient. They had been in the vanguard of the earlier volunteers from Russia before World War I and had become expert at tree planting and reforestation work. The Old Workers constituted the executive committee and their decisions were generally implemented. Contact with the Zionist organization was made through them. They used their authority in a no-nonsense way, insisting on strict discipline, requiring us to report to work on time as well as to work diligently on the project. We expected that the relation with our mentors would be more sympathetic. Gradually we began to understand some of the reasons for their outward show of toughness as we heard their stories of the hardships suffered under Turkish rule during the First World War. The Turks feared the Jews, especially those from Russia and other enemy states, were sympathetic to the Allies. Some were even accused of being Allied spies and were imprisoned and tortured. In the first three years of the war thousands of Jews were deported and taken by Italian and American ships to refugee camps in Egypt.[2]

In 1917 as the British army under Field Marshall Edmund Henry Hynman Allenby advanced into Palestine, the Turks evacuated the remainder of the Jewish population to the north in the Galilee, where shortage of food and the lack of shelter created havoc with the health of the evacuees. A plague of locusts descended on the entire region, destroyed the crops, and stripped the fruit trees. Hunger was ever present and many new immigrants died of starvation in the "Promised Land." These experiences had molded the attitudes of these older settlers, as the Depression molded those of many older Americans today. They constantly criticized and lectured us "kids." Although we strongly resented this, we did try to please them.

The Old Workers also had some special privileges in their living arrangements. The two single men shared a room; the married leader and his wife had the remaining room at one end of the barracks. At the start of the project everyone was so exhausted by the end of the day that as soon as dinner was finished, we fell on our beds and slept. On Saturday mornings, our day of rest, however, we would be awakened by the married couple's love making. Our vivid imaginations reacted to the sounds and giggles coming from the room. Needless to say our pulse rates quickened; we were sexually aroused and ran out of the barracks to take a long walk.

[2]In this war Palestine, which had been under Turkish rule for four hundred years, served as a base for the Turks and their German allies in their attempts to launch an attack upon the Suez Canal and Egypt, and together with Syria it had to provide the supplies required by the Fourth Turkish Corps.

As time went on and we got used to the hard physical work, our evening leisure time became more enjoyable. There were lively discussions at the dining table. The main concern of most of the group was how and when their dream of becoming farmers would materialize. Hopes were high and the optimism of youth prevailed. Spontaneous hora (circle) dances even during the dinner, as well as the evening, culminated our talks.

This project lasted from August to December. One evening Abraham Harzfeld, the director of the entire agrarian project, came to talk to us. His shocking news was that there were no more funds for our project and most of our group would be reassigned. Only a small corps would remain on Mount Carmel to maintain the planted areas. He consoled us with this philosophical advice: "There is a biblical saying that without being down below, one cannot reach the heights." He then began to sing these Hebrew words, over and over in the rhythm of the hora: "Oy, Oy, Aliyah—Yeridah Tsorech Aliyah." Translated: "You cannot go up without first going down." We joined him in the song and began to dance slowly in a circle with arms around each other. It was a memorable but sad evening.

We were given our choice of several projects to join. One was a new road being built in the north, connecting the ancient city of Tiberias to the rail junction of Zemach at Lake Kinneret. The road followed the south side of the lake about five miles. From our friends who were already working there we learned that the main job was to crush the huge rocks and boulders into small stones suitable for a roadbed that was to be topped later with asphalt. In ninety degree heat, the work was back-breaking and exhausting. Pioneers lived in tents, we heard, and the food was meager; at best the place was primitive. If there was an attraction to this project, it was the feeling of being part of a continuing, rich, ancient heritage, attested to by the ancient stone buildings and the age-old synagogues of Tiberias. Some were still in use. Of historical interest were a number of burial markers of the scholar-rabbis of Talmudic fame.

Another project offered us, which we decided to take on, was that of draining swamps near Atlith, a poor and small pioneering settlement at the foot of Mount Carmel near the sea, established a decade earlier by Romanian Jews and a Russian sect, "Subbotnicks." The term "Subbotnick" was derived from the Russian word Sub-bota, which means Saturday. They observed the biblical command to keep Saturday as a day of rest, believed in the redemption of Palestine as predicted in the Bible, and followed Jewish religious rituals. These people had come from the Ukraine and immigrated to Palestine during the period of the Jewish second aliyah in 1904. Atlith had one unpaved street with about twenty houses on both sides, with storage sheds interspersed for communal use. There was a one-room school house, where a young teacher and his wife lived as well as taught.

The children of the Subbotnicks learned Hebrew as their mother tongue. Even though Russian was the language spoken in their homes, the children spoke Hebrew outside. As it often happens with immigrant families, the elders had difficulty in mastering a new language. This was true with the Subbotnick families. On many occasions the parents had trouble communicating with their children and complained to us that their children didn't understand them. In all, there were about fifteen children, ages three to fifteen years. Their studies included the reading and writing of Hebrew, geography, biblical and modern history of Palestine, and bar mitzvah preparation. On Friday nights and Saturdays the school building was used as a place of worship by the villagers. Our group did not attend these services; our attitude toward religion was not traditional, but neither were we atheists. We believed we were expressing our faith by rebuilding the homeland and preferred to spend our free time outdoors swimming and exploring the nearby historical areas. Adjacent to the school was the communal bath house. Hot showers were available on Friday afternoons, following the age-old tradition of cleansing the body in preparation for the Sabbath. The rest of the week, cold showers were available. Several outhouses were located back of the houses at a "respectable" distance.

The many swamps surrounding the village had resulted from underground seepage and winter rains left to stagnate in the ground depressions, which became the breeding places for the malaria-carrying mosquito. Nearly everyone was afflicted with this dreaded disease. It strikes suddenly with a high fever, leaving the patient exhausted and weakened. Just as the attacks come suddenly, lasting several days, they also disappear as quickly, though certain types of malaria (malaria Tertiana) can remain active throughout the lifetime of the patient. The only treatment at that time was quinine tablets that were always in short supply.

Atlith involved another big readjustment for our group of sixteen boys and girls. In the beginning we were on our own without any "experts" to guide us. Tents were sent to us, but we did not know how to erect them well enough to withstand the strong January winter winds. They held up the first two nights but on the third morning we awoke to find the tents blown away. Gone also were our meager belongings! With much difficulty we retrieved our tents and from this miserable experience we learned how to erect them so they would stand up to the strong sea winds. Luckily we were allowed to use the kitchen and dining facilities in the village community hall. The girls had become more experienced in preparing the food, and more items were added to the variety of our daily meals—canned beef imported from Australia and fresh vegetables such as cucumbers, tomatoes, eggplant, and feta cheese from the neighboring Arab village. On Fridays our sabbath meal was roasted chicken or lamb—the "gourmet" highlight of our week.

As soon as minimal living arrangements were set up, we turned our attention to our work of draining the swamps. The Pioneer organization sent an instructor to advise us on the rudimentary details of this project. He stayed with us the first week since none of us had any knowledge of this work, leaving an instruction sheet with a rough sketch of the location of the drainage ditches. In principle, the concept was to direct the flow from the higher ground towards the sea. We were fortunate that there were several villagers who had successfully drained their own land. With their help, we laid out a plan of action. The practical approach was to dig a number of narrow ditches leading to larger ones that would be directed to the Mediterranean. We were provided with the standard short-handled hoes to make the shallow canals. This was truly a backbreaking experience. Unlike the work on Mount Carmel, we never really got used to this demanding work. The satisfaction, however, was that we were contributing to the elimination of malaria in that location.

Through our labor, the benefits of which were soon clear to the villagers, the early social standoff changed between the villagers and ourselves. Their background was so different from ours. They were farmers, we were students; they observed the religious practices; we did not. Yet romances began to flourish and one of our group, Gashri, "the shy one," fell in love with a beautiful Romanian girl, married, and remained in the village as a farmer. The efficiency of our work was hampered greatly by the constant bouts of the malaria that affected many of our group, including me. As mentioned earlier, quinine pills were the only preventative, but it took me several months to learn to swallow pills. At first I tried to crush them in my mouth, but the bitter taste was too repulsive. However, as soon as I stopped taking them, I shivered with malarial chills.

Usually on Saturdays and holidays and whenever else there was a work stoppage we left our ditchdigging and headed for the Crusaders' ancient fortress on the beach that was built in the eleventh century. It was not completely in ruins, though its walls and roof were open in large part to the elements. The salty sea breezes and the winter rains had produced a damp, mouldy atmosphere in those crumbling sandstone walls. During World War I three Americans in their thirties, who had come to Palestine with the Jewish Legion lived in these unhealthy ruins.[3] Their living conditions in these ruins were primitive, and they were frequently sick with dysentery, malaria, or some other ailment. These "diehard idealists" chose to remain after the war and start a fishing enterprise. They acquired the necessary fishing gear, several small boats and nets, and went out early every morning for the catch, casting their nets in a wide semicircle at a considerable distance from the shore. Eight or ten of us would row out in two large boats to join them just before sunrise. Anchored about half a mile from shore, we would cast our nets together and pull in a catch of mackerel, groupers, and gray mullet, as well as herring. Generally there was enough fish to sell to the villagers. Each venture out onto the water in the dark hours of early morning was a mysterious and exciting occasion, especially when the catch was successful. There came a time, however, when malaria laid the Americans low, and they had to cut back on their predawn expeditions. We offered to help them row the boats and pull in the nets; actually, we proved skillful enough to go out on our own while the three fishermen convalesced. Our eagerness to help them was a certain morale booster while they were ill, and our growing expertise as fishermen was a source of pride for us.

Our living conditions and social life were better here than on Mount Carmel. Fortunately, we were allowed to use the small community hall for social affairs. On Friday evenings after dinner, dancing the hora and singing old Hebrew melodies or improvising new ones were the major entertainments. Often the three or four neighboring Arab village leaders (*mukhtars*) were invited to our social gatherings, and we would all dance the traditional hora together. The mukhtars taught us variations of their Arab dances, which were similar to the hora. Our relationship with our Arab guests was friendly and warm, so friendly that they offered to our leader Iser Kulik to "buy" some of the girls in our group for their wives or concubines. They were surprised when they were refused, since the price they offered was considerably

---

[3]The idea of a Jewish Legion to fight on the side of the Allies was primarily conceived and successfully implemented by Vladimir Jabotinsky who came from Odessa, Russia. After the Kischinev pogrom in the Ukraine in 1903, he became an ardent Zionist and organized self-defense groups. He was very proud when the Jewish Legion was finally formed in 1917. It consisted of Jewish volunteers from Britain, America, and Palestine. Known as the Thirty-eighth Battalion of the British Royal Fusiliers, this company fought in the Palestine campaign, being the first to cross the Jordan River.

more than the price they would pay for a good camel, and a wife usually commanded a lower price than a donkey or an ordinary camel. I didn't believe it, but the
story goes that greetings between Arabs invariably started: "How is your donkey?
How is your camel? And how is your wife?" It took a lot of friendly diplomacy to
explain that our girls were not for sale. I might add that we had no intention of
parting with any female member of our group—there were four of them to eighteen
of us, a tense situation for the males. The lack of feminine company had a depressing
effect on all of us. One mitigating factor was the hard physical work we performed
that made the sex urge less intense. However, the young Romanian wife of the
village teacher was a constant sexual irritant. Invariably when we returned from our
labor to the community house for lunch, she would be lolling on the school house
steps, the buttons on her blouse open to show more than a glimpse of her full
breasts; her legs spread apart wantonly. Back at work, we teased each other constantly about her, and she was the object of many improbable fantasies.

I have joyful memories of the hiking trips our group took to various parts of the
country. One such trip was a seventy-mile journey from Atlith to the northernmost
kibbutz, Tel-Hai. The occasion was to commemorate and inaugurate a monument to
Joseph Trumpeldor who a year earlier on 1 March 1920 fought off, with a small
group of defenders, a much larger force of Arabs intent on destroying the settlement.[4]
In the retreat from Tel-Hai to a stronghold farther north, Kfar-Giladi, he was fatally
wounded. His last words were "It is good to die for our country." Within a year he had
become a hero to the Jewish settlers. Twenty of our group started the seventy-mile
trip in the early morning hours. We made the journey on foot, with minimal necessities in our knapsacks. The road led north through Haifa, then through desolate
undeveloped areas, finally reaching Tiberias on Lake Kinneret late at night. This
sixteen-hour trek was exhausting, but a high adventure for our group. My companions settled down to sleep on the shore of the lake. I was fortunate that my aunt
Hannah, the nurse, lived in Tiberias in a small house. Even though she did not expect
me, I tapped on her window and we met again with joy as well as surprise. After a
hurried snack and a short chat about my adventures, I fell asleep as soon as I touched
the couch in her living room. The next morning I rejoined my companions to continue north to the hilly and mountainous regions of the Jewish village Rosh Pina and
on to the ancient city of Safed in the upper Galilee. From there we passed desolate
areas inhabited by Bedouins whose black tents were silhouetted in groups against
the sky. The trip was planned so that the night was spent in a hospitable kibbutz,
recently established by the young Pioneers. The living arrangements were meager—a
wooden building for kitchen and dining, tents for sleeping. The kibbutz members

---

[4]Joseph Trumpeldor fought in the Russo-Japanese War in 1905 where he was wounded and lost an
arm. He was the first Jew ever to hold the rank of commissioned officer in the Russian army reserve corps.
In 1912 he migrated to Palestine and helped establish a settlement at Migdal. He also served under the
British in 1915 in the Gallipoli campaign after World War I. When the French forces withdrew from the
upper Galilee in 1920, the Jewish settlements in Metulla, Giladi, and Tel-Hai were being attacked by Arab
bands. Trumpeldor organized a defense corps of about fifty volunteers (some from the American Jewish
Legion). They held out heroically for two months at Tel-Hai.

gave us their best tents, doubling up with their fellow workers, and shared with us their meager food supply, a real sacrifice in those pioneering days. There was always reciprocal hospitality between members of the various kibbutzim. At the end of the third day we finally arrived at Tel-Hai exhausted, dirty, and hungry, "slept like dead" for twelve hours, then were awakened by the shouts of other new arrivals.

All of us wanted to hear the details of the Arab attack and strategy of the defendants who against great odds had withstood the siege for several days. Our first surprise was the smallness of this outpost. It consisted of one large fieldstone building protected by an eight-foot stone fence. The entrance was through a solid wooden gate. During the day we were pleasantly surprised to meet nearly thirty of my travel companions from the Russian boat. It was a joyful reunion, with everyone anxious to tell one another what they had been doing since we had been separated. The variety of work assignments was truly amazing. Some had joined the road building corps to construct a road from Tiberias to the railroad station at Zemach, about eight miles to the east and at that time the northernmost part of the railroad line. Others had been sent to build new housing in the older settlements. For most it meant learning a new trade—building the wooden forms for the concrete beams, masonry, plastering, and other construction crafts. As I listened to their stories, I almost wished I had joined that second group. (As it turned out, a year later our own group became a construction group.) The others listened almost with envy to our stories of planting pine seedlings on Mount Carmel slopes to create forests. However, they did not envy us the assignment of draining the swamps in a malaria-ridden village. It was exhilarating and almost unbelievable to see the transformation in all of us in the year since our arrival in Palestine. We were tanned, toughened by work, self-reliant men and women. The Tel-Hai celebration was held under the starlit sky to inaugurate the monument, which was in the form of a life-size lion of carved stone.

Speakers claimed that holding on to this northern outpost had demonstrated Jewish fighting ability for once and for all and had discouraged the Arabs from further attacks on these isolated settlements. For the newcomers, it meant confidence in their ability to defend themselves in their new land. After a solemn moment of silence, we all burst into song. Spontaneous hora dances lasted till the morning hours, emotion and sentiment ran high, and we all slept on the ground where we dropped utterly exhausted.

We spent another day exploring the northern border with Lebanon and the most northerly kibbutz outpost of Kfar-Giladi. It was to this outpost that the wounded Trumpeldor was carried by his comrades after the retreat from Tel-Hai. Then the trek back—walking a different route through older pioneer farm villages of Poriah, Balfuriah, and Mesha where the hardworking settlers struggled to eke out a living. These villages were settled by strong-willed idealists who had come to Palestine in the late nineteenth and early twentieth centuries. They were determined to make a livelihood from farming, anticipating the difficulties. The villages consisted of fifteen to twenty families, each with its own plot of land, several cows, some chickens, a wagon with a mule, and minimal primitive farm implements provided by the Jewish National Fund. Vegetables and grain struggled to grow in this arid soil.

On the way back we passed through the narrow ancient cobblestone streets of Nazareth. For us in the year 1921 it seemed as though the world had stood still for two thousand years. We were surprised to see the tradesmen plying their crafts in hole-in-the-wall shops, using the age-old traditional methods of hammering and shaping the metal. Carpenters made short-legged tables and stools as well as cabinets; coppersmiths produced household utensils—coffee urns, copper eating and cooking bowls, pestle and mortar implements for grinding coffee and grain. And there were small stands of freshly baked pitas (small rounds of unleavened dough) and fresh vegetables such as eggplant and tomatoes. Olives and goat cheese were also in abundance. Freshly butchered slabs of lamb hung on big hooks from the wooden rafters of other stands, attracting in addition to the customers, the ever-present flies. The coffee houses were everywhere; here men passed the day playing backgammon and smoking their nargilehs spiked with hashish. These were the customary social gathering places for lively conversation and political discussions from which women were by tradition excluded. The male participants in this setting were generally attired in the kefiah headdress and loose white robes, creating a dramatic contrast with the black-clothed and veiled women.

The main source of income in Nazareth in 1921, as it is today, came from tourists and groups of Christian pilgrims coming to pray at the Church of the Nativity. The favorite tourist items were prayer beads, bible covers, or camels and religious figures carved from the native olive wood. For our part, we admired the craftsmanship of the metal work, but we did not have money to buy any of the items. After spending the morning in the city, we feasted on the cheap food bought in the market—pitas, cheese, chickpeas, and olives. We left Nazareth with the feeling that we wanted to come back and spend more time exploring this ancient and historic city. Despite the Arab-Jewish unrest and tension of the past year, we had friendly experiences. There was much more to explore, but because we still had a long way to walk, we could only promise ourselves to return another time.

From here we proceeded southeast to Mount Tabor, about a two-hour march. This mountain rises majestically in a half spherical shape about fifteen hundred feet above the surrounding fertile valley of Jezreel, which was later to become the "bread basket" of the country. At the very top was a newly built monastery for Polish monks. To reach it we had to climb a winding narrow cliff path. Looking down through the clear and invigorating air we could see tilled farmlands. The valley was becoming green and fertile through the efforts of the Jewish settlers, opening our eyes to the potential of our efforts. We spent several hours with the monks on Mount Tabor, who received us warmly. We managed to converse in both Polish and Hebrew, in imperfect broken phrases. They showed us around their modern, well-kept quarters. Their favorite Hebrew word was *yoffi* (beautiful). After a light snack of bread and olives, we started down the path on the last leg of our journey home.

Soon after we returned to Atlith, rumors reached us that our swamp- draining project was about to be terminated by the Zionist organization because of shortage of funds. Actually, the only funds required were for minimal food, some clothing replacement, and a few piasters for pocket money, and we were all the more frustrated because of the importance of our work to the health of the villagers. Meanwhile several Jewish entrepreneurs came to the village to investigate the possibilities of establishing a salt plant and a rock crushing quarry. The salt would be produced by evaporating the seawater in shallow ponds near the shore. The quarry would be located a short distance away, at the foot of Mount Carmel. We wanted to stay in Atlith but these men were willing to pay mere subsistence wages, taking advantage of our situation. We angrily rejected their offer and decided to rely on the guidance of the Zionist organization for future work. Meanwhile, we waited for our next assignment, spending our time fishing and swimming in the Mediterranean and reading the few available Hebrew newspapers.

After several weeks passed, two of my close friends Shimon and Daniel and I decided to satisfy a childhood dream and go on foot to Jerusalem, a distance of about eighty miles. Our luggage consisted of a change of underwear, an extra shirt, and some bread and olives for emergencies. For lodging and regular meals, we were confident of the hospitality of the kibbutzim along the way and the camps of the special "Labor Corps," a volunteer group of young people under the jurisdiction of the central Zionist organization. Their age group ranged from eighteen to twenty-five, about the same as ours.

Our past experience with the kibbutz hospitality justified our expectations as long as the distance between stopping points could be covered in a day's tramp. We usually walked six to eight hours, allowing a few rest periods. It was difficult for us to anticipate what the Bedouins along the road would do. The Arab effendis had been spreading tales among the population that the new Jewish immigrants would take away their property. Moreover, we did not know whether the Arabs we met would be friend or foe, so the first night on the march we spent a sleepless night in a ditch by the road, fearful and hungry, having eaten all our emergency rations.

The night passed without harm, and the morning sun brought better spirits. We tramped south to Hadera, a third of the way between Atlith and Tel Aviv. Hadera was one of the early agricultural villages which had been drained of swamps. Groves of eucalyptus trees, which are not only fast growing but absorb vast amounts of water, had been planted in strategic areas around the village. This greenery in the dusty landscape made Hadera an inviting and welcoming sight. (In later years the mature trees were also the source for pulp used in paper manufacturing, the beginning one of the many new Israeli industries.) Fortunately for us there was a Labor Corps camp nearby, with about a hundred young people living in tents and continuing the tree planting in the immediate area. Here we were welcomed, our spirits and energies revived. After showering we devoured a meal of eggs, olives, and pita bread. We slept well in one of their tents.

Our next destination was Petah Tikvah, at that time the major center for oranges and lemons grown on privately owned Jewish land. In contrast to the kibbutz philosophy of shared work and communal living, these fruit growers were primarily interested in high profits based on the cheapest labor (obtainable usually from Arabs). Here the well-to-do landowners lived comfortably in solid sandstone houses, cool in summer and warm in winter. We had no personal contact here and tramped through on the road to Tel Aviv, never dreaming that a few months later we would be laboring in these very orchards along with the Arabs.

Although for me this was the second visit to Tel Aviv, it was a welcome and exciting stopover in an otherwise hard and tiring journey for all of us. We spent part of our meager funds for a substantial meal in a tiny eating place, run by a middle-aged Jewish woman. We gorged ourselves with the chopped eggplant salad, slices of baked lamb, pita bread, and finished off with delicious Turkish coffee and honey-covered little cakes. We then walked around the few paved streets—Herzl, the beginning of Allenby, the Rothschild Boulevard.[5] We had two goals in mind: watching the well-dressed and attractive girls go by, and reaching the sea. This later turned out to require a formidable effort. Even though the actual distance between city and shore was a little over a mile, the area in between consisted of high sand dunes interspersed with the black Bedouin tents. Scrambling up and down dune after dune was an exhausting effort after the day's long march. We felt rewarded, however, when we could strip off our shorts and sandals on the deserted beach and plunge naked into the Mediterranean. Back in the city we found the Pioneer House, where we had first been welcomed upon our arrival in the country, and arranged to spend the night there.

Our walking tour continued the following day, past the ancient city of Jaffa to the old crusader city of Ramleh, passing the nearby large English army camp of Sarafand. From here on the road began to climb toward the mountainous area around Jerusalem.[6] Our only chance of overnight lodging on this route was in the small settlement of Har-Tuv, located in an isolated area, almost hidden away in the low mountain range, off the main road. Only youthful optimists would leave the road and attempt to find it with the vague directions we had been given in Tel Aviv by Pioneer advisors who had visited this place previously. We started to climb up the rocky slopes to the northeast. After several hours, we realized we were lost. There was no path, not even a sign of habitation as far as the eye could see. By luck, an Arab shepherd with his flock came over a ridge. With the little Arabic that we knew we were able to ask directions, and just before sundown finally found the place. The risk was justified by the warmth of the welcome we received from the farmer's family with whom we spent the night. The man and wife, about sixty years of age, were from that first sturdy pioneer group that had come before the turn of the century. As happy as we were to find them, they were even happier, for they saw in young settlers like us an echo of their own hopes and dreams.

This couple had come from a small village in Bessarabia (Russia) and wanted to settle close to Jerusalem. The Jewish National Fund, which owned this land, allocated it to them for cultivation. The attraction of this isolated area was a water well. They told us of the hard times they experienced in the beginning, clearing rocks to create arable terraces in which to plant tomatoes, eggplant, cucumbers, and other vegetables. A number of olive trees had been planted near the house and managed to grow. They built a small stone farmhouse, but they had difficult times when the severe cold mountain weather and rains in winter created a shortage of food and bare essentials. In addition, unpredictable locust invasions from Africa devastated the crops, especially the one of 1915–1916. Somehow, their difficulties had not affected their stamina and their ability to remain warm human beings. They demonstrated this by offering us overnight lodging in their limited quarters, which was a godsend to us.

[5]Theodor Herzl originated the idea of establishing a Jewish state in Palestine. His ideas were published in a book "Judenstaat," in 1895. Allenby, a British general, led his army in victory against the Turks in Palestine in 1917–18. Baron Edmond Rothschild was the great benefactor in the early years of the first villages, establishing a major wine producing industry, as well as a number of agricultural settlements.

[6]Jerusalem is situated twenty-five hundred feet above the Mediterranean Sea level. On the east, it is thirty-eight hundred feet above the Dead Sea and the surrounding valleys.

Because I was the youngest and reminded them of their own youthful beginnings, they took a special liking to me.

The next day we said goodbye to these wonderful people who had given us both physical and spiritual strength by their example, and with their detailed directions we found the main road again easily. At noon we stopped at Bab-El-Wad (Gateway of the Ravine), which provided a watering place for donkeys and camels and a small run-down inn for the human travelers where we bought feta cheese and pita bread for the final stretch of our journey. From here we climbed on continuously over a mountainous and tiring road, past little Arab villages with their stone houses built into the cliffs along the road. Just before reaching Jerusalem the road dipped down to a small plateau leading to the Jewish settlement of Motza. (A decade later this place became a health recuperation center for the members of the Histadruth Labor Organization.) Our stop here was short and pleasant, with a rest and a light snack. We pushed on, anxious to reach Jerusalem still an hour away, by evening. It was getting dark when we reached the city; our first priority was to find a place to sleep. When we had left Har-Tuv the farmer told us about a hostel in Jerusalem for young travelers run by an ultraorthodox Jewish sect. At first we were not interested since we did not observe religious practices and were not religiously inclined. However, finding ourselves stranded in the darkness of the city, we decided to look for this place. We finally found the building down a narrow side street. The hostel was filled to near capacity by a large number of young boys who were also being given religious instruction. As much as we knew about their opposition to the establishment of a Jewish homeland in our time (they believed that the revival of the Jewish state would come with the Messiah in the future), we were shocked by their hostility to our beliefs. Our different outlook created heated arguments and a tense atmosphere. We decided to avoid further confrontations and to spend as much time away from them as possible.

We were entranced with the surroundings and history of this ancient city and spent several days exploring the old walled section. Judaic, Christian, and Islamic cultures all left their imprint everywhere—the Wailing Wall, the remnants of the Temple of King Solomon, the Mosque of Omar, and the Church of the Holy Sepulchre. Going through the Jaffa Gate to the Old City, we sank into a sea of people, sounds, smells, colors—all this in a jumble of ancient winding cobblestone streets, just wide enough for a donkey and two people to pass. We stared at every kind of merchandise—foods, clothing, household utensils of copper, silver jewelry, religious ceremonial objects, made by native craftsmen. These were made and displayed in the hole-in-the-wall shops lining both sides of the narrow street. We walked through a patchwork of sun and shadow, as the light was diffused by the canvas awnings attached to the numerous stone arches like flying buttresses over the streets that were built originally to reinforce the walls of the buildings on both sides of the street. The sounds of peddlers calling out their wares and the voices of the merchants and shoppers bargaining loudly mingled with the braying of the donkeys and their tinkling bells hit our senses. We were emotionally overwhelmed as we felt the ancient past reaching out to us. Our arduous trip was well rewarded.

We began the return trip to Atlith on 1 May 1921, early spring in Palestine, the best and the most exhilarating season. The air was fresh and cool, delightful to breathe, and the sun was just warm enough to feel comfortable. Like The Three

Musketeers, we three eighteen-year olds started out singing, often with arms linked, on the long hike back to Tel Aviv. Had we looked at a newspaper in the last ten days, we would have read that the Arab nationalists were preparing for a series of attacks on isolated Jewish settlements as well as on Jewish population centers throughout Palestine. It was generally known that the British were planning to "turn a blind eye" to these discords so as to keep the two segments of the population at each other's throats—the divide and conquer strategy. As it turned out later, our ignorance was our salvation. We hiked along in high spirits, one or another of us dashing off along one path here or there, looking for a shortcut and rejoining the others on the main road in an exuberant mood of hide-and-seek. Half way to Tel Aviv, as we were walking together on the main road for once, an Arab truck driver stopped and offered us a ride to Tel Aviv. Although we were surprised by his friendly gesture because of general Arab animosity, we were happy to accept his invitation and climbed into the back of the truck. After a polite exchange in our broken Arabic, we started to sing again as we rolled along. On our route was the all-Arab city of Ramleh. Instead of taking the bypass, as we expected, our driver drove straight into town to the main square. There we found ourselves in the center of a milling crowd of several thousand Arabs. Our driver then ordered us to get out, saying that he had changed his mind and decided not to go on to Tel Aviv. It never occurred to us, in our festive mood, that we would be the targets of the Arabs' hostility. Even when some youngsters started to throw stones at us, we still thought it a playful gesture. With linked arms we started to walk on through the crowd, still singing our marching songs in high spirits. The crowd slowly parted and let us pass. Away we tramped, out of town, and reached the British military encampment at Sarafand in an hour or so. Only then did we hear from the anxious people there that a day before the few Jewish families and the only storekeeper in Ramleh had been murdered by the Arab mob. The well-known Jewish writer Joseph Chaim Brenner, who lived nearby, had been killed by a mob that morning and many young people from the surrounding area were being sheltered in the British camp for protection. Among them were a number of our friends, who knew that we were starting back that day from Jerusalem and had given up hope of ever seeing us alive again. At our sudden appearance there were tears and happy cries, prayers, and hugs. The one question on everyone's lips was "What saved you?" One theory was that the Arabs, seeing us happy and singing at the top of our lungs in the face of certain death, believed that we were lunatics, and their moral code forbade them to harm crazy people. Had we panicked and started to run, this theory went, we would not have returned to tell the story.

The Arab riots against the Jews continued for another week. Jewish settlers traveled around the countryside only in armed groups. We three joined one of these caravans of about twenty people to get back to Atlith. When we arrived we found both the villagers and our own work group apprehensive. In the past we had considered ourselves relatively secure because of our friendly Arab neighbors, but now they were under mounting pressure by Arab nationalists to attack all settlers. As for us, we had no defense plans. Our single precaution was to place an armed guard at the entrance to the village. We took turns at being on guard duty every four hours even though none of us were experienced in handling a gun. If a menacing group of Arabs came in sight, the guard was to fire two shots in the air. At that point, all were to run to the schoolhouse where we would defend ourselves with the very few pistols we had available. Most of us would have to depend on homemade weapons—daggers, knives, metal bars. After three uneventful days and nights, we were awakened by the warning shots. The sounds of horses and wagons mixed with Arab shouts could be heard in the distance. Everyone ran to the schoolhouse as planned and armed themselves with their improvised weapons. As it turned out, these passing Arabs continued on their way peacefully and most of our Arab neighbors remained friendly, but the incident showed us how helpless we would be in the face of a real attack. After a few weeks the situation normalized and we went back to our routine, though we did keep one person taking turns on watch around the clock.

Life became exciting again when we heard that four girls were arriving to join our group, two of them sisters of our members. We young men speculated endlessly on what they would look like and which of us they would find attractive, and our small group hiked five miles to the small wooden shack that served as a railroad "station" to welcome them. It was a happy occasion, and we forgot about our fantasies of glamorous girls when we met. They were ordinary-looking girls, but with a heartwarming idealism. Sonya especially appealed to me. Her face reminded me of Leonardo da Vinci's Mona Lisa. She was the sister of Yedidia, my close friend and guiding spirit of the group. His main interest was the study of the history, philosophy, and goals of the Zionist movement. His knowledge of Hebrew, which he had learned from his father in Grodno, was nearly perfect. He had a logical mind, a prodigious memory, and the ability to express himself beautifully in Hebrew. The scholars who were then attempting to adapt Hebrew for everyday use as a modern language were hard at work compiling a dictionary. However, there were comparatively few in Palestine who had attained Yedidia's facility. Most of the immigrants, regardless of when they arrived, were struggling with Hebrew as their second language, and one more often heard English, Yiddish, Polish, German, and Hungarian than the language of the Bible. Yedidiya's fluency strengthened our own interest in and enjoyment of speaking Hebrew in our daily life.

Many leisure hours were spent discussing our precarious work situations in Atlith, the safety of the village, and the British opposition to the establishment of the Jewish state and its probable effects on our future in Palestine. Most of this talk took place during meals or during our free evening hours, on the Sabbath, or on rainy days when we could not work. When I took walks with Sonya alone, I was too shy to let her know how attracted I was to her. For one thing, she was an "older woman" of twenty-two, while I was eighteen. Sonya was friendly but seemed to feel nothing more for me, and for the two years before I left to return to the United States we were comrades. Thirteen years later in 1933 when I returned to Palestine from the United States as an architect, I met her at Yedidia's home in Jerusalem. An outgoing and self-assured woman, she was now a nursery school teacher in a kibbutz near Haifa. We recalled our days in Atlith and had a good laugh about our youthful inhibitions and shyness.

During 1933–1937 when I had a small architectural office in Tel Aviv, we met occasionally at Yedidia's home. When Sonya learned that I was getting ready to return to the United States she wrote that she would like to see me and we arranged to meet in a restaurant in Haifa. It was a warm and friendly get-together with nostalgic reminiscences of our Pioneer group dating back fifteen years. Never in my wildest dreams did I anticipate what was to come next. "Please take me with you—I'll be a good wife, a lover, a friend—I've always loved you . . . !" Too shocked at this unexpected revelation, I was speechless and helpless to respond or to assuage her feelings. The interval of fifteen years since our pioneering days had wrought personal changes in me. How can one explain the different impact of time and experiences on each of us? It was a sad parting.

Although there was work left to be done in Atlith, the budget for this phase of our group's work was depleted. We were offered other nonskilled jobs in the orange and lemon groves of Petah Tikvah. Our group decided to accept the offer and left Atlith. The work involved irrigation of the groves. Carefully laid out rows of trees were crisscrossed with irrigation ditches connected to the main water supply. People were stationed in strategic locations with special short hoes to remove any obstacles to the flow of water in the ditches. Work like this was backbreaking in the subtropical summer heat, and the cooling breezes were blocked by the trees in the orchards. What kept us from complete collapse was the lemonade we concocted by mixing irrigation water with the juice of the lemons we picked from the trees. We readily accepted the popular notion that lemon juice would kill the germs in the unfiltered water. No one became ill, probably a matter of luck.

In Petah Tikvah we realized for the first time in Palestine that our work had no connection whatsoever with our cherished ideals. In the months that we worked there we felt like outcasts. We were hired through the central workers' exchange run by the village. Each evening the orchard owners would appear at the exchange to hire whatever number of laborers they needed for the following day. There were always more workers than jobs. Those without work would show up early at the exchange the next morning and stand around hoping that someone would fail to show up. It was a humiliating situation for us. Our work day was long and we were too exhausted at night to attempt to socialize with the Jewish villagers. The owners of the groves felt that they had made a contribution to the cause of a Jewish homeland by hiring us at a rate slightly more than they paid their Arab laborers. They had no other interest in us and there was no social relationship. We lived alone in our tents near the groves. We told ourselves this was a temporary phase—that we were at least learning the fundamentals of fruit growing, which gave us a feeling that we were still fulfilling our commitment to rebuilding the land. In our tent quarters we felt the absence of women even more sharply than in Atlith because there were no other distractions. To make matters worse, two married couples joined our work group, and every time they went to their tents, whether during the two-hour lunch siesta or at bedtime, everyone's eyes followed them enviously.

When the summer was over, the Pioneer organization offered us a chance to join a construction group called Kvutzat Habanoim in the city of Haifa at the foot of Mount Carmel. All of us except for a few who decided to try their luck at getting work in the private sector, accepted the offer. This first year in Palestine left us with mixed feelings about the leadership. That this would be our fourth work assignment in one year showed the inability of the central organization of the Pioneers to make long-range plans. At times we had the feeling of being forgotten by those who had sent us here. We had almost no contact or communication with the organization. At the same time the move to Haifa had a special appeal for me. As for work, it meant an opportunity to learn the different construction trades and I was eager to get started. Besides, the surroundings were familiar from my first work assignment, and I loved the Carmel mountains and the naturally formed harbor of Haifa with its many foreign ships anchored in its blue Mediterranean waters.

Moving to Haifa was a simple matter. Our personal belongings were few. My only presentable "holiday attire" which I had carefully preserved from my highschool days, was a pair of long trousers and a military style jacket remodeled from an officer's uniform. My other clothing, such as underwear and shorts, was threadbare. Our work clothes consisted of khaki shorts, white cotton shirt, and sandals. One truck was sufficient to carry our group of twelve, our tents, and all our personal belongings. Within a couple of hours we were at our destination, a construction site on the lower slopes of Mount Carmel that is now a thriving business district called the Lower Carmel. Our living conditions here were poor. We pitched our now-ragged tents near the construction site. Moreover there were no showers to wash off the stone dust with which we were covered from head to foot by the end of the day. The waters of the Bay of Haifa were only a twenty-minute walk away, but at the end of the day it was too long a hike. To complicate matters, we became infected with head lice, a common condition among the native workers. The remedy was to wash the hair in kerosene. We at least tried to keep our hands and faces clean. However, when we all developed an itchy skin rash over our bodies, especially on the genitals, we threatened to quit unless showers were installed. With the installation of showers, sanitary conditions became at least tolerable.

The project to which we were assigned by the organization was the construction of a number of two-story buildings. Each contained eight two-bedroom apartments. It was to be a learning experience in becoming efficient stonecutters and stonemasons under a special arrangement with a private Jewish contractor. The starting wage was one piaster (five cents) an hour, to be increased in minor amounts as the work progressed. The earnings were paid directly to the organization, which in turn distributed the wages to each of us.

As newcomers in the construction group, we were given the unskilled jobs—mixing mortar, building scaffolding, and carrying the building stones to the masons. As time went on I was made apprentice to an Arab stonecutter, one of many who were our instructors. The rough stones were brought from a nearby quarry and we apprentices cut them to required sizes with chisel and mallet (special square head hammers). Other apprentices then lugged them on their shoulders to the masons on the scaffolding. The closing space at the end of each row was measured and the dimensions of the last stone were called out by the mason in a loud voice to the stonecutters below. He would wait on the scaffold for us to cut and deliver those stones. The stone blocks that we used were quarried nearby in the Mount Carmel foothills. This stone was of medium hardness, had a pink coloring, and was easy to chisel. It was satisfying to see the emerging shape under the steady blows of the hammer.

For two months I sat in the meager shade of a gnarled ancient olive tree, cutting and chiseling stones for the standard size courses, those which go around the building uninterrupted by any building openings. This work required great exactness and refinement of execution. After several months I was able to train others in the art of stonecutting, while moving up to become a bona fide stonemason. We were fortunate to have Muhammad, an Egyptian master mason, to instruct us. He was a tall, lean man, about fifty years old, with red turban and white flowing robe. He had married a Palestinian Arab and lived in Haifa. He delighted in seeing our group of young people learn the tricks of the trade so quickly and he praised us for completing the buildings ahead of schedule. For our "graduation exercises" we spent a week in a stone quarry nearby to drill holes for the dynamite, place the charge, light the fuse, and run to safety. You could say that we knew our material inside out by the time we finished our course with Muhammad, and interest in our work increased accordingly. As I learned several years later when I was in architectural school, this "hands-on" approach was also one of the principles of the Bauhaus school of architecture based in Germany in the 1920s and continued in Chicago under Mies van der Rohe. It was to influence me later in my own architectural practice.

Our work in Haifa came to a halt when we completed the apartment complex. Building funds for these projects were depleted and the Pioneer organization was looking around for other construction projects in the area where we could utilize our new skills. While waiting for a new assignment, we spent several months working on the nearby Technion high school building. The school, financed by German Jews, had been started in 1913, but upon the outbreak of World War I only the structural framework and the stone exterior and interior walls were complete. Our job was to chisel the rough surfaces of the interior stone walls to prepare them for plastering. Today this building is part of an extensive campus complex of the Haifa Technion, an institute of technology comparable to the Massachusetts Institute of Technology in the United States. By the time we finished this work, we received our awaited assignment. We were pleasantly surprised to learn that we were going to Rishon-Le-Zion (First-of-Zion), eight miles southeast of Tel Aviv to build houses for some newly arrived Jewish families from Yemen. This pretty village lay at the foot of towering sand dunes, with the blue Mediterranean beyond. It had the appearance of a prosperous community—small villas attractively landscaped dotted a main street lined with palm trees. We soon learned that it had taken many years of hard work and struggle for the settlers to create this comfortable place. The first settlers came from Russia in 1882, and bought nearly a thousand acres of land, mostly sand dunes from the Arab landowners. There they were without water, and no money was left after the land had been paid for to buy drilling equipment for wells. All water had to be brought in wooden barrels from the nearby settlement of Mikveh-Israel in a camel-drawn carriage. Later, mules replaced the camels. In desperation, the settlers sent emissaries to the various European Jewish communities to describe their plight. In Paris, Baron Edmond de Rothschild was contacted and he responded not only with money for the wells, but also with cuttings from his vineyards. The Baron's continued interest resulted through the years in making Richon-Le-Zion an important wine-producing center, once the varieties of grapes suited to the sandy soil had been developed.

Our project, which had been given priority by the Zionist organization, was to build small private houses for the Yemenites who were living temporarily in tents. The men worked in the vineyards and wine cellars while some of the women were employed in the village as house servants. In all, fifteen new families came to settle in Richon-Le-Zion in 1922. What made this project exciting for us was the knowledge that we were helping to create livable quarters for people who had been second class citizens for centuries in their native land of Yemen. There they had not been allowed to own land or be farmers. Here, in addition to housing, they were provided with health clinics and education services. No manual labor was beneath their dignity. Small of stature and dark skinned, they were hardworking and intelligent. For the most part these Yemenites were skilled gold and silversmiths, and they were also adept in weaving, engraving, calligraphy, bookbinding, painting and carpentry, pottery making, and tailoring. Their skills were, no doubt, one of the reasons for their survival throughout the centuries. From 1920 to 1948 only small numbers of Jews were able to leave Yemen. Most had to abandon their belongings and bribe their way to reach the embarkation port of Aden. From there the Zionist organization provided transportation to Palestine. A quarter of a century later, between 1948 and 1950, nearly the entire Jewish population of fifty thousand people was transported by plane from Yemen to the newly established state of Israel. Thus their belief in the biblical prophecy "On the wings of an eagle ye shall return to Zion" was realized.

The site for the Yemenite houses was on the outskirts of the village, near the vineyards. We pitched our tents nearby and erected two wooden barracks—one a dining and meeting hall and one for storage of the building equipment. Two construction foremen from nearby settlements came to teach us and supervise the various building operations. We were provided with a wagon and two mules to carry water to the site, for both building purposes and personal use. The wagon was also our means of transportation to Tel Aviv to pick up special building items, as well as for occasional pleasure trips. The soft sandstone quarried nearby was easy to cut and shape into building blocks. In addition to our special skill as stonemasons, we had to learn plastering, roofing, and some carpentry to complete the houses. We had to dig the foundations, mix the concrete by hand, and pour it in place. No heating was provided—lighting would be by kerosene lamps. We managed to do a fair job, except for the roofing. This trade required more learning and skill. The houses were the beginning of what was eventually to become a Yemenite quarter—a poor man's neighborhood in an otherwise affluent village.

Although the Yemenites' earnings were very low, their houses were kept spotlessly clean and whitewashed, with pots of flowers hanging from every wall and window. They created small vegetable gardens in the limited one-quarter acre plots of land allotted to them and it was fascinating to see what a strong sense of design was reflected in the plans of these little gardens. All the gardens at the backs of the houses were interconnected in a continuous pattern (a plan which I later followed for my own home in the United States). Their cleanliness and beauty was reflected in their folk songs, one of which asked "What is a fly doing on my pure white wall?" and "Please leave my house!"

They were observant Jews, spending the Sabbath as a day of rest and prayer. Their festive occasions centered around the family celebrations of births, circumcision, holiday rites, bar mitzvahs, and weddings. Men and women danced in separate circles, the women in colorfully embroidered blouses and skirts, which they had brought with them from Yemen, wearing silver necklaces, rings, bracelets, earrings, and silver ornaments in their hair. In all, these families were a happy group, enjoying their status as a free people in their ancestral homeland.

My memories of Rishon are marred by one unhappy development. I awakened one morning with a very high fever in a village where there were no doctors. Shulamit, one of the girls in our group, served as a nurse "by appointment," without any background or qualifications. Her remedy for any ailment was to serve the patient two fried eggs—a great luxury for us. Those two eggs were supposed to cure everything. When several days of eggs did not help and my fever rose higher, a doctor was summoned from Tel Aviv. He promptly diagnosed my illness as typhoid fever.

The makeshift ambulance that was to transport me to the nearest hospital in Jaffa fifteen miles away, was a farm wagon bedded with straw and drawn by one horse. The hospital for contagious diseases, located on the outskirts of Jaffa, was run by Arabs and administered by an elderly English nurse with a staff of several Arab male ward attendants. By the time the wagon with the iron-clad wheels bumped me over the cobblestone roads to the hospital, I was semiconscious. I was put in a large ward with about twenty other patients who were suffering from a wide variety of contagious diseases—syphilis, tuberculosis, among others. Shulamit, who had come with me, was not allowed to remain in the quarantine ward—No Visitors Allowed— and left in tears.

Unfortunately for me and for the four other Jewish patients stricken with typhoid fever, our time in the hospital coincided with Arab riots in Jaffa. In this hospital the treatment for typhoid fever was to give the patient one glass of milk every four hours. For some reason, the five Jewish patients received one glass of milk every twelve hours. We suspected this was a deliberate plot by two hostile attendants to starve us. What saved me and the others was Shulamit, who returned one night later, at the risk of being caught and quarantined herself, and learned how we were treated, "You looked like corpses!" she told us later indignantly. She filed a complaint with the British government health authorities, and conditions improved immediately. It took several weeks for me to recover my strength. For two others with typhoid the change came too late.

Strangely enough, I do recall one humorous episode from this hospital time. Not all the attendants were hostile. There was one named Hadj Mahmud, called "Doc," a kindly older man. His ambition had been to be a doctor, but in his youth he was stricken with glaucoma, which left him almost blind. His duties included taking the patient's temperatures rectally, posing a twofold problem—first to find the rectum and then to read the figures. We accepted his services good naturedly and tried to assist him. Another recollection—as we tossed in our beds, half starved and with burning fever, we would talk about the wonderful foods that our mothers used to prepare for us, and we yearned for a miracle that these treats would suddenly appear before us. Sharing these memories helped keep up our spirits. My return from the hospital was celebrated with great joy, especially by Shulamit, my savior. This time her fried-egg specialty helped, but even with my stamina it took more weeks before I could go back to my normal routine.

In Richon-Le-Zion we were socially isolated from the villagers. Occasionally we met young people, but our diverse backgrounds discouraged any closeness. The local young people were the children of the middle-class owners of the vineyards and orchards. We felt that since all their needs were provided by their families, their personal lives were unproductive. Our ideal, however, was to earn our livelihood through our own physical labor. What also set us apart was the contrast in the way we dressed and looked. The villagers were well dressed and groomed. Our holiday and Sabbath clothing was limited to a white shirt, khaki shorts, and sandals. Although we were clean shaven, our haircuts were few and far between. There is no doubt that this contributed to our isolation. In some ways we were partly responsible for the lack of communication. The one place where we could have mingled with the villagers was a small synagogue where services were held on Friday evenings and Saturdays. However, we did not attend these services since we were nonobservant.

We did manage to inject some excitement and fun into our daily routine by illegal nightly forays into the vineyards. There we could get our fill of the wine grapes, which were luxuries for us. The vineyards were guarded, so to avoid detection we would mimic the howling of jackals to frighten away the guards. So perfect was our imitation that our group became nicknamed the Jackals. Eventually the owners put an end to our little game by adding more guards.

Bread for our meals, which came like the rest of our food from Tel Aviv, was delivered by a new immigrant, Avrahami, who lived in the village. He always arrived late in the day, by which time we were so famished that we devoured it all, including the next morning's allotment. Avrahami had his own worries and problems. His ambition was to develop a small chicken farm on a tiny plot of land adjacent to his house where he lived with his wife Hannah and three-year-old son. Hannah had come from a middle-class family in Poland, a protective environment without household responsibilities. Her life in Palestine demanded a completely new and terrifying adjustment. She knew nothing of cooking or housekeeping, nothing of farm animals. Avrahami saved enough to buy a rooster and hen to start his flock and left Hannah in charge. One Friday night when he returned in time for the Sabbath, Hannah met him with joyful news: "I have a wonderful dinner for you tonight!" After he washed and readied himself for dinner, he was waiting for Hannah to bless the Sabbath candles, and looking forward to her surprise delicacies. He was horrified when his wife brought to the table his prized hen, nicely roasted. His dreams of a chicken farm vanished in that moment. We consoled him with one of our own stories of mishaps and frustrations and encouraged him to try his luck again.

In the spring of 1923 our work in Richon was finished. By this time the General Labor Federation or *Histadrut* had established a special division, *Solel-Boneh*, to handle general construction projects. Through this division the British authorities learned about us. Because of our reputation as a reliable and experienced construction team, we were recommended to build a residence for the new English governor of the Ramleh District. Ramleh, about twenty miles from Tel Aviv on the way to Jerusalem, was the old Arab town where I had my miraculous escape during the riots two years earlier. Although we were happy to be chosen for this prestigious project, we were worried about being so close to Ramleh, a traditional hotbed of riots and violent demonstrations against the Jews during Ramadan and other Muslim religious holidays. However, we accepted this challenging project and pitched our tents as close to the British encampment as we could. Our fears were not unfounded, as it turned out; later, during one of the religious processions the crowds had to be prevented from attacking us by a cordon of armed British soldiers carrying rifles.

As soon as we were settled in our tents, the Solel-Boneh supervisor Jacob Strauss rode up on horseback to get the project started. One tent on the site was allotted to him. He was an engineer educated in Germany, a heavy-set man in his midforties, wearing a semimilitary khaki outfit and a tropical helmet. This military image presaged action, and action there was. The site became a beehive of activity.

Caravans of camels brought sacks of sand, crushed stones, and cement for concrete. Donkeys labored under blocks of stone, water cans, and other building materials. Our group was increased by a large number of Arab stonecutters and stonemasons. The noise was deafening—the hammering of the stonecutters, masons shouting orders to the hod carriers, braying of donkeys, shouts of the camel riders, and the continuous and loud arguments among the workers. The governor had ordered the building completed within a year, as he planned to be married in the fall and bring his bride to his new house at Christmas.

As hard as we tried, the rainy season starting in November prevented us from keeping to the schedule. Some days the rain lasted two or three hours, but there were times when it poured for several days. From March on, when the rains stopped, we tried to catch up by working long hours. By the end of the year the building was completed to the satisfaction of the government superintendent. Despite the official approval, we were worried about the waterproofing of the asphalt roof. The use of asphalt for waterproofing was comparatively new in Palestine and there was no one to show us how to apply it. We did some tests during a few days of light rains, but this was not conclusive.

The governor arrived with his bride on schedule for Christmas, and that night the rains came in torrents. The roof waterproofing held quite well everywhere except for the master bedroom. The following morning he might well have ordered our whole team before a firing squad. Instead, he sent to England for experienced roofing contractors, while we patched it up as best we could.

In a few weeks we put the finishing touches to the governor's house and again we found ourselves waiting around for another building project. Our remaining duties were to clean up the campsite and take latrine sewage to a dump away from the camp. Our day of recreation was the Sabbath, when we would borrow donkeys from the neighboring Arabs and ride to Ramleh, and sometimes even as far as Tel Aviv, a two-hour journey. We would stop at one of the many Arab roadside vendors to enjoy the lamb kabobs grilled on the spot and wrapped in pita bread. The donkey rides were not too comfortable, but at least they accommodated a person of average height. A humorous sight was that of our tallest member sitting astride his donkey holding up his feet in front. He had "built-in brakes" because he could stop his donkey anytime he wanted by merely putting his feet down. Few of the rest of us had this sort of control over the animal's movements. One hazard in riding a male donkey was its violent behavior when detecting a female, even at a considerable distance away. The rider would then be thrown off; this discouraged some of our group from joining us on these trips.

There was no tent large enough for us to even get together to talk. However, when we did have a group discussion, which happened often, it concerned our growing dissatisfaction with the continuous work shifting from one project to another, the poor living and sanitary conditions, and the lack of communication with the Histadrut organization. We found ourselves arguing and differing over our goals to the point where we were all on edge and irritable. One outcome of this was the decision of Yedidia Yanovsky, the main theoretician of our movement, to leave the group. This came as a shock to all of us who had respected and accepted his guidance for the past two and one-half years. However, after much persuasion and the prospect of an interesting project, he agreed to stay on.

The Histadrut organization soon embarked upon a new venture involving us—the building of a suburb in the Judean Hills on the outskirts of Jerusalem to be called Tel-Pioth (hill of beautiful views). The place truly deserved its name. Rising thirty-eight hundred feet above the Dead Sea, it commanded magnificent views of the sea, the old sections of Jerusalem, and the surrounding valleys. We were surprised to learn that the houses here were to be built of sand-lime bricks, used in the Tel Aviv construction projects. We had expected that the building would be of the hard Jerusalem pink stone, as required by the Jerusalem building code. However, because the suburb was outside the city limits, it was allowed to be built of bricks. For us it meant learning a new facet of the construction industry and added a new challenge and opportunity to learn bricklaying, a trade that was to become a major factor when I started my life in the United States. Again we pitched our tents, this time in the mountainous landscape of Jerusalem. The tents provided dubious protection from the weather and were unbearably hot during the day and unbearably cold at night. The worst months were November, December, January, and February. The cold and damp from the rains were all-pervasive. After much complaining, the organization told us about a large unoccupied Arab house owned by an absentee landlord, located in a thicket of pine trees nearby. It did not take us long to clean it up, whitewash the walls, and fix the broken pump in the outside water well or to build a wooden outhouse some distance from the rear of the house. Kerosene lamps were used for lights. As was typical of most of the buildings—especially housing—there was no heating system.

We soon resembled a big closely knit family with all the advantages and disadvantages of such living. In all, there were thirty of us—eight girls and twenty-two boys. Six newcomers, including a girl, joined us in Jerusalem. They were interested in construction work and had asked to be assigned to our group, which had remained basically the group of Grodno Pioneers. In our summer "tent city" there were so few girls that their attention was sought by many suitors. In the evenings the boys would visit the girls in their tents. There were three girls assigned to a tent, which made courting difficult, since there was no privacy. Still, it seemed to me that the girls were the ones who chose their favorites. I was attracted to Sara, the sister of one of the original group members who had joined us in Jerusalem. Coming from a farming village near Grodno, she radiated wholesomeness and good looks. We hit it off well and our relationship, short of being intimate, was a happy one. There was an unwritten understanding among the three occupants of the tent that if one had an evening visitor, the other girls would stay away. One newcomer to our group, Aaron, a handsome fellow, immediately was sought after by all the girls. It didn't take very long before our Don Juan centered his attention on a very attractive and sexy girl, and a torrid love affair developed that ended in a joyous wedding ceremony—the first in our Jerusalem group. After a short time the couple left our group and tried their hand at starting a small farm on their own initiative. We later learned that this marriage broke up soon thereafter. The backbreaking work and the lack of financial support from the Agricultural Department drained not only their physical stamina but their marriage relationship. In spite of the hardships, he remained on the farm; his wife left him and went to Tel Aviv for nurses' training, and about ten years later she married my good friend Yedidia.

The brick houses we were building were of a higher quality than the stone ones in Haifa and those planned for the Yemenites in Rishon-Le-Zion. They were spacious one-story villas, architect-designed, built for government officials, bankers, professionals, and generally well-to-do people. Here we had to learn another branch of masonry brickwork. Our experience with stonemasonry served us well. Within a short time, with the help of a master mason from Tel Aviv sent by the Pioneer organization, we became proficient bricklayers. We were deservedly proud when the new owners complimented us on the fine workmanship.

A nearly tragic incident occurred during the construction operation. Arab workers were hired to help us with the foundation and carpentry work. Things were peaceful until one Arab got into a violent argument with a member of our group that ended in a fist fight. When the Arab broke away in the hubbub, several of us pursued him for about a quarter of a mile to the nearest village where we lost him. The village seemed almost deserted. All the men were either away in the fields or at work elsewhere. As for the women and children, we avoided any contact in order not to frighten them and we soon returned to work. As it turned out, this incident became a political scandal. The next day the local Arab newspaper announced that a group of Jewish immigrant workers had raided the village, raped women, and beat up anyone they could find. We immediately contacted the British authorities to deny these accusations, but despite these denials the British sent a squad of English and Arab policemen to our job site to arrest the culprits. With them came two elders of the Arab village to identify the pursuers. The elders falsely pointed to two of our best construction workers who had not been present or even part of the group that had chased the Arab. They were promptly handcuffed and carried off to a Jerusalem jail. To show how lightly the police really took the whole affair, however, they allowed the two men they had arrested to be exchanged for two other workers who were less essential for our building operations. In the next two weeks our leaders met with the elders of the village and both sides concluded that there had been a gross misunderstanding and that the fighting incident was blown out of proportion. The elders agreed to drop their charges so that the arrested men could be released immediately. We initiated discussions on how to avoid such confrontations in the future, explaining our peaceful intentions and desire to work together with them for the benefit of all.

The result of our overtures was an invitation by the elders to a party in their village to celebrate the "peace." Since the Arabs celebrate these events with men only, it was best for us to attend without the girls in our group. Ten of us arrived just before sunset. At the outskirts of the village we were met by several elders who led us to the garden of the *mukthar,* the village head. There we sat on small rugs in a semicircle. Part of this garden was planted with vegetables and part with flowers. About a dozen villagers joined us. As is customary, we were served strong Turkish coffee, and were also offered "arak" (an alcoholic drink served to non-Muslim guests). Conversation was difficult since they spoke only Arabic, and since our knowledge of Arabic was minimal we could manage only the usual polite courtesies and inquiries about the health of family members. We all were glad when one of the men stood up and invited us to join in a festive circle dance. It was a good ending to the meeting, and we all were pleased with the positive turn of events as we returned home.

My good personal relationship with the Arab co-workers led to an invitation by one of them to visit his home in Bethlehem on a Saturday. There was an unofficial understanding that Jews were not to visit that city, though I don't recall whether we knew that at the time. On the Saturday of our visit my friend Gershon and I mounted donkeys and set out on the two-hour journey to my Arab acquaintance's home. We enjoyed the picturesque road through a number of Arab villages, and past the Tomb of Rachel, venerated by both Arab and Jews. As soon as we entered the city, the hostile looks of the passersby, then derogatory remarks by a few Arab men, and finally the action of some children who started to throw stones at us, made it all too clear that we were unwelcome. Alarmed, we were ready to turn back when our Arab host appeared in the distance. Seeing our situation, he ordered the small but unruly crowd to disperse, apologized profusely for the behavior of his townspeople, and led us to his house. The main room was circular with a dirt floor. The only openings were two small windows on opposite sides of the room to let in some rays of light and for ventilation. This draft also fed the fire our host now started over a few coals in the middle of the room to brew the coffee. Meanwhile, several of his neighbors joined us and we all sat cross-legged on the floor around the fire. The smoke made our eyes tear, and everything appeared through a haze. In addition to the thick, strong coffee served Turkish style in tiny glasses, our host served "Arak." To serve the drink he cut several cucumbers in half, neatly carved out the inner part, and used them as glasses. He also sliced a watermelon in an ingenious way so that when he was through with his slicing operation, he could press his hand on top of the melon and it neatly fell apart so each person could take his portion. A stack of rounded pitas, the unleavened bread that is a diet mainstay of Mideastern people, was tossed expertly around the boiling coffee pot to each person sitting around the circle. Our conversation was cordial but formal—inquiries about personal and family health and other generalities. As we left, the host went into his little garden behind the house, picked out some fine eggplants, tomatoes, and cucumbers and presented them to us as a parting gift. He then walked with us to the outskirts of Bethlehem. As the twilight was setting over the hills of ancient Bethlehem, our emotions were high. What a contrast to our feelings of a few hours before. This visit brought to mind the wisdom of the biblical saying: "How good it is for brethren to dwell together!" It was a unique and gratifying experience in human relationship.

By this time we had completed the building of ten villas. Because there was a slowdown in new building contracts, some of us were assigned to a project of building stone houses in the suburb of Ein-Karem, on the opposite side of Jerusalem. To avoid having to look for new living quarters for ourselves, we hiked to our new project each morning and back late evening, a journey which took us several hours each way. The highway looped around the city and made a complete semicircle to the new work location. We found a shortcut by following a direct path over the mountains and through the intervening valleys. The distance saved was considerable, but the resulting exhaustion of climbing up and down the hills greatly reduced our efficiency at work. After a box lunch, which we carried, we had our siesta in the several tents temporarily erected near the site. The hot summer sun made the tents a furnace, further adding to our exhaustion. This work lasted several months and we were glad when this assignment was over, even though it meant another wait for work.

4

AMERICAN
IMMIGRANT
Detroit, 1923–1925

When I left Grodno for Palestine with my friends, my brother Sol had also become frustrated with the political chaos around him. In 1922 he was drafted into the Polish army and that was the deciding factor to run away. He crossed into Russian territory and from there he escaped to Germany, making his way to Berlin. I recall Sol's first letter from Berlin in which he told me of his financial difficulties. His dire financial straits made me realize the tremendous contrast in the directions of life taken by each of us. In our Pioneer group we were generally satisfied with the minimal basic needs of food and shelter. Money, as such, played no role in our daily life. The pocket money allowance was a pound (five dollars) a month and was generally spent on sandals and clothing. Most of us continued to use the clothing we had brought with us from Grodno, even though it was worn and threadbare. I was anxious to be of some help and sent him five pounds (twenty-five dollars), which I had saved. From Berlin Sol was helped to come to the United States by a maternal aunt and uncle who had emigrated from Bialystok, a city near Grodno, and were established in Detroit. They also wanted me to come to Detroit, though at that time I could not imagine myself leaving my friends and abandoning my ideals of rebuilding a homeland.

During my third year in Palestine, work in the building trades spurred my interest in further education in a school of architecture, but there was no such school locally. If I were to study in any of the European universities, I would need money to pay my way. Economic conditions in Europe in the early twenties were so bad that there was little chance of my getting a job that would pay enough for my studies. It was 16 March 1923 as I celebrated my twentieth birthday when unexpectedly I received a letter from Sol in Detroit urging me to join him.

His invitation sounded very tempting. He was certain that with my Russian high school diploma I would have no trouble being accepted in the nearby University of Michigan, which had a School of Architecture. He also thought that with my experience in the building trades, especially bricklaying, I would be able to earn enough money to pay my way through school. As for living arrangements, I could stay with him at my aunt's house until we could find larger quarters in the neighborhood. Going to the United States, being close to my brother and other relatives, seemed to hold the best promise for the future. After much thought and soul search-ing, I made my decision to leave. Making up my mind was only the first step, however. It was a long and complicated process to get an entry visa to the United States in 1923. The immigrant quota was small and very restrictive and only special categories such as clerics, students, craftsmen, and professionals were allowed. My last chance to receive a visa was to apply as a student. I went to the American consulate many times, dressed in my best wornout trousers and my old military jacket from my father's store in Grodno. With my wild and bushy head of hair, I probably looked more like an anarchist than a young student. The consul finally issued a conditional visa stating: "The applicant states that he is proceeding to the United States for the purpose of higher education. However, he is going at his own risk." The risk was the possibility of being turned back at Ellis Island.

When I told my friends about my decision they were dismayed, but they accepted it with understanding. They arranged a farewell party at a home in Tel Aviv the night before my departure. The evening was a mixture of gaiety and sadness. Everyone crowded into the small two-room apartment where we talked, danced, and drank wine until daylight. We shared our memories of the past three years, especially the narrow escape from the Arab mob at Ramleh. I felt that I was letting the group down by leaving, but I was anxious for new experiences and new horizons. I sensed a painful mixture of both good will and envy among my friends. By morning it was an unsteady but cheerful group that went with me to the dock to wave goodbye.

I was shocked when I boarded the ship. The first leg of my journey would take me from Tel Aviv to Marseilles, where I was scheduled to board a train to Cherbourg via Paris, and from there set sail for New York. Sol had bought the tickets through an agent for a combination passenger-cargo French liner, which called for a berth in a four-bed cabin. Instead, the purser led me to the steerage in the hold of the ship where hundreds of Palestinian Muslims going to South America were tightly packed into three tiers of bunks. There was hardly any space to move about, and the smell and filth were intolerable. My protests were to no avail. In desperation I offered the purser five English pounds, half of my entire fortune. He responded by taking me to the crew's quarters which were on a deck below. There I was allotted a hammock for sleeping. In all there were about ten hammocks suspended from the beam above. There was sufficient, but not very appetizing food. Canned meat, cheese, and olives were served every day. The best part was the French hard-crusted breads that were baked on board the ship. Because the weather was warm and the sea calm, I spent most of the uneventful seven-day journey on deck, walking up and down and talking to the sailors. From them I learned that the shipping company did a thriving business conveying workers fleeing the unemployment and hard life of Palestine for jobs in South America. The ship made short stops in Port Said and Alexandria, Egypt, then on to Marseilles. The French port was clogged with ships carrying every sort of goods and the port district bubbled with activity. Many of the emigrants rushed to the red-light district along the waterfront, where prostitutes from open store fronts offered their services for a few francs. Competition for business was keen whenever a new ship arrived. One can only guess how much venereal disease entered the new country along with these emigrants.

An agent from the company that had issued our tickets met me and several others as we disembarked and took us to a small hotel near the railroad station. This was clean and adequate for a night's stay, with a common shower and toilet at the end of the corridor. In the morning I took the train for Paris. As soon as I got off the train I was immediately confronted with a new world—quaint streets, wide and beautiful boulevards, and lively people in the parks and sidewalk cafes. I walked all day long without stopping except to eat the famous French *jambon* (ham) sandwich with its excellent crusty baguette. When I reached the Eiffel Tower in the late afternoon I was exhausted yet pleasantly surprised to see the Lebanese student and his parents whom I had met on the train from Marseilles to Paris. They were also on their way to the United States. We managed to communicate in my broken Arabic and his broken Hebrew. His parents, who seemed to be well-to-do, knew Paris well and invited me to join them for the rest of the day and evening. We dined together in a good restaurant, and I made another ecstatic discovery—the joys of French food. For the past three years in Palestine, food had meant only satisfaction of one's hunger— with the basics of bread, eggs, olives, fruit, vegetables—all doled out in minimal amounts. I never thought that a meal could give so much enjoyment. As the French do, I carefully sopped up the last drop of sauce with my bit of the bread. As the evening ended, my Lebanese friends and I parted in high spirits.

The travel agency had paid for lodgings in an unattractive cheap hotel and early the next morning I was on a train to Cherbourg with a group of immigrants. We reached Cherbourg only to learn that our ship would be five to six days late in arriving. This time, fortunately, we were given better hotel accommodations. The reason for this improvement, I surmised, was the company's recognition that they were dealing with European immigrants and not middle-eastern laborers, who were the majority of the cargo on the trip from Jaffa-Tel Aviv to Marseilles. The days passed slowly exploring the interesting old town near the port area, watching the six- to eight-foot tides wash in and out, my first such experience, because on the Palestinian beaches the tides were hardly noticeable. There was time to get acquainted with the other travelers and to make friends. One of them was Dr. Garies from Estonia who was also going to Detroit (I played an important role in his first years in Detroit, but this is another story).

Many men in our group were enticed by pimps who roamed the waterfront bordellos nearby. I was frightened and disgusted even by the thought of going with them, but if I had had any fleeting temptation, my Estonian doctor made sure that it remained fleeting. Instead, together we visited the library and the small but interesting museums and explored various parts of the city. We kept returning to the dock whenever we heard of the arrival of a ship. One morning a ship arrived from the United States. As the passengers disembarked, we eagerly surrounded them and bombarded them with questions about life in the United States. One Polish immigrant was anxious to talk. According to him, America was no place for people looking for the good life, and the food was bad. "Nothing tastes good like in Europe—the bread is sour, the fish tastes like grass, the fruit is awful, but worst of all the people are nasty." We later learned from an official that this man had gotten as far as Ellis Island, where he was detained for three months because of trachoma, an infectious eye disease. This incident created an anxious feeling that something similar might happen to us, but when all the documents had been checked and rechecked and all formalities completed, we boarded the ship with an excitement and anticipation hard to describe.

Once on board everyone became immersed in his own worries, the most immediate being the strict health controls at Ellis Island. The nine-day voyage to New York took place in a subdued atmosphere. The sounds of many languages reverberated in the air. Most of the immigrants on this ship came from Eastern Europe. There were Poles, Estonians, Lithuanians, Latvians. Yiddish was spoken as well as the language of each country. Many of them were families with children. There were also a number of older people coming to join their relatives who had preceeded them a few years earlier and were now established in their adopted country. Among the passengers was a Jewish businessman from New York returning from a visit to his family in Poland. He took an interest in me when he found out that I was coming from Palestine. He was astonished to learn about the pioneering work being done to reestablish a Jewish homeland. He asked how he could help me, and I told him that I was worried because I did not have the fifteen dollars I needed to show before being allowed to disembark, a requirement I had learned about during the voyage. After bribing the purser on the boat from Tel Aviv, my entire fortune, at this point, amounted to five dollars. He offered to lend me the necessary money, and since I had no security to give him in return, I insisted that he take my tefillin (phylacteries).[1] Although I was not religiously observant, these tefillin in a beautiful velvet pouch embroidered in my parent's shop had a great sentimental value for me. They were all that I had as a memento from home. He reluctantly accepted the phylacteries. In a few weeks he returned them to me by mail with his good wishes for my future.

When not worrying about the Ellis Island doctors, the immigrants talked about where they were planning to settle and the welcome they might expect from their relatives, many of whom they would be meeting for the first time. In my own case, except for my brother, I didn't know any of my relatives in Detroit—my mother's brother and his wife and a number of cousins. My uncle Louis was in the real estate business and my cousin Jack owned a haberdashery store. My brother had learned English very rapidly and was working in his store as a salesman. I was entering into a new mysterious world, but because I was coming to my brother and family members, I had no fears and mentally prepared myself to meet whatever situation would arise. The self-confidence developed in my three years in Palestine was serving me well as I approached the new land.

Our arrival in the "land of opportunity" on a misty April morning was not the festive event we had been anticipating. In the distance we could discern, with joy and trepidation, the Statue of Liberty. We docked some distance from Ellis Island and immigration officers came on board. After a preliminary examination of our papers, groups of immigrants were put into small boats to be taken for final processing on the dreaded island. As we landed, we were taken to a large hall lined with examining rooms. From there we could hear cries of despair from rejected immigrants—some with physical disabilities, some with diseases—many were found to have tuberculosis and trachoma, an eye disease that leads to blindness and very prevalent at the time in Egypt and the Middle East. In later years the physical examinations were done

---

[1] Tefillin are two tiny square leather boxes containing slips on which are written certain scriptural passages. One of the boxes is worn on the head and one on the left arm. The one on the head symbolizes our intellectual closeness to God; the one on the left arm, closest to the heart (the seat of emotions), our love for God. They are worn by males during the daily prayers (except on the Sabbath and holidays).

at the point of departure before visas were issued, but in 1923 this was not the case. Then came my turn. I passed the medical exam easily. The next hurdle was my student status. Because the American consul had not personally supported my statement of intent to study in the United States, I was fearful that the immigration officer would be suspicious of me. I had my high school diploma that helped my case, but what really impressed him—and he didn't believe it until I proved it to him—was my declaration that I was fluent in six languages: Russian, German, French, Polish, Yiddish, and Hebrew. He made me read passages from prepared test sheets in each of these languages and was finally convinced of my true statements. I also felt good about having fifteen dollars, the sum required of each person immigrating to the United States. In all, I stayed at Ellis Island for a half-day. Through all this excitement I forgot about food although I seem to recall that sandwiches and coffee were handed out.

Once processed, each immigrant had a tag pinned to his coat with his name and destination. An immigration officer escorted us by ferry to the Battery, the southernmost tip of Manhattan nearest to the railroad station. Special cars were designated for immigrants. I was placed on a train going directly to Detroit. It was a relief to have this unnerving ordeal over with and to have crossed the final barrier separating me from my road to a new life. As I made myself comfortable on the train, my exalted feelings were soon jolted by an unexpected experience. No sooner had the train started moving when a vendor approached each passenger and put a tiny bag of peanuts in front of him or her. All of us took for granted that this was the way the American government welcomed its newcomers, with free peanuts. Another hour passed and our joy increased when the same man placed a small box of candy in front of each of us. The "angel" then disappeared for another hour. During his absence most of us were still pleasantly surprised by such generosity of the American government. As time passed and the salesman didn't reappear, we timidly started to open the chocolate boxes. Then came the real letdown. The man showed up again, this time with a money changer attached to his belt and asked for $2.00 from everyone who had unwrapped his box—which meant most of us. This incident left us upset and wondering whether we made the right choice in coming to a country where such tricks were practiced on unsuspecting newcomers. The effect of this experience was a sobering one for the rest of the journey. The twelve-hour train trip to Detroit was tiring and gloomy, with everyone immersed in his own thoughts and concerns for the immediate future.

I arrived at the Michigan Central Station near downtown Detroit in late afternoon. Hundreds of well-dressed people were milling about; loud speakers boomed out the arrival and departure of trains. For the first time I felt self-conscious about my patched-up military jacket. I was also feeling rather lost in this crowd, since no one was there to meet me. I had not sent a telegram to my brother relaying the time of my arrival because when we were transferred from Ellis Island to the New York Central railroad station and put on the train, we were rushed along to be on time for the departure. Also, I did not know how to go about sending a telegram. I wasn't too concerned because I thought it would be exciting to surprise my brother and relatives. Ready for this adventure, I walked out through the great glass doors of the station and saw a streetcar coming with a sign in large letters, "Detroit." I immediately boarded it, confident and proud that I could manage by myself without knowing a word of English. I later learned that all streetcar signs read "Detroit," with smaller lettering indicating the particular destination. At any rate, this streetcar was going downtown, where I got off in the middle of heavy traffic, with no idea where to go from there. I wrote down the address of my aunt, with whom my brother was staying and showed it to a policeman directing traffic. The policeman walked with me to the proper streetcar and told the conductor where to let me off. It was 504 Englewood, just off Woodward Avenue, one of the main thoroughfares, about four miles from downtown.

When I got off I found a pleasant middle-class neighborhood, with tree-lined streets and well-kept homes. With mixed emotions and deep apprehension, I started down the street. After several blocks the magic number 504 appeared. With bated breath I rang the doorbell. After what seemed an eternity, the door opened and a black woman stared at me with amazement. Nothing had been said about my arrival, and when she saw an unkempt, young stranger with a knapsack (not to mention my jacket), she was ready to slam the door in my face. When my aunt came to see what the commotion was about, her first words in a mixture of Yiddish and broken English were, "My poor, poor boy! Did you think that black woman was your aunt?" I had heard that the Americans thought all new immigrants were "greenhorns"—ignorant and stupid persons, but I didn't expect to experience this attitude from a relative. Also the words "poor, poor boy" shocked me because I never thought of myself as being poor, for in Palestine old clothes and worn shoes never meant being poor. I was ushered into the living room that was furnished, as I later found out, in the 1920s American fashion—an oriental carpet, upholstered love seat, and several easy chairs. Window curtains were elaborate patterned lace and two floor lamps with fringed shades and a coffee table completed the furnishings. Several large family pictures were hung in the living room over the couch. After three years in a tent, this was quite a change for me. The maid served coffee, tea, and homemade cake, a great treat, while Aunt Fannie telephoned my brother at work with the good news. She showed me around the house, switching on the electric lights, turning on and off the hot water taps, and so on, to demonstrate the wonders of American technology. We had enjoyed all these technological wonders at home in Grodno, but I thought it best not to say so and was properly impressed. My brother Sol arrived within an hour, and we had an emotional reunion with tears and embraces. Sol, still unmarried, had changed very little in the past three years. He looked as young and dapper as ever, and in my eyes, even more so in his up-to-date American outfit. He wore a striped, dark blue double-breasted suit, a starched white collar shirt, and a silk-patterned necktie. What a contrast to my worn military style jacket. As the news of my arrival spread, my American cousins Jack and David, Aunt Fannie's children and their wives, joined the gathering, anxious to hear all about my experiences as a Pioneer in Palestine.

The next day started the process of my "Americanization." First there was a trip to the barber, then to the clothing store and shoe store. At the end of the day I didn't recognize myself . . . I even had on a necktie, the despised symbol in our kibbutz which we called in Hebrew "dag moluach" or the "salted herring." The wearing of a necktie signified in our eyes a person who did not make his living with physical work and hence had little in common with the kibbutz philosophy of life. Salty herring was a term used to express our derogatory feeling. I felt somewhat uncomfortable in my new outfit, although when I looked at myself in the mirror I was pleasantly surprised.

In the first few days, Sol and I began to think about a change in living arrangements. It was good for Sol to have stayed here the first year, but to have two young men to be concerned about we felt would be an imposition on Aunt Fannie. There were a number of rooms for rent in the neighborhood, and after several weeks we moved across the street. This arrangement gave us more freedom to come and go. Close ties with the family continued with the regular Friday night Sabbath dinners. I began to think about the kind of work I could do to earn a living and, at the same time, get experience in American construction practices, for I had definitely decided by this time that I wanted to study architecture. My family was shocked when I told them that I wanted to start as a manual laborer in the construction industry, but when they understood that this was temporary and would serve as a preparation for my future study of architecture at a university, they were satisfied. The next day I bought a pair of overalls, work boots, and white canvas gloves. My cousin Jack and I drove to one of the construction sites on the west side, in the Linwood-Chicago Boulevard area where luxury apartments were being built.

Jack explained to the foreman that I had just come from Palestine, had worked there as a mason, and was anxious to start on any sort of the work. My main handicap, he added, was that I did not speak English. The foreman hired me as a water boy, carrying drinking water by pail to the thirsty masons on the scaffolds. I also dragged heavy planks for scaffolds to other areas as the work progressed. Just a few days of this hard and boring work had a depressing effect on me. The family also disliked seeing me coming home dirty and exhausted at the end of the work day. In discussing this problem, everyone agreed that to become a bricklayer I would have to join the union. Jack volunteered to take me to the union headquarters and talk over my problem. When the union representative asked whether I belonged to a bricklayers union in Palestine, I produced the only card I had, which was membership in the General Workers Organization, the Histadrut. Although the card was in Hebrew, the union man accepted my explanation and issued me a union apprentice card good for three months, after which I was to take a bricklayers exam. This was a lucky break for me since the usual waiting period for an apprentice before taking the exam was four years. If I passed, I would receive full union wages, one dollar fifty per hour, one of the highest rates in the construction industry. Even my new apprenticeship rate of ninety cents was higher than what was paid in the carpentry, plastering, and mechanical trades. In the auto industry the average rate for union male workers was eighty-six cents per hour for a fifty-hour work week.

The union local assigned me to a location in the Linwood and Clairmount area where luxury apartment buildings were under construction. The first step in apprenticeship was getting adjusted to the American techniques. I learned that there were two master bricklayers, one placed at each corner of the wall. They would first build up the corners plumb and level to the required height. A cord line then would be stretched between the corners for each brick course. Between the corner men, there would generally be six to eight bricklayers filling in the entire course in line with the cord. They had to finish before the corner men would raise the cord for the succeeding course. At the bottom of the scaffold was the foreman whose job it was to see that the line was moving upward as fast as possible. His yells of "line up" sounded all day long. In an eight-hour work day under this pressure each man laid between 1,400 and 2,000 bricks, an exhausting effort. For comparison, in the 1980s a bricklayer lays about 500 bricks per day. This lower production level was brought about through the continuing efforts of the union to improve the working conditions as well as to provide more employment for its members.

In early September 1923 my three months of apprenticeship were over. The foreman was reluctant to raise my wages to full union scale because of possible resentment among the bricklayers who might be jealous of my rapid advancement. I decided to leave this job and answered one of the many ads for bricklayers in the newspaper. I was hired to work on a Catholic seminary complex in the same neighborhood. My crew was made up of mostly Irish, Poles, and a few blacks. We were to build the chimney stack of the power house for the entire complex. The higher the stack rose, the more difficult the work became, as the flimsy and inadequate scaffolding shifted dangerously with every gust of wind, making us cling to it in terror. The work generally was backbreaking and exhausting, but I had been conditioned to hard outdoor work by my three years in Palestine. There was also a "bonus": free time, although unpaid, when it rained. In the morning, or at any other time of the day, the foreman would send everyone home after an hour wait for the weather to clear. This was much like a vacation time—involuntary and unpredictable—but it allowed me time to read and study.

At this time I decided to enroll in special evening classes for immigrants in one of the public schools nearby. The teacher Mrs. Ryman took a personal interest in us and arranged get-acquainted meetings with American students. Her idea was to have each American student "adopt" a new immigrant as a special friend. Because of my high school background and my knowledge of several languages, she chose Clemence Van de Sande as my sponsor. She was from a Dutch-Italian family. Her upbringing taught her to help others and to welcome them into her home. Clemence, who was eighteen and a senior in high school, was not only kind and understanding, but was also very attractive. At a time when an immigrant was usually isolated from social contacts with American people, her father (who might be said to have adopted me) and her brothers took me to their Presbyterian church services, and included me in their family gatherings. I was a special favorite of Clemence's mother, who called me her "little prince." With all these new friends, my English improved rapidly and when Mrs. Ryman offered to give me free private tutoring in addition to the classes, I progressed even faster. My friendship with both Mrs. Ryman and her lawyer-husband lasted many years.

Along with my language classes, I enrolled for evening courses in blueprint reading, which were offered by the Detroit Institute of Technology. The instructor Frank Riley, an engineer in his sixties, was construction superintendent for the new Buhl office building in the downtown area. Teaching the evening course was his hobby. He was devoted to his students and took a personal interest in all of us. In his classes I became familiar with the American building system, the terminology, available materials, standard sizes, measurements—it was completely new to me. There I was introduced to the two-by-four wood stud—the mainstay of residential construction in Detroit. Mr. Riley also taught the estimating classes and elements of foundation design and drafting techniques. He recommended me as a bricklayer for the Buhl building when my job at the seminary was completed. We became good friends, a warm relationship also lasting many years.

My work on this twenty-seven story high-rise building in 1924 provided many tragic as well as unusual experiences. Little attention was paid to the workman's safety in the construction industry in the early twenties, as I mentioned earlier. Insufficient and unsafe scaffolding and lack of barricades around floor openings, elevator shafts, and other openings were the norm. There was a predictable fatality formula in the trade—one killed for each floor built. If one floor was built without mishaps, the workers "expected" two accidents to occur on the next floor. In one instance, a worker fell through an unprotected elevator shaft twenty floors to his death. Work stopped only briefly in the vicinity of the incident. The pressure exerted by the foreman to resume work pushed the shock of the fatal accident momentarily away. Other accidents occurred on exterior scaffolding. One-plank scaffolding was substandard even in the 1920s when scaffolding of at least two planks wide was required. The workers suspected that the contractors would rather pay for the accident insurance, which was cheap, than to provide proper scaffolding, which was expensive. At this project, where almost two hundred workers of the various trades were employed, there was always an ambulance kept waiting at the street level for the daily casualties.

I remember especially one incident at the Buhl building. I was assigned to work with a master mason applying terra-cotta ornamental facing around the steel columns on the first floor. He would set the terra-cotta facings to the front, while I backed up his work on the interior with brick. We did not realize that the derrick used to lift the heavy terra-cotta sections had been placed on planks that had been laid out earlier for a truck roadway leading into the interior of the building. The work progressed without incident for a few days, until a truck drove over the planks. The weight of the truck on one end raised the planks and tipped the derrick. It fell a few inches from me and crashed onto the head of the stonemason, killing him instantly. A tragic note was added to the man's death. When three of his close friends went to notify his wife of the fatal accident, they found a birthday cake with candles lit and the family waiting for him. It was his fifty-fourth birthday.

A second incident at the Buhl building nearly ended my bricklaying career and my life. The decorative terra-cotta on the outside of the windows had to be pointed up with mortar (to fill in the cracks between the adjoining pieces). These windows were on the upper floors, eighteen to twenty stories aboveground. The contractor did not want to build special scaffolds outside each window. Instead he devised an inexpensive substitute. A plank extending out the window and resting on the window sill was anchored down to the floor inside the building. It was on this projecting single plank that the bricklayer was expected to walk out on, slowly turn around, and begin work. Because I was short and light, I was assigned to this task. I climbed onto the plank, walked slowly out, and turned around cautiously to face the window. A laborer inside the opening would hand me a small pail of mortar and a special pointing trowel. With my back to the street, the pail on my left arm, I put the mortar on the trowel and started to point up the joints. The first few days things went smoothly. I learned to balance myself on the single plank, measure my steps, and concentrate on my work. One morning while stretching my arm up to reach a higher spot over the window, I bent backwards slightly too far and for a fraction of a second tottered in the air. Some instinct must have helped me jerk forward again and regain my balance. It took me a whole week to recuperate physically from a badly strained back and emotionally from that frightening ordeal. My brother and aunt were very disturbed by this harrowing experience, and there was much talk about changing jobs to a safer place.

While I was considering a change of occupation, an unexpected advancement in my status came about, as a direct consequence of this near accident. Mr. Riley offered me a very important job. The Buhl building was built around a courtyard, which was to provide daylight to the surrounding offices. For maximum reflective light in the ten-story courtyard, walls were to be faced with white glazed bricks. The laying of these bricks required special skill because the mortar joints were very thin and were called "buttered" joints—each brick was "buttered" with a thin layer of mortar before being laid. The superintendent assembled a team of six qualified bricklayers, older men, experienced in this type of work. I was the seventh and the least experienced. The team was composed of three husky Irishmen, two Poles, and one Italian. This was a friendly group, anxious to teach me the fine points of this special work, and with their help I soon learned the intricacies of this type of brick-work. After we had been at the job for several days, the union steward showed up and announced that according to union rules a group of seven bricklayers required a foreman. All the bricklayers stoutly refused to assume this promotion, even though it meant an additional ten cents per hour, or one dollar and sixty cents rate for the foreman. One of the men finally hit on a solution: "Let Louie be the foreman!" Horrified, I protested vehemently that I did not know enough about the work to take charge of the operation and that I would be embarrassed to give orders to men twice my age. "Never mind" said they, "We will teach you how to be a foreman and you'll soon find out why we don't want the job." For a week they helped me master this new skill. Then one of the men developed a nervous quivering in his right hand and could not align the brick courses properly. When Mr. Riley saw the situation, he told me that it was my duty to dismiss the man from the job. To soften the blow he promised that the man would be transferred to less exacting work in the same building. While I was hesitating, the man himself approached me. He had foreseen that his handicap would lead to his dismissal, and this, he said, was the reason why neither he nor the others had wanted to be foreman. I began to realize what responsibility meant in decisions involving co-workers.

My relationship with most of the fellow bricklayers was generally good, though some of them resented that I never accepted their invitations to join them at a nearby bar after work. I explained that I had to save every penny I could for my tuition—evening classes now and eventually college. They argued that by saving money for education, I was not contributing to the economy of the country and that what I spent at the bar would help keep America prosperous. There was more to this than their joking words conveyed of course—perhaps resentment of my ambitions or that I saw myself differently. Discussions at work on the scaffolds centered mostly on sex lives with wives or girlfriends. However exhausting our work, it did not seem to affect the supply of sexual fantasies and desires. One man used to brag that for the last twenty years of his marriage he had never missed one night of lovemaking. The lunch break was one-half hour, but most of the workers emptied their lunch boxes in about fifteen minutes, to leave time for girl watching on the street below, with guesses as to which girl was a virgin, as well as giving ratings for sex appeal.

Meanwhile my night classes in English with Mrs. Ryman were helping to improve my vocabulary. All I heard during my working hours was talk peppered with profanity. Son-of-a-bitch, shit, and other four-letter words were used repeatedly. It was one of my embarrassing moments when I asked Mrs. Ryman the meaning of these words. She had a good laugh at my naivete. The evening courses with Mr. Riley at the Detroit Institute of Technology had taught me the technical terminology, giving me the background for the first year of the university architectural course.

5

ARCHITECTURE STUDENT 1925–1929

It actually seemed that my dream in Palestine might become a reality after all. In August 1925, after two years of construction work, I had saved enough money to register for the fall semester at the University of Michigan, the only university that offered a bachelor's degree in architecture in the state at that time. I put on my best American suit and, with my diploma from the Russian gymnasium in Grodno safely tucked in my pocket, I took a bus to Ann Arbor to apply for admission to the College of Architecture. With trepidation I watched my papers being examined by the registrar. To my great delight, he accepted my documents from Grodno and even allowed me college credit for some language, mathematics, and literature courses, a total of one semester out of the standard four-year course. However, in September when I was trying to get settled in Ann Arbor, my enthusiasm flagged. Over and over, in neighborhoods near the campus, I was told that there were no rooms available even though "For Rent" signs were displayed everywhere. After numerous rejections, I finally realized that nothing was for rent to Jewish students. This revelation was shocking and disillusioning; in my innocence I had glorified Ann Arbor and assumed that as the home of a great American university it would reflect the same ideals. The word "university" in my mind signified "temple of learning" in surroundings free from prejudice and biased beliefs. I finally found a small rooming house farther from campus where three upperclassmen and another freshman already lived. Our landlady was a wrinkled elderly widow, who was strict with her roomers. She kept her house in perfect order but rarely smiled.

My first year was difficult, and it may be surprising that the hardest thing of all was probably putting up with being a freshman. First-year students had to wear special caps called "pots" and were harassed in all sorts of ways by upperclassmen. A freshman could be stopped at any time of the day or night and "ordered" to sing, or crawl on all fours, or perform other demeaning acts. In my rooming house the three upperclassmen, for lack of other entertainment, were always scheming to play some trick on me and the other freshman. Once they told me they had arranged a blind date and presented me with two tickets to a concert. The blind date turned out to be my cross old landlady. After the first shock and disappointment of this "date," we decided to enjoy the situation as best we could. For me, the music helped get over

71

the embarrassment of the fifty-year difference in our ages. For my date, the concert was a pleasant surprise that she actually enjoyed. This joke provided material for weeks of kidding and teasing.

My adjustment to the academic life was not difficult, even though I was more than seven years away from my high school days and four or five years older than my classmates. Much more distressing was the attitude of some of the Gentile freshmen toward Jews. The first greeting I received from the student who was to share a double-drafting table with me was "Hello Abe." Fortunately, this was not typical of the rest. Even though I had endured some racial slurs when I worked with the bricklayers, I did not expect anti-Semitism from fellow university students. The warm camaraderie we developed in Palestine and the pride we took in working for an ideal had made me contemptuous of prejudice. After the initial hurt feelings had subsided, I decided to concentrate my energies on studies. Consequently, I developed long-standing friendships with my instructors that lasted years after graduation. Professor Nelson in the English Department saw greater maturity in my assigned compositions than in those of the American high school graduates. Also my spelling of English was unexpectedly good because of my knowledge of Latin and French, and this always amazed him. John Fisk, my math professor, found time to discuss not only trigono-metric and calculus problems with me, but also subjects relating to world problems and politics. On occasion Professor Titcomb, who taught architectural design, invited me to visit his home to see his collection of prints and books. His approach in teaching design was in the classical idiom, which followed the style of Greek and Roman buildings, and was prevalent in the design of public and government proj-ects. However, he also encouraged innovative ideas, which was fortunate for me because I had been attracted by the contemporary ideas of the Bauhaus School that had recently emerged in Weimar, Germany.[1] The Bauhaus movement proclaimed its principles in 1919. "Architects, painters and sculptors must recognize anew the composite character of a building as an entity. . . . Together let us conceive and create the new building of the future, which will embrace architecture and sculpture and painting in one unity." This integration of the arts in buildings reflected my thinking, which I put into practice when I opened my own office.

In our English and math classes there were some assignments to prepare, but most of the work consisted of design and drafting projects that were done in a large drafting room at the school. We often spent much of the afternoon and evening there, sometimes until the early hours of the morning. In these years part of my architec-tural education consisted of copying and rendering (in color) the Greek orders of architecture—Doric, Corinthian, and Ionic. It was a thankless task: in my desire to achieve perfection on these renderings there was no limit to the last-minute touches. What was missing was a more creative and forward-looking philosophy on which our designs could be based. On the positive side though, the long nights spent in the drafting room laboring over our drawings eventually created a friendly atmosphere in which the students got to know each other and carried on lively discussions on

[1]In 1925 the Bauhaus was transferred to Desau and in 1933 it was closed by the Nazis. In 1937 a new Bauhaus—the Institute of Design—was founded by Laszlo Moholy-Nagy in Chicago. This center, under Mies van Der Rohe, was to become the extension of a new direction in architecture and industrial design.

every subject imaginable. Coffee and doughnuts were brought in regularly, each student taking turns as host. On some occasions, either because of exhaustion or revulsion against the dull exercises we were working on, the room "exploded" in horseplay. Using the drafting boards as shields, one group would try to drive the other out of the room with a barrage of missiles—erasers, pencils, drawing materials. The university administration retaliated by closing the drafting room at ten o'clock in the evening, which really was a punishment since it did not allow sufficient time to complete the design assignments.

Some practical jokes played by the students on each other were cruel. The finishing of a set design problem was always a festive occasion, anticipated with relief and hope for a good mark with a few days of rest before the new assignment. A finished project was laid out on the drawing board on the last night, ready for the critique by the jury. The jury of three design professors stopped at each board, examined the renderings, and made comments on the quality and the techniques of the presentation. The students followed the jurors around and were encouraged to ask questions. On one occasion, just before the jurors arrived, I went to my board and saw my finished design lying there splattered all over with ink spots! When my classmates saw my despair they were hilarious. The ink blots were made of plastic superimposed over the drawing.

Deadline pressures of the weekday assignments were lightened somewhat on the weekends. There was an occasional movie on Friday night. It took my classmates several months to persuade me to go to a football game. I was sure it was sheer foolishness, but once I attended a game and saw the colorful crowd, the marching band, and the rest of the exciting hoopla, I was hooked on the game for the rest of my life.

Occasionally, I traveled to Detroit on weekends to visit my brother Sol. After his haberdashery closed at nine o'clock Saturday night, I would pick him up, and we would stop at a deli for a corned beef sandwich, and then go to a late movie. On Sundays the two of us would have a leisurely breakfast with Dr. Meyer Glick and his family, with whom my brother lived. Their house was near Palmer Park where we sometimes went skating. Hotdogs and coffee were a real treat on those cold Sundays, and I would return to Ann Arbor on the late bus, rested and ready for the work of the week ahead. In Ann Arbor one of my favorite diversions was ushering at the Hill Auditorium concerts. There were many applicants for these jobs, but fortunately I was recommended by my classmate Bob Blakeslee, the head usher. In addition to enjoying the excellent symphonic and concert artist's programs, I also was permitted to go backstage to meet and talk with the soloists, and sometimes, with the conductor. I especially remember how excited I was when I learned that one of the Chicago Opera singers, Rosa Raisa, was born in Bialystok where some of my maternal relatives were living. I introduced myself, and her face lit up when I told her that my mother also came from Bialystok. She was anxious to hear any recent information I had on her native city.

In looking back at my freshman year, my English studies remain one of the highlights. The themes of my compositions were generally interesting to the professors because I wrote of my experiences, quite different from those of the average freshman. My knowledge of French and Latin, as well as German, helped me to express philosophical thoughts clearly in English. Another positive development was my membership on the gymnastic team. It brought back the good memories as well as the physical skills of the Maccabi gymnastic club of my high school days in Grodno. Unfortunately, I had to drop out of the team at the end of the freshman year because of the heavy academic work load.

On the negative side, there was my remaining feeling of isolation from my classmates. Reasons for my reaction were several. I was four years older than most of them. In Europe and the Middle East I had had many varied and even some dangerous experiences. Most important, however, was the fact that social life on campus was dominated by national fraternity and sorority cliques. Membership was very restricted. Jewish students as a rule were not accepted as members, which excluded them and many others from campus social life. This limited their opportunities to establish lasting friendships with students of different backgrounds. In my freshman architectural class of one hundred (all men but one) there were only two Jewish students. In the 1920s few Jews chose to study architecture or engineering because they knew that they would have difficulty finding jobs in these fields because of prevailing prejudice. This depressing feeling of isolation drove me to fill in whatever free time there was with optional freehand drawing and watercolor painting classes in the art department of the architectural school. The instructors there, unlike my classmates, were interesting and friendly. Professor Jean Paul Slusser, the head of the art department, liked my watercolors and encouraged me to develop my talent further, which cheered me considerably.

During the first summer vacation I stayed with my brother in Detroit in Dr. Glick's home. I went back to bricklaying work immediately. I was fortunate that I could count on getting work whenever I needed to save money for living expenses and the next year's tuition. My earnings for the twelve weeks of summer work amounted to about six hundred dollars. This was sufficient to cover the tuition fee of seventy-five dollars, the room rent of five dollars, and forty dollars a month for food and incidentals. Although the working day left me tired, I still missed the companionship of friends who would enjoy and share common interests. Evenings were dull and depressing, except for occasional dates with my friend Clemence. I remember walking the streets around downtown Detroit, feeling very lonely and dejected. I resisted the temptation to strike up an easy acquaintance with some woman at a bar to relieve my loneliness. One evening in my wanderings I came across a sign that read: Detroit Society of Arts and Crafts. Curious, I walked in and the receptionist referred me to a young sculptor, Samuel Cashwan, who was teaching a class in life drawing and sculpture. He asked me to stay until the class was over and then we had a long discussion on the value of studying art as a part of an architectural education. We both believed art should be an integral part of the total building design—in interior as well as exterior surroundings. We sensed an immediate closeness in our values and in our personalities, and so began a friendship that has lasted over sixty years. I readily accepted his invitation to work in his studio on Jefferson Avenue. From then on all my evenings, weekends, and free time were spent studying sculpture in his studio.

Sam Cashwan was about my age—in his early twenties—and had come to New York City as a boy with his family from Kiev, Ukraine. After studying art at the

Architectural League, he went to Paris to work with the famous sculptor Antoine Bourdelle. Returning to the United States, he joined his family in Detroit where they had settled. He became the head of the sculpture department of the Detroit Society of Arts and Crafts; this position enabled him to have his own studio and accept private commissions. Cashwan allowed me complete freedom in my studies with him. Twice a week we drew from nude models, my first such experience. I was apprehensive that I would be embarrassed or physically excited in a life class—being close to the model, able to examine the varied and often beautiful intricacies of the female body. However, I was so engrossed with making a presentable drawing that the model could have been any object. I also modeled from plaster casts of portraits or figures. In the use of clay for sculpting figures from models, I experienced a joy in the tactile pleasure of transforming the pliable material. This began an exciting period of utilizing my newly developed skill. I found no shortage of volunteers to model among my friends or their children, and in the months ahead there were a succession of portraits—Betsy, Lillian, an Indian friend, Asad, Clemence, and the children Nora and Maida. A number of years later I made a portrait of my father, which became a lasting, cherished memory for me.

Cashwan had "magic fingers" and worked with intense nervous energy. When a clay figure finally satisfied his high standards, it was cast in plaster. I quickly learned the procedure and acted as helper, assistance which he heartily welcomed. Cashwan's natural talent had been recognized by many awards and scholarships. One of these scholarships took him to Paris where he won a gold medal from the French National Academy of Art for a large white marble figure called "Interlude," now part of the Detroit Institute of Arts permanent collection. I also assisted him in designing appropriate bases for several of his public commissions located on Belle Isle. These were my first architectural projects involving the design of a base for a figurative composition. During the summer I made two clay portraits of children. It was a great satisfaction (and surprise) to me that my head "Nora," daughter of an acquaintance, was accepted in the Michigan Artists Annual Show at the Detroit Institute of Arts that fall. The chaotic disorder so typical of an artist's studio did not take away from the warmth of the atmosphere on Jefferson Avenue. There was always classical music played in the background on an old phonograph. Cashwan's wife Vera came often to keep us company and brought a supply of homemade cookies. This chance encounter and the resulting friendship with Cashwan and his family made what started out to be a dull and depressing summer one of my most enjoyable and productive experiences.

Back in Ann Arbor that fall I began to realize the importance of my summer's work in sculpture. I knew I wanted to learn more about the other visual arts, so I chose for school electives life drawing and watercolor painting. Once a week the class was taken out into the countryside to paint from nature. We had a talented and understanding instructor, Professor Alexander Mastro Valerio, who encouraged his students to develop their own style and direction, assisting only in the technique and theory of color and perspective. Yet I missed the experience in the three-dimensional visual art—sculpture—I had enjoyed so much with Cashwan. My expectations of spending the next summer in the same studio were dashed when he showed me the eviction notice he had received from his landlord. The building was to be torn down and he had to be out by the first of the year. He would be moving to another studio, but he assured me that I would be welcome to join him wherever he might be. During frequent weekend visits from school that fall, I helped him finish his projects. Articles not worth keeping were set aside. What I did not know was that he intended to have a big "burn up" New Years Eve party. The highlight of the party, attended by many of his friends, was the breaking up and throwing into the large fireplace the useless pile of "junk," as well as the old wooden derelict chairs, benches, and tables. It turned out to be an unforgettable party mixed with sadness and hope, with many farewell speeches and toasts to the future.

One catastrophic incident occurred in my junior year that nearly changed my future life. I cannot believe (and neither can anyone else who knew me then or now), that I would be capable of such reckless foolishness. In my third year of school, architectural design was the most important course to pass. At the end of the semester when the professor collected and marked all the completed designs, he kept them locked in his room on the second floor for safekeeping before the grades were announced. The curiosity of the students, including mine, reached a fever pitch, each one daring the other to climb up the outside of the building and enter through the window to get a look at the marks. Late at night with another student I climbed through the window, entered the room, and looked at the marks. News of this stunt reached the authorities the following day and after long deliberation by the architectural staff, my companion in the crime was expelled and I was put on probation. That I was a foreign student and in the top scholastic rank probably saved me from expulsion. Had I been expelled, I doubt whether any other school would have allowed me to complete my education.

I particularly enjoyed the classes in our senior year associated with the studies of structural and mechanical engineering (heating and cooling). The new science of acoustics had just been added to the architectural curricula. We all had a good laugh in class one day when the professor declared that good acoustics in an auditorium depended on the proportion of men and women present. His thinking was that women had twice the sound-absorbing capacity of men.

In the advanced courses, even though the contemporary designs I submitted were accepted by my professors, the dean of the school, a man named Emil Lorch, thought otherwise. He called me into his office and told me he did not care for the modern approach I followed. He also stated that he thought he detected the possible influence of the style of ancient synagogues. It was clear that he disliked any hint of such a derivation in a design and that his dislike was based on its Jewishness, which was enough for disapproval. On another even more revealing occasion he called me into his office "just to talk." He told me that he was worried about the "Purple Gangsters," a group of Jewish criminals active in Detroit, as well as with the underworld activity of Jewish individuals elsewhere in the United States. I was so amazed at his emotional tirade that all I could say was "What does this have to do with me, an architectural student?" He did not answer, but said he was glad to see more Jews going into the profession and assured me that, personally, he had no prejudice against them. I walked out of his office, shocked and speechless. To me, architecture was and still is a forward-looking and positive profession, devoted to creating a better living environment for all people, an environment in which prejudice certainly has no place. Prejudice also showed itself in what should have been a joyful, rewarding event. Because of my scholastic record I was eligible to become a member of the national honorary architectural fraternity, Tau Sigma Delta. The induction always took place at the end of the spring term, but I was to graduate in January. My fellow students were surprised when I did not receive notification of election by the fraternity committee and they offered to find out the reason. A week later I learned they had been told I had completed the four-year course in three and one-half years and that I would not be on the campus for the spring graduation ceremonies so I was not eligible for the honor. The excuse was so obviously absurd that when it was exposed, the committee reversed the decision.

It was January 1929 when I graduated from architecture school. I was determined to visit my parents and relatives in Poland once my education was completed. It had been nine years since we parted, and I knew that once I started to work as an architect it would be difficult to take time off for such travel. I wasn't worried about getting a job in an architect's office since the economy seemed to be booming. (No one in their wildest imagination could predict the stock market crash later in the year that would create financial havoc and hardship throughout the country.) I had to leave in April since I especially wanted to spend the spring Passover holidays with the entire family, which meant I reluctantly would have to forego my graduation ceremony and the Tau Sigma Delta induction in Ann Arbor.

Sol and I were anxious to make this visit we had been planning for several years. Both of us had become American citizens at the end of the required five-year residence, Sol in 1927 and I in 1928. When I left Poland in 1920, Lithuania had sovereignty over the Grodno area. I held Lithuanian citizenship and was not subject to the draft for the Polish army. By 1921, however, Grodno had become Polish territory, and Sol had been drafted into the Polish army. He left the country to avoid military conscription and now was afraid of being caught and forced to fulfill his Polish army service if he returned. We had heard that Russia and Poland reserved the right to conscript returning former citizens into the army.

6

EUROPEAN INTERLUDE AND THE GREAT DEPRESSION 1929–1933

Alone with my two suitcases filled with gifts for the family, I took a bus to New York City. There I would board a ship to Cherbourg, France, for the first leg of the journey. In New York I was looking forward to staying with my friend Gershon, a former Detroiter who had moved there and was recently married. When I arrived I went with my bags to his apartment in midtown Manhattan. He greeted me warmly and introduced me to his wife, an attractive and stylish young woman. The small apartment was tastefully furnished and gave the impression of comfortable living. We spent a pleasant evening catching up on news of our friends. When the hour was nearing midnight, and no suggestion was made that I stay overnight, I left for the nearest YMCA. I was surprised and hurt at this lack of hospitality since this was a new experience for me. In Israel, hospitality meant being invited to stay overnight, whether in modest city apartments or in tents of the kibbutzim. As I had several days of free time before my ship left, I made an effort to see the art museums, the ethnic sections of the city, the Lower East Side, Chinatown, the Bowery, Wall Street. The Metropolitan Museum of Art made a great impression on me—the Egyptian, Babylonian, Assyrian, Greek, and other ancient art collections, as well as the contemporary sculpture and painting were overwhelming. It was exciting but exhausting to try to soak in so much in so short a time. I promised myself to continue this learning process and return whenever I could.

By the day of my departure, from leisurely tourist I had become again the worried traveler. To save my limited funds I decided to go to the docks by subway. With my two heavy suitcases in hand, I struggled through the turnstiles and stood up the half-hour trip in the crowded car. It was a great relief to reach the boat and get settled in my cabin in tourist class. To my surprise my cabinmate was a student from Ann Arbor who had lived next door to me for three years. We had never met before. The passengers formed a motley crowd—salesmen, French women who had married American soldiers in the First World War returning to visit their families, many Italian immigrants on a visit back home, some college students out for adventure. The main fun of the trip was watching romantic involvements develop among the most unexpected couples and gossiping about them freely in the lounge, discussions lubricated by visits to the bar. There was also some frolicking in the balmy evenings on the upper decks with people (including me) stretched out next to each other in deck chairs, with lap robes offering privacy for all sorts of "undercover" activities.

At Cherbourg we boarded a train to Paris. Because most of us knew each other now, the trip resembled an outing with friends. A young French woman, wife of a G.I. who was returning to visit her parents, sat next to me. Although our conversation was lively on the surface, it had undertones of romance. An incident changed this innocent atmosphere. On one of the train stops to Paris, a street vendor who was selling Persian woven blankets approached our compartment window and, taking for granted that we were man and wife, started to expound the special qualities of the blanket, how nice and warm it would be when we snuggled under it together. These suggestive remarks immediately produced a different atmosphere between us; we held hands and hoped for a possible meeting in Paris. By the time we reached Paris, a feeling of guilt got the upper hand and we parted as friends. I also avoided renewing my contact with the two girls I knew from my "undercover" acquaintances on that boat because of the tales they had told of their past sexual experiences. These implied cured venereal diseases, though both appeared to come from upper-middle-class homes, and I would have thought them "nice girls" had I not heard their stories.

The first thing I wanted to do in Paris was to look up a distant cousin, a medical student at the Sorbonne University who lived in the Latin Quarter. He was related to me through my mother's family; his family lived in Bialystok. By the time I found my way to his neighborhood it was late evening. In looking for someone to direct me to his address, I came across an elderly man reading a newspaper in front of a street lamp. I walked up to him and in my broken French asked for directions. He looked up and said in a few French words "I can see that French is too difficult for you. Choose any of the European languages. I happen to be a professor of western languages at the Sorbonne." When I explained to him in English that I was looking for my cousin who lived in the area and that I could not find the street in the complex labyrinth of the Latin Quarter, the professor said "I'll take you to him." After he led me through a maze of streets, he stopped at an old run-down five-story building. Here my cousin lived on the top floor. We walked up darkened stairways and knocked on his door. To my deep disappointment there was no answer. The professor took it calmly. "It is already eleven o'clock, so I'm sure your cousin should definitely be here by midnight," he said. "Let's go out to have an aperitif. There is a little Hungarian cafe nearby and we can chat and listen to violin music." And so we did. After an hour of pleasant conversation we went back to the apartment. This time it was Aaron, a young man about twenty years old, who opened the door. The professor announced formally, "I have the honor to introduce you to your cousin from America." He then told me that he had enjoyed my company, and without giving me time to thank him and express my appreciation for his kindness, he took his formal leave. Aaron seemed very moved by my unexpected visit and embraced me warmly. His small studio apartment was a typical student's sparse lodging—one large all-purpose room for studying, eating, and sleeping with a small kitchenette containing a gas stove and sink off this room. The shower and toilet facilities were down the hall and shared with other students. He hastened to make a pot of coffee, and (this time) I was invited to stay overnight. Even though we both were tired, we talked for several hours about our families and mutual acquaintances and made plans for the next day. It was my second visit to Paris and I was beginning to feel quite at home. After we visited the Louvre and the Rodin museums, I could see that Aaron was not an art enthusiast. He finally confessed that what he really wanted to do was to go to an American movie, which he could not afford on his meager budget. This was my opportunity to play the role of the big-spending American host.

The next day I took a train to Warsaw. My brother Wolf, his wife Pola, and their five-year-old son Samuel met me at the station for our first reunion in nine years. The neighborhood where they lived was nearly all Jewish. The streets were crowded with hurrying people. Peddlers with handcarts or horses and wagons were calling out their wares. They sold everything from fresh fruits and vegetables to pots and pans and old clothes. They offered to buy anything from potato peelings to antiques, whatever the tenants wanted to sell or get rid of. Many Routenstein relatives lived in this neighborhood or nearby. Three of my paternal uncles had married Warsaw girls and raised their families there. The oldest uncle, Ephraim, had a special embroidery shop where he and several assistants produced insignias and epaulettes for the higher military ranks, a business like my father's. He was also a respected elder in the main synagogue. My other two uncles were struggling merchants. My brother Wolf lived with his wife and his two young sons in her parents' fourth-floor apartment. His mother-in-law Mrs. Gurwich was a domineering woman who kept tight control of the entire household. Wolf was a bookkeeper and with his modest income could not afford his own apartment. Besides, whatever savings he was able to accumulate were spent on his gifted son's musical education. Their financial sacrifices paid off when years later the boy was accepted in the prestigious Conservatory of Music in Warsaw, where he was the only Jew. The Gurwich family, father and two sons, manufactured a high-quality candy. (In 1941, when the Nazis occupied Warsaw and herded all the Jews into the ghetto area, their expertise in candy making prolonged the Gurwichs' lives for a few years.)

There were only two days before the start of the Passover holidays. Wolf, Pola, and Samuel were preparing to come to Grodno with me. We went on a shopping tour together to buy a new set of Passover dishes for my parents. These dishes, according to Jewish dietary laws, were to be used only on Passover. I also bought gifts for my parents and my sisters Elsa and Riva, who were living at home. My brother Yakov and his wife and their five-year-old daughter were coming from Suwalki, a border town near Germany, to join us for a family reunion on the Passover holidays in Grodno. I had gifts for them as well. A joyful and tearful reception awaited us at the train depot in Grodno. My parents, sisters, and many family friends were there. My father had aged considerably in the nine years, his hair grayer, but he was looking spry and cheerful, and as always was rather quiet. My mother, never showing her fragile health, was tender and kind, her eyes shining with happiness. My two younger sisters whom I had left as children were now pretty teenagers. Only my older sister Riva looked serious and appeared lonely amidst all the merriment. As for me, I had come back to a Shangri-la of love and belonging. I realized how much my visit meant to each of them, as well as how much they meant to me.

As happy as I was to be home, it was sad to see how the general situation had deteriorated. My father's military store was still operating under the Poles, providing similar services as they had for the previous Russian and German occupation forces. It was a hand-to-mouth operation. In Warsaw Wolf acted as a buyer for the small

amount of merchandise my father needed. Yakov had opened his own military sup-
ply store in Suwalki about eighty miles north of Grodno. My youngest sister Rosa, as
I mentioned previously, was on her way to Palestine as a Pioneer. My sisters Elsa and
Riva had no hope for a decent future in Grodno, either for a job or getting married.
Neither had a dowry, without which beginning a married life—renting an apartment,
or starting even the smallest kind of business—was out of the question.

After I had left for Palestine my family moved to an apartment over their store.
It was always kept neat and tidy, but for the Passover holidays every nook and cranny
had to be cleaned and floors scrubbed so that not a crumb of bread (called *hometz*)
remained in the house. The new dishes we brought delighted my mother. All were
now ready for the festive first and second evenings (seders) of Passover when the
youngest of the family asks the traditional four questions, the first of which is, "Why
is this night different from all other nights?" My father presided over the table laden
with the special herbs and foods, symbolic of the exodus from slavery in Egypt: the
bitter herbs a symbol of the bitter conditions of the four hundred years of bondage;
the matzos, unleavened bread, reminders of the hasty departure; the mixture of
chopped nuts and apples darkened with wine representing the mortar of the bricks
the Israelites used. My father read the Haggadah telling the story of the Passover
holiday, with everyone singing the traditional songs and raising the wine glasses four
times in toasts.

It was May and for several days I stayed close to home, telling stories about my
adventures in Palestine and the United States. Here and there I had free time to look
for interesting subjects to sketch in the "old neighborhoods" of my childhood—the
courtyard of the old apartment, the banks of the Niemen River. I had brought with
me small sketch pads about four inches by six inches and a small metal watercolor
set that could fit into a coat pocket. It was a pleasant surprise for the family to see
their familiar places through my sketches. When I did start to look up my high school
classmates in town, I discovered that almost all were gone. Most had emigrated.
Albert, one of my high school classmates who did remain, came to see me. He was
the son of a wealthy flour mill owner. This family, two sons and three daughters,
lived in comparative luxury, and Albert, a handsome and eligible young man, had
the pick of the beautiful girls. He, like everyone else, was curious about life in
America. He was surprised that I had not married an American girl, while I was
surprised that he had not married yet either, since there were so many attractive and
eligible girls around. Albert complained that their mothers were exerting so much
pressure on him that he could hardly bear it. One mother was so determined to
marry her beautiful daughter to Albert that she made arrangements for intimate late
evening rendezvous in her own home. Albert confessed to me that she had almost
succeeded in trapping him, but her attempt backfired as the affair became a matter of
open gossip for the entire Jewish community. (I met Albert again twenty years later in
Mexico City, where he immigrated and had become a wealthy man through banking
and investment in Mexican industries. He had married a young wealthy Mexican, a
Catholic girl who had studied in a convent school in New York, so in the end he did
escape the mothers of Grodno.) Along with hearing about Albert's romantic adventures, I wanted to find out what had happened to a girl named Sarah with whom I
had once been infatuated. I remember her as slim and blond, very attractive and
feminine. She was called by the endearing name of Sorele. She was still living in

Grodno with her parents, and as I approached her house my heart was pounding. The door opened and there she stood, looking as lovely as I had remembered her, though now a full-bodied, mature woman. It was a reunion with kisses and tears. She told me that she had been married the previous month and that her husband had left for Argentina to establish himself in business, after which he would send for her. During this visit I spent as much time with Sorele as possible under the circumstances. It took no time at all for us to realize that we were still greatly attracted to each other. During our long walks, hand in hand, in the gardens of the park and along the banks of the Niemen River, our passionate feelings became almost uncontrollable, but she held back. She told me that "If I am unfaithful to my new husband with you, when you leave I will not be able to hold back with anyone else." I soothed myself with the chivalrous thought that I cared too much for Sorele and her future to cause her guilt and pain—but who knows if the lack of privacy was not the determining factor? These small communities were like fish bowls and we could hardly carry on an illicit affair there on the river bank.

After this romantic interlude, I visited relatives and friends of the family and several high school friends. We took long hikes through the pine and birch forests along the Niemen River to the resort village of Lososno, about twelve miles away. We stopped midway at a farm we all knew, where city people could get a special treat—milk fresh from the cows, with fresh baked black bread and homemade butter. Life in America was the main topic of our conversation. My friends' lives were uneventful and monotonous. Most were unemployed and there was a general feeling of frustration and hopelessness. In my family my sister Riva was partly occupied with tutoring students in German and French. Elsa, on the other hand, spent much of her time visiting with her friends. Sometimes they went to movies or an occasional theater performance. Few could afford to continue their education after graduating from the gymnasium, and even if one could do so, very few Jews were admitted to the Polish universities, which had a limited Jewish quota. There were some jobs for young Jews as clerks in the stores or offices, but city and government jobs were reserved for Poles. There were several girls in our group to whom I was attracted, and under normal circumstances the dating that I did would have led to a serious relationship, but I suspected that the enthusiasm of these girls toward me was stimulated more by their desire to marry an American citizen and emigrate to the United States than by my personal charm. At any rate I was not home long enough for such matters to come to a head.

Throughout my stay my mother kept busy preparing my favorite dishes. The appetizing aromas from the kitchen, special meatballs and potatoes fried with onions, chicken soup with matzo balls, potato pancakes, cinnamon flavored yeast coffee cake, all brought back pleasant memories of childhood. During my visit my father and I went to Sabbath services in the Great Synagogue of Grodno, where he served as an elder. I was given the honor of reciting the weekly portion of the Torah. My father was very proud that I had not forgotten the Hebrew text. Most of his time was spent in the store. Our conversations usually took place around the dinner table. The main meal was around two o'clock, and at the end of the day there was a late supper. My father was amazed to learn that Sol and I owned a car, which to him was a symbol of great wealth. He could not comprehend that in the United States owning a car was possible for almost everyone with a job. Sol and I together, saving for two years, were able to buy a new Model T Ford for five hundred dollars. Then I told my father about our tragedy: three weeks after we had achieved the American dream of becoming car owners, our new car was stolen in front of a friend's house. It was like losing a member of the family, I had told him. This situation was so new to my father, like a catastrophe from another world, that he was horrified. I hastened to assure him that after the required four-week wait, the insurance company had provided a new Model T, and he could relax again.

In June, towards the end of my three-month visit, I started to brush up on German and French as I was planning to visit Austria, France, and Italy on my way back to the United States. My older sister Riva, the language teacher, was my tutor. The lessons seemed more like refresher courses to me as I had a good high school background. I was soon able to carry on simple conversations. Part of my success with languages was due to Riva's excellent training. (She herself had attended the University of Toulouse for two years.) Sol and I thought that she should join us in Detroit where she could find work as a secretary for some international corporation. When I discussed this with her, she was enthusiastic, and I promised then and there that we would work on it when I returned to Detroit.

The last few days before my departure were the hardest to bear as my parents put up a brave front and tried to carry on their daily routine as though nothing was going to change. But the departure day arrived. The station was a brisk twenty-minute walk through two main streets. Two horse-drawn carriages were hired to carry the immediate family and baggage. The rest of the relatives and friends followed on foot, walking about as fast as the carriages. Waiting for the train to arrive was painful. Minutes seemed like hours and I must admit that I was impatient to get all the sad partings over with. Friends of my sister and my parents stood in small groups, conversing together. They tried to lighten the sadness of my parents, so evident in their faces. They, meanwhile, watched me intently and seemed to resent any moment I spent chatting with others. In the back of our minds we all had the same fearful thought, Would we ever see each other again? Finally the train arrived. In contrast to my last departure in a freight car, this was a shiny, newly equipped passenger train. This was one aspect that cheered my parents, who remembered well the first parting. So it was that when I boarded the train, after saying the final good-byes, I was torn between a desire to be with them, but at the same time, anxious to leave this hopeless environment. As the train pulled out of the station, I saw my parents through misty eyes, bidding me farewell. I stopped in Warsaw again to see my brother Wolf and his family before going on to Vienna.

One of the highlights of this visit was going with Wolf to swim in the fast flowing Vistula River on the outskirts of the city. Wolf was an excellent swimmer and we cherished the short and pleasant outing. On the third day of my stay, which was the Sabbath, we all went to the Great Synagogue. My uncle Ephraim honored me by calling me up to the bimah to recite the blessings for the weekly portion of the Torah, which the cantor read from the scroll (the first five books of Moses). My reading pleased my uncle, who feared that "the American melting pot" might have "melted" my Hebrew. Another sad parting at the railway station, with Wolf, his wife, and five-year-old Samuel. Sol and I wanted to help him come to the United States, but he refused. What he wanted was a loan to start his own bookkeeping business—this was his dream—but I had no such funds available. He also felt he had to stay near my parents to help with the store.

I recalled the tumultuous departure from Warsaw nine years before with my Pioneer friends and our arrival in Vienna. This time Vienna had a much friendlier welcome for me. Instead of a "reception" in a delousing station, I went to a fine hotel with furniture upholstered in red velvet, almost too luxurious for my taste. A few days of sightseeing in this beautiful city and then on to Venice. This time there were no curious children following the immigrant with tattered clothing, but there was one curious incident. On the train from Vienna a young man in his thirties who was from India sat next to me. It was his first trip outside his country and he felt helpless. He was worried about where he was going to stay and all the other travel details. He made real the expression "to travel light"—he had a large briefcase containing two shirts, two pairs of socks, and a set of underwear. A very expensive camera completed his luggage. I wanted to be helpful, but not to the extent of being his "nurse-maid," and I tried to discourage his dependency on me. However, chance worked in his favor. When we arrived in Venice, we went to the same hotel. I had my room reserved, but he did not. There were no vacancies in the hotel, and somehow I found that he was sharing my room. As soon as we closed the door, he undressed and started to wash his underwear, shirt, and socks. I decided that there was not much I could do without causing an uproar, so I left him doing his laundry. I wandered for a while through parts of the city where I thought I would be free of his company, but he found me after a short time in an out-of-the-way piazza. After a two-day stay together in Venice, our schedules called for taking the same train to Rome. On the train ride I brooded over various schemes to get away from him and finally told him that I was going to stay with friends in Rome. This solved the problem of sharing a room with him again, or even staying in the same hotel. At the station we said good-bye and parted. Two days later, however, we met at the Coliseum. He ran up to me and embraced me as a long-lost friend. He also gave me his address in India—he said he was the son of a Maharaja and invited me to be his guest anytime I was in India. I have not yet taken him up on that.

In Rome the new sights I had read about exceeded my expectations. St. Peter's Cathedral, the Vatican, and Michelangelo's Sistine Chapel were the highlights, though I missed much of the exquisite details of St. Peter's Dome, as my attention was focused on a young Italian girl standing next to me. I thought that she was like a Leonardo da Vinci portrait come to life. I followed her without attracting her attention for several hours—to the Arch of Titus and to the Catacombs, where I lost track of her. The "earthy" attraction of that day was in contrast to the visit to see Michelangelo's Moses the next day, a truly spiritual experience for me. Another happy memory of my stay in Rome was of the pension where I stayed. My room faced the gardens of the Villa Borghese. The family treated me like a friend and did everything to please me. Each morning their twelve-year-old son, who had the face of a Michelangelo child angel, brought me a breakfast tray. Outside, a strolling violinist played his one song "O Sole Mio" to awaken me. A tossed coin was his reward; he was my favorite "alarm clock." I find myself often recalling this short but delightful stay. My memories of Rome still remain vivid in the many sketches I made exploring the city. Invariably when I would find a promising subject to sketch, it would attract youngsters from the neighborhood, curious to see what I was drawing. I still have warm feelings about these youngsters. I recall a touching incident. One day when surrounded by these young children, I needed to refill my water can. When I showed them the empty can, they all ran to get water. Within a short time they returned, each with a can of water and each feeling they were helping with the painting.

I took the train to Florence to see the famous Renaissance buildings I had studied in the History of Architecture classes. The impact of the buildings, especially the Pitti Palace, overwhelmed me—and even the lodgings to which I had been directed turned out to be a former palace being run by a widow as a pension. The original furnishings had been left intact—paintings, wallhangings, marble statuary, and gilded wall paneling. I felt as though I was a guest in the palace instead of a paid visitor. It was a perfect setting for a romance, and all the ingredients were on hand; staying in the next room was an attractive American girl who also had just arrived. We hit it off right from the start and planned our sightseeing ventures together. She was a rabbi's daughter from Philadelphia and was brought up with strict moral standards. We both resisted temptation to become more than mere fellow sightseers.

Paris was the last stop on my way back to Detroit. After the Louvre, the Rodin, and the Luxembourg museums, I spent a day visiting the artists' quarters in the Montparnasse area. I wanted to contact Jacques Lipchitz, then a struggling sculptor in his thirties. He had come to Paris as a young man from Druskeniki, a resort town near Grodno. His young brother Paul had been in my gymnasium graduation class, and when I was visiting at home he had asked me to contact Jacques, which I promised to do. However, Jacques was not in his studio and I didn't get to meet him at this time. (It was not until 1966, thirty-seven years later, that we were able to meet at Hastings-on-the-Hudson near New York City. He had become a world renowned artist, surviving the Nazi occupation of France by escaping to Spain and later to the United States.) I wandered into other studios that were grouped around a large open court in his building. The artists were friendly and one painter invited me to have a coffee. I learned from him how hard the struggle was for artists to survive in the current 1929 economic slump. It was difficult to get works into galleries and there were few buyers, especially for new, unknown artists. It was evident from my new friend's surroundings that there was little money for even basic necessities. Again as the "rich" American in Paris, I invited him to spend the evening with me at the Cafe de Dome, a place frequented by artists. The discussions on cubism and impressionism lasted until early morning. I learned about important galleries to visit, some out-of-the-way museums, and interesting old neighborhoods not usually seen by tourists.

Browsing among the artists' stalls along the Seine River, I replenished my sketching supplies—a metal watercolor box with a water flask small enough to put into a coat pocket. Every stop was an invitation to make a quick ten- to fifteen-minute sketch. These sketches developed my skill and focused my attention on details that otherwise I would miss. (Sixty years later, sketch pad and watercolor kit go into my pocket whenever I leave for a trip.)

Sol had driven the ten-hour trip from Detroit in our reliable Ford auto to meet me in New York. We spent a few days with friends, relaxing and swimming at Jones Beach. Sol was depressed to hear about conditions in Grodno, and both of us tried to think of ways we could be of help. I had much to tell him, especially about our parent's precarious economic situation. We talked of bringing them to the States, but because of the unhappy experiences some of our friends had in bringing over their parents, the idea didn't appeal to us. In many cases the immigrant parents lived isolated in an apartment and saw their children infrequently. Sometimes the parents found companions from their hometown, but this "transplanting" could be a very difficult and often lonely experience. In some instances parents were even contemplating returning to the Old Country. We could not, of course, foresee in the fall of 1929 the catastrophe of the Holocaust. Who could have imagined such tragic events?

I got back to Detroit to find a euphoric atmosphere and every expectation of continued prosperity. Tales of "killings" on Wall Street abounded, as well as of many "instant millionaires." I got a job with the prestigious architectural office of Albert Kahn Associates as a draftsman, but not for long. The stock market crash came and with it began the Great Depression of the thirties with its unemployment, bread lines, broken families, and suicides. Shantytowns filled with homeless men sprouted up along the Detroit River. Albert Kahn Associates and other major architectural firms laid off most of their staff, retaining only the key people. There were no unemployment insurance laws, and workers were left to fend for themselves.

For a short time I worked for Frederick Howell, an English-born architect who specialized in custom-designed homes. I was his only assistant, so that I had to learn the whole range of architectural services from conceptual drawings through final working drawings, letting of contracts, and supervision of construction. My salary was thirty-five dollars per week, less than half of what I earned as a bricklayer, but I considered myself very lucky, especially since construction had nearly come to a halt and there was no demand for bricklayers. At that time graduate architects were happy to start in architectural firms as apprentices either without pay altogether or at a stipend of five to ten dollars a week. The demand for custom housing diminished rapidly and in eight months I was out of work. It was a time of hopelessness and despair for most young men, but our situation could not compare with the tragedies in families with children who were used to a decent living standard. Under the strain many breadwinners simply disappeared, and their deserted families had to depend on the meager support from state and city public welfare departments. The lines outside soup kitchens and shelters became longer each day.

My interest in art came to the rescue in these depressing times. I rented a one-room studio on the third floor of a walk-up building in the 1300 block of East Jefferson Avenue, not far from the city center and just north of the Detroit River. It had two high dormer windows with a view of the sky. The furnishings consisted of a cot, an easel, a small table, and two stands for clay. For paper, clay, and paint supplies, there was a large storage closet. The toilet facilities were in the hall, serving my studio and a large room across the hall that was used for exhibitions by the artists in the building. Periodically we staged art shows on Saturday nights, with the public and press invited. These art openings usually ended in a great party. Most of the money from sales was used to pay for wine and food. My watercolors and pencil sketches were priced from five dollars to thirty dollars. Even the most successful show would not come close to making any of us rich. Other artists had their studios nearby, and the area was known as Detroit's "Latin Quarter." The Quarter was comprised of half a dozen older rundown apartment buildings. During the Depression many middle-class tenants could no longer pay their rents and moved out. The landlords were anxious to get some income from the property, and the attraction of these buildings to artists in the thirties was the low rental—about twenty dollars a month, which included heat and light. The caretaker of our building acted as custodian of the premises, knew the artists personally, and watched out for strangers. Artists would go together to the river to sketch the shacks made of scrap materials built by homeless men along the riverfront. These satirical paintings made the shantytown a symbol of the Great Depression. The *Detroit News* published one of my paintings entitled "Modern Living Quarters in Detroit," and a still life of mine was accepted in the annual Michigan Artists Show at the Detroit Institute of Arts. These acceptances gave me confidence at an otherwise bad time: if I could not be an architect, too bad—perhaps I was really an artist, after all.

We in the Latin Quarter worked a lot from nude models. There was no shortage of volunteers for the glamor of being sketched by an artist. On one occasion my model brought along a girlfriend. They had recently graduated from high school and were unemployed, so they posed for two-figure sketches. What made these sketches unusual was that I combined the best features of both, the torso of one model with the legs of the other. Later, when the sketches were exhibited, each girl claimed the figure as her own portrait. The daughter of a friend, Tanya, a lovely teenage girl who was eager to model, can be described in the words of my diary of those days: "Is it just an alluring trick of fate, or will it mean happiness and recovery from the terrific slump I have been going through lately? Something tells me it is going to be 'paradise'! How unexpected! Only yesterday I thought of her as a possible model—would her mother permit her to pose in the nude? I have a persistent but hazy fantasy about her as a lover. Lovely, fragrant body, already a woman at fifteen. The conversation with her mother—I remember her worried face when she said, 'But don't you think that posing will take away her last vestiges of modesty and nothing will be left of the maiden shyness that is still necessary to have?' Watching the mother's sorrowful face, I almost regretted the arrangement." Quite unexpectedly, when the modeling sessions started, I became so absorbed in trying to draw the image of her body on canvas that my sexual fantasies became of little importance. After several modeling sessions she no longer showed up for our appointments. I was shocked to learn later from one of my friends that she was disappointed I had not made any sexual advances and had found a lover elsewhere. In our Latin Quarter, where artists, models, friends, visitors, and art lovers were together constantly sharing similar interests, it was natural that affairs would flourish. Some relationships were a passing fancy; others ended in lifelong attachments.

At one Saturday night artists' party I was introduced to Mary, a visitor from Washington, whose sister had a studio in our building. Mary was a delegate to the National Educational Conference being held in Detroit. We were immediately attracted to each other and found that we had many interests in common. As we talked about our hopes for the future, I told her about my fear that any lengthy absence from the practice of architecture would be disastrous for my professional future. I had begun to think seriously of going back to Palestine where there was much building activity in progress. My friend Yedidia and others were writing, urging me to come. However, I was delaying making any changes. Mary, on the other hand, was a well-paid administrator for a national educational association and was happy with her work. Despite our diametrically opposed situations, we felt very close to each other. In the evening Mary said she wanted our relationship to be complete, and we spent a memorable night together, thinking that we would probably not be together again. She returned to Washington. In the year that followed we wrote to each other until the announcement of her marriage to a prominent federal official in Washington. In 1933, just before my departure for Palestine, I visited Washington. Mary and her husband received me warmly. They introduced me to a number of congressmen and government officials at their club. We again talked about Palestine and of my hopes to open an architectural office in Tel Aviv. This was probably the first time most of these politicians had heard an up-to-date first-hand account of British-mandated Palestine that was to become the new state of Israel fifteen years later in 1948. In 1935, while I was still in Palestine, I heard nothing from Mary and wondered what had happened to her. To my dismay, my letter to her was returned with a note from her housekeeper: Mary had died in childbirth. The day this news came the family with whom I was sharing an apartment was celebrating the birth of a baby, a coincidence that made this sad news even more poignant.

Since returning from visiting my family in Poland, the thought of bringing our older sister Riva to Detroit persisted. The delay in making the plans was not the lack of funds—we had sufficient savings to pay for her travel expenses and to help her get settled. The only way that she could enter the United States under the quota from Poland was as the wife of an American citizen. In the back of our minds we hoped we could introduce her to one of our bachelor friends with whom she might "hit it off." Harry Lawson, a writer, was interested in going to Paris to meet her, and we were willing to pay his expenses. There was no obligation to marry unless both liked each other. Language was no barrier since Riva was fluent in English as well as French and German. Fortunately, the couple seemed to like each other and they were married in Paris in a civil ceremony. Their first few months in Detroit seemed happy, full of expectations and hopes for a new life. However the marriage did not work out and they were divorced.

It was a difficult adjustment for Riva. After her divorce she offered to keep house for Sol and me. We rented a three-room apartment on Taylor Avenue for twenty-five dollars a month. Riva slept on a couch in the living room and Sol and I shared the one bedroom. In the beginning she occupied herself with the housekeeping chores. She was able to create a warm attractive atmosphere with very little money. Even more important, she knew how to prepare all the special dishes my mother used to serve. For an educated woman, however, with a thorough knowledge of five languages and a deep interest in world affairs, household duties alone were not sufficient for a satisfying life. After several months, she was happy to be hired as a French teacher in a private school.

The first summer of the Depression (1930) had some positive and happy moments to be remembered. Because apartments were standing vacant by the hundreds, our landlord allowed us to leave our furniture in the apartment on Taylor for July and August, rent free, while we and several friends rented a cottage at Lake Orion about thirty miles away. While working in the city we stayed with our good friends the Glicks. Upon returning to the city in September the landlord allowed us an additional two months free rent, a privilege accorded new tenants. Life at the cottage, with minimum expenses, was temporarily free of worries. Whatever money was needed was drawn from our meager joint earnings. Sol and I came on Sundays and for our vacations. Riva was our "manager." The free days, for the most part, were spent in boating, swimming, and reading. On Sundays the cottage was filled with friends from the city, some of whom stayed on for several days. And I had time to make watercolor sketches, hiking miles to find interesting subjects before discovering that what I was searching for was at the doorstep of our cottage. Lake Orion itself consists of a number of small islands that could be reached only by boat. To explore the waterways was always an intriguing adventure.

Employment opportunities were still scarce when in the fall of 1931 the U.S. government rapprochment with the Soviet Union brought to Detroit a technical mission to work with the Ford Motor Company to assist in designing automobile factories and other industrial complexes for Russia. The advertisement in the local papers called for engineers and technicians with knowledge of the Russian language. Although my knowledge in the technological field was limited, I applied for the job because of my knowledge of Russian. I was hired and assigned to translate complex automotive engineering manuals into Russian. For half a day I struggled with my first assignment and decided I was not sufficiently familiar with the Russian terminology. When I told the supervisor that I was quitting, his reply was "Don't be a fool. None of us knows more than you do. Try again." Luckily, after several difficult days, I was transferred to the architectural department that was working on designs for auto factories for various parts of the Soviet Union. There were about twenty of us in this department, mostly Russian engineers and architects, several Detroit architects, translators, and office managers. The language barrier and a delay in getting final approval from the department heads in Russia slowed down our progress, and the work lasted until 1933. At the end of two years the Soviet mission, called Autostroy, was ready to transfer the major design operation to Russia, leaving only a skeleton crew in Detroit. The Americans on the staff were invited to go there too, and a number did. The Russian offer of a contract at high wages with a promise of good living accommodations for several years seemed very attractive.

In essence, our work at Ford's was the forerunner of a much larger deal between Ford and the Soviet Union. In addition to the engineering technical services, Ford assisted in securing the services of the large industrial architectural firm, Albert Kahn Associates of Detroit. This firm set up an office of several hundred professionals in the Soviet Union. The office remained there for five years, completing a large number of automobile factories. I chose to remain in Detroit. If I were to make any move, it would have been to Palestine where I still was in contact with close friends from the Pioneer days.

While working at Ford for the Autostroy, I witnessed a tragic incident in Detroit labor history. The offices of the Soviet mission were located in the huge River Rouge Ford plant in Dearborn in a two-story renovated office building just back of the main entrance gate. From the windows facing Miller Road, the main artery, we saw an unusually large crowd approaching. Demonstrations and protest marches by unemployed auto workers took place frequently at the gate. However, this Hunger March of 7 March 1932, organized by the Unemployed Councils, had a special sense of urgency. A rally had been held in Detroit the day before and on the following day five thousand unemployed workers marched down Miller Road toward the Ford employment office. They were confronted at the outskirts by the Dearborn riot police who demanded their marching permit, which they did not have. When ordered to turn back, the workers tried to push their way forward. The police responded with tear gas and high pressure water hoses. At the same time the Ford security police appeared with guns drawn and started to shoot into the crowd. Four people were killed and a fifth died the next day. Among those killed was a seventeen-year-old boy. The newspapers reported that nearly a quarter of a million people took part in the public funeral procession up Woodward Avenue to Woodmere Cemetery. According to the Detroit newspaper accounts of events the week after the killings, over fifty people were arrested for being on private property (the Ford grounds) and rioting.

7

ISRAELI ARCHITECT
1933–1937

With the completion of the Autostroy project in Detroit in early 1933, I again started to look for work. Construction was nearly at a standstill, and no bricklaying jobs were available. My sculptor friend Sam Cashwan recommended me to a design firm specializing in automotive hardware. The assignment was to develop new ideas for door handles and other various hardware items connected with the automobile. Because of the Depression, all the highly paid designers had been laid off and the management was looking for low-pay help. I found myself the only person in what had previously been a department of about fifty people. Despite my inexperience, I did develop several interesting designs, my main contribution being an innovative plaster casting method for preliminary studies. Still, it was a complete departure from the work for which I was trained. Being alone in a large room filled with forty-nine empty drafting tables, benches, and desks, without anyone to discuss and share ideas with became depressing and boring. I made up my mind to quit this job, even though I knew I would have difficulty finding any kind of employment in Detroit, one of the hardest hit industrial cities in the nation. At the same time I was receiving letters from my friends in Palestine urging me to return. They were confident I would have no trouble finding employment in the continuing building activity there. After much soul searching and inner struggle, I decided this was the time to make the move. It was a hard decision to leave Sol and Riva, since we were a very closely knit family. However, I considered it a temporary move.

To accumulate sufficient funds for travel and for several months of living expenses in Palestine was not easy. Much of our savings had been lost in the October 1929 stock market crash. However, Sol and I continued to add to our savings in the bank over the next several years. In April 1933, when I was ready to take my departure, our bank closed and I could not withdraw my money. (The Detroit area was experiencing runs on the banks since January 1933, as people lined up to withdraw their savings to live on during the long drawn-out period of unemployment. In 1931, 1932, and 1933 there was neither social security, nor unemployment benefits. The local and state welfare funds were depleted and aid was minimal. On 5 March 1933 Franklin D. Roosevelt, by presidential decree, ordered all banks closed.)

The only asset I had now was a life insurance policy, and I immediately applied for a loan on it. After waiting with trepidation for several days, I received a check for $600.00. I cashed it immediately, which was not a day too soon.

After Riva and Sol saw me off at the bus station for the night journey to New York, I planned to rest on my overnight trip. It turned out differently. I was seated next to a young attractive woman and as soon as the bus got underway and the lights dimmed, we struck up a conversation and before long the subjects ranged from her childhood experiences to her home life and the problems of her marriage. Many times in my contact with people, whether old friends or casual acquaintances, they have confided their personal experiences, often including the most intimate personal details. So it was on this trip. The bus trip to Philadelphia lasted twelve hours, and as the lights on the bus were dimmed, the conversation with the woman next to me opened up. It reached the closeness of a longtime acquaintance or even friend. I remember being awake the entire trip. In the morning, as the bus reached the hotel stop and we started to bring in the baggage, the closeness of this encounter "melted away" as by magic. From here I took a bus to New York and the Italian steamship. The itinerary called for a stop-over in Naples, with visits to Pompeii, then by rail to the port of Bari on the east coast of Italy. From there, another ship would take me to Jaffa. The two-day stay in New York waiting for the ship was lonely and sad. Surprisingly, the voyage to Naples turned out to be a romantic one. I found myself seated in the dining room at a table with other young people, men and women of about the same age. They were mostly American-born Italians coming from different cities to visit their relatives. Our conversation was lively, and we soon became well enough acquainted for special friendships to develop. The atmosphere on the ship was similar to being on a desert island in some ways. This led to the pairing off of many couples. My table companion Nina was a lovely young Corsican woman who was on a visit to her relatives. She was married, traveling alone. We were strongly attracted to each other immediately, but as much as we wanted to be alone together, there was no opportunity for privacy on the five-day voyage. On the last evening before reaching Naples, our group arranged a gala champagne party. At this party Nina removed one of her rings and placed it on my finger—a symbolic and touching gesture and it seemed that it was the finale to our short, but highly emotional relationship.

The following morning the passengers went by train to Bari, a port city on the Adriatic Sea, across the Italian peninsula. There a ship was to take us to Jaffa. A somewhat scary but interesting incident happened in this city. As usual, I carried watercolors with me and did fast sketches whenever time and place allowed. Strolling along the waterfront I picked out a spot and started to paint. Within a few minutes two carabinieri (Italian police) were standing behind me examining my sketches. Unbeknown to me, the building I was sketching was a part of Mussolini's military installations that were forbidden to be photographed or sketched. I was taken to the military police headquarters and after an hour of explanations and proof that I was not a spy, I was allowed to leave, but I had to leave my sketches with them. This incident put a damper on my sightseeing. I was glad to board the ship for Jaffa that evening. The atmosphere was one of seriousness of purpose and high expectations, unlike that of the previous trip from New York to Naples, where a happy-go-lucky mood prevailed. Most of the passengers were immigrants going to Palestine. In tune with the mood of the others, I spent most of the trip in conversation with an American on the consular staff at Amman, Jordan, which invariably ended with his voicing his strong opposition to the idea of making Palestine a Jewish homeland and eventually a Jewish state. I felt he was merely expressing the policy of the American oil companies involved in oil explorations in the Arab countries of the Middle East. The U.S. State Department at that time did not want to antagonize these Arab rulers by supporting the idea of a Jewish state.

I had written about my arrival to my cousin Sonia, who lived in Tel Aviv with her husband Daniel and young daughter Gentila. Her husband was the head proofreader for the Labor Party daily newspaper *Davar*, which was published in Hebrew, the official language. The other two official languages were English and Arabic. Yiddish was the dominant language spoken by the immigrants, the majority of whom were from Russia and Eastern Europe at that time. Although many considered Yiddish, written in the Hebrew alphabet, a dialect mixture of middle-high German and Hebrew, the Yiddishists were proud of their rich heritage of literature, theater, and music. On the other hand, the ideal of Zionism was not only to return to the land but to revitalize biblical Hebrew into a modern language. The Hebraists gave top priority to compiling a vocabulary of new words and concepts for use in modern life. Daniel was a brilliant linguist, equally proficient in Hebrew and Yiddish. The irony of Daniel's position was that he belonged to a group that ardently promoted the use of Yiddish as an official language in the new homeland.

Besides Sonia, the others who were to meet me at the boat were my sister Rosa, who was living in Kibbutz En Shemer near Hadera, and Yedidia Yanovsky of Jerusalem, who had been the leader of my Pioneer group in Palestine. Rosa had joined the kibbutz in 1932, married, and had two small children. Yedidia had studied architectural engineering in England and was working for the British government as an engineer. The time for disembarking at Jaffa arrived. Because the British restricted quotas for immigrants, each passenger was interrogated on board ship by the authorities in a long, tedious questioning period. The mandatory government had sharply restricted Jewish immigration, a policy set by the British Colonial Office to appease the Arabs. Not only was the quota small, but the immigrant had to show proof that he had five thousand dollars of savings. In my case, my Aunt Fannie in Detroit had personally vouched for this amount. My status at entry was as architect and businessman.

The procedure of getting ashore had not changed in ten years. Because Jaffa had no port installations, the ship had to anchor a considerable distance from the shore. With several other passengers, I was put into a small boat with my baggage. The boats taking us ashore still had to maneuver through the rocky remains of the ancient port. Memories of ten years earlier, when I first arrived in Palestine covered with coal dust from the Russian freighter, lingered in my mind, although this time I came trained and prepared for a profession.

My sister met me with joyous tears, and Yedidia expressed the hope that this time I had come to stay. Sonia suggested I stay at her apartment, a fourth-floor walk up in the older section of Tel Aviv, until I could rent a room. A two-horse carriage was loaded with my hand baggage, as well as a 600-pound trunk full of my books. The logistics of how to bring the trunk to the fourth floor was solved by a Yemenite porter. This slightly built man had unbelievable stamina and strength. Ropes around the trunk were anchored to his forehead—protected by a wide leather belt—and this 120-pound man carried that trunk up a four-story flight of stairs! I was amazed to find that Sonia's apartment contained only three rooms—two bedrooms and one spacious combined living and cooking-eating area. The family unhesitatingly set up a cot in this all-purpose room to accommodate me, a warm expression of hospitality. They wanted me to stay until I found a job. In a few days, however, I rented a room with a family.

My main concern was to find work, immediately. Yedidia told me about the Levant Fair being planned in Tel Aviv. One of the organizers, Shlomo Yaffo, was from Grodno. He and two partners were in the business of promoting trade fairs for Palestine and arranging for trade pavilions in other countries for the fledgling Jewish industries. Yaffo, a very cheerful man, received me warmly when I called. He knew my family by reputation, and I had heard of his father, Bezalel, who was a Zionist leader and writer. When he heard about my professional background and qualifications he offered to hire me on the spot. So eager was I to start working that I accepted his first offer of ten English pounds a month (fifty dollars), much lower than the going rate for architects. There were eight architects and engineers working in the Levant Fair, immigrants from different countries and backgrounds. Most had recently arrived. Lurie was a quiet-spoken German architect engineer in his thirties. Joana was an Austrian architect, a woman who worked out her designs on oversized paper with charcoal and looked like a chimney sweep at the end of the day's work. Gernicki was a Polish architect who had come to Tel Aviv several years before and by now considered himself almost a native. Staff member Frannie was an electrical engineer who had recently arrived from Poland. Chief designer El-Hanani was an emigre from Leningrad whose background was chiefly in painting and graphics, an artistic type with long hair, penetrating eyes, and handsome features. He stimulated us to develop interesting and exciting shapes for the various pavilions, all of which had to be submitted for approval to those participants who did not have their own architects. Our main problem was to translate his imaginative sketches into working drawings from which the pavilions could be constructed. Frequently our designer's dreamlike concepts could not be executed and after much arguing and endless discussions we had to make substantial changes in his concepts.

Chief engineer Zilke, also from Germany, was a tall, lanky fellow in his fifties. His engineering decisions were final and he ran the office like a military establishment. His discipline had its advantages since deadlines would have been overlooked by the staff. The working atmosphere was very casual and followed the European style—tea at ten and four o'clock with philosophical discussions in between. It is still amazing to me that the fair opened on time. As I learned from later experience, many important tasks generally remain unfinished just days before the official opening of an exhibition or fair. Then it becomes a matter of crews working around the clock. And lo and behold, on opening day the fair is ready for the official ribbon-cutting ceremony.

The site for the Levant Fair was on the coast several miles from the center of Tel Aviv, where the River Yarkon flows into the Mediterranean. A rough road was built to connect the city to the exhibition grounds. The fair became the hub to which the city eventually gravitated. This temporary road within a short time was transformed into the city's main thoroughfare with new housing, shopping, and recreational facilities. It was grandly named Disengoff Street in honor of one of the mayors of the city. My role was to assist the local architect Minzker in planning the five-thousand-seat outdoor amphitheater in which the opening festivities were to take place. Because Minzker was busy with his own private practice, he left most of the surveying work and supervision of the complex seating layout to me. As there was no one in authority to advise me, I had to make my own decisions. Fortunately the management was happy with the results, advanced my rank in the office, and increased my pay by two pounds (ten dollars). The Levant Fair was the first important international fair in Palestine. All the major European countries participated, the most important of which were Austria, Belgium, France, Great Britain, Italy, Sweden, and Switzerland. Palestine was represented by the British Mandated Pavilion, the Jewish National Pavilion, and pavilions erected by the City of Tel Aviv, the Palestine Industries, the Farmers' Federation, the Histadrut (General Labor Federation) and the Women's International Zionist Organization (WIZO).

The ribbon was cut in the colorful opening ceremony on 26 April 1934, and British high commissioner for Palestine Lt. Gen. Sir Arthur Wauchope welcomed the multitudes of visitors. Foreign exhibitors mingled with the local population to create a cosmopolitan atmosphere that was exciting and exhilarating. Large evening crowds were attracted by the symphony concerts in the centrally located amphitheater. Ethnic outdoor restaurants did a brisk business. The fair's attractions were a welcome change for the hardworking, pioneering population. Beneath the festive mood, however, was the ground swell of resentment against the British restrictions on new Jewish immigration. An incident indicative of the tension took place during the opening ceremony. At the end of the British high commissioner's welcoming speech, one of the laborers who had been finishing the landscaping near the entrance gate, ran up to him with a spade in his hand. The guards rushed up and seized him, assuming that the man was trying to attack the commissioner. Before they had a chance to drag him away, he cried out that he only wanted to ask the commissioner to get him an entry visa for his wife and children who were still in Poland. Everyone around breathed freer and the commissioner promised to look into the matter.

With the completion of the Levant Fair, I started to consider opening an office of my own. During my work at the fair I had come to know a number of local developers who asked me to design apartment buildings. I moved to a two-room apartment that served both as living quarters and an office. It contained a desk and two drafting tables in the office, one for me and one for a part-time draftsman. Structural and mechanical work would be designed by consulting firms. There was seldom more than one building to design at a time, so life moved at a leisurely pace, a welcome change from the pressure of the fair deadlines. Breakfast at a seashore restaurant and the morning paper, a short visit to the construction site, and a swim in the Mediterranean occupied my mornings. My impressive looking briefcase contained a few construction documents, a swim suit, and a small towel. Two to four was siesta time and four to seven was spent at the drawing board, together with the draftsman. Sometimes there were interviews and business consultations in the late afternoon. I spent many evenings at some sidewalk cafe. Among the crowd were friends and acquaintances who either passed with a greeting or joined the table with or without an invitation. The sidewalk cafes served as the social meeting place for most people. What contributed to this outdoor way of life was not only the typically small and cramped living quarters, but also the mild and balmy semitropic climate of the country. I found this life-style agreeable and satisfying. Perhaps part of this was because deep in my mind I considered my stay in Palestine temporary. At the same time I knew I was getting valuable experience in my profession.

As new apartment projects were commissioned, my days became busier. The conceptual designs and final working drawings were done in my office. Bids had to be obtained, and supervision of the jobs was also part of my daily routine. In Tel Aviv and in the country generally, building activities in the years 1933–1937, just prior to World War II, continued at a furious tempo. There was a desperate need for housing. The city zoning code allowed three- and four-story apartment buildings. In Tel Aviv all the buildings were of structural concrete framing. The solid wall panels were built with silicone bricks that were locally produced. (Lime and sand were abundant for brickmaking.) The exterior finish of the walls was of special stucco (plaster). To provide variations in texture and color, marble chips of different colors were mixed with the stucco. When it was partially dry, it was washed over lightly with water to expose the chips. Concrete was the favorite material because it was a local product and there were plentiful supplies of sand, gravel, and crushed stone. Only the steel reinforcing rods had to be imported. The designs were of simple, geometric forms, devoid of ornamentation. These were influenced by contemporary European architects such as Eric Mendelsohn of Germany and others from France and Belgium. A number of Jewish students who had studied architecture in European universities applied the new modern trends in their building designs. One innovative feature for this subtropical climate was to leave the first floor open, supporting the upper floors on concrete columns. This allowed the ocean breezes to penetrate the street level spaces, keeping the air moving in the area and cooling the building.

Running an architectural firm, as the case was with many other professionals, had to be done with minimal facilities. (It was rumored that it was the British political policy to slow down the development of Jewish enterprises in Palestine.) I had no typewriter and no phone, since it took years to get a telephone once an application was made. I had to go several blocks from my office to a secretarial service to have a letter typed and to a public phone to make a business call. Communication with clients, contractors, and suppliers was mostly done in person, walking to their offices or homes; sometimes I took a bus, and in exceptional cases I borrowed a friend's car. There were very few cars in Palestine in those years. Because there were few companies that did architectural blueprints, the architects in Tel Aviv devised their own primitive but effective method for reproducing their drawings. A drawing was put on a special frame, then pressed on a photo-sensitized paper, exposed to the tropical sunlight for a few seconds, and rushed back inside the room to be inserted in a developing box. Added to this daily hassle was a major problem—getting approval of architect's plans from the city building department. The plans had to be submitted to two departments; one for technical review, the other for aesthetics. Because of the large number of applications for building permits and insufficient personnel to process them, it took months before a permit was issued. I quickly learned the importance of knowing the right person to get my application put on top of the pile.

Regardless of the obstacles, the happy day for the groundbreaking of my first large apartment building project came. According to the building code, a basement and three floors were allowed. For economic reasons, I needed to add another floor. I raised the basement ceiling one-half floor above ground level so as to admit sufficient light for additional apartments (an innovative design at that time). About a month later, when the pouring of the concrete for the first floor was in process, a buildings inspector and two policemen arrived on the job and ordered the pouring to be stopped. Although the plans had been approved, the building department had received a complaint that the code was not being adhered to. The contractor refused to obey their orders and argued that the work stoppage would bring a huge financial loss to the owner as well as the workers, but to no avail. One of the policemen stationed himself on the concrete mixer to enforce the stoppage. Fortunately, it was close to lunch hour, and inspector and policemen left for lunch. Immediately work was resumed and that critical section of the pouring was completed. During all this commotion, I feared this might be the end of my brief career as a Tel Aviv architect. All was not lost. When the inspector returned after lunch, he left a stoppage order. On the advice of my friends, I went to the city appeals board. One of the members of the five-member board was a young American engineer who knew me personally and was sympathetic to my design approach. An hour of heated argument ensued. Some members argued that an exception for me should not be allowed, as an example for others. In the end I was allowed to continue the structure but with a warning to follow the building code to the letter in the future.

I felt that I could handle just about any problem from then on. However, there was one situation for which I was not prepared. As in any building boom, there were all sorts of promoters of unrealizable schemes. An Italian engineer approached two of my friends to plan a housing project outside Tel Aviv. He was the inventor of a new type of building block that could be used in masonry wall construction. These hollow blocks were manufactured in exact shapes and dimensions so that they could be laid without mortar. At regular intervals of six to ten courses, liquid cement was to be poured through the openings in the blocks to stabilize the wall. It seemed a feasible idea although it had not been tested. The problem was that the newly invented machine to make the blocks had to be imported from Germany at high cost. Herman Strauss, a well-to-do refugee German lawyer, agreed to invest. The other, a young Palestinian Jew, David Habib, experienced in construction, was willing to participate. I would be the architect and would also furnish drawings for the promotional material. The Italian engineer succeeded in raising sufficient money to promote the project. He had taken full-page advertisements in the main newspaper in Alexandria and Cairo, Egypt. In both of these cities there was a large well-to-do Jewish middle class. He hoped to attract a number of buyers to invest in the apartments, either for rental or for a vacation home. But the response was minimal. There was no money to buy the expensive machinery and the land on which to build. As a consequence the project fell through. As for me, I learned the valuable lesson of being more analytical, both of the promoter and in the validity and testing of his ideas. Even though I had invested considerable time in preparing the plans and the renderings for promotion purposes for which I was not paid, I actually was relieved when the project was dropped. At least no more investor's money would go down the drain.

Although I had to do most of the work of my business myself, there was no great pressure. Commissions did not come in at steady intervals. The fees I charged were competitive and were only sufficient to cover my modest living expenses. I had to supplement my earnings by working evenings for Magidovitch, an established architect for whom I did conceptual drawings and perspectives. A perspective drawing is a presentation, generally in color, showing the building as it will appear when completed. This work requires special skill and art training. There were only a few architects who could do this. The pay of ten piastres an hour (fifty cents) for this job was nearly double the regular hourly pay for architects. In this office I met Shimon Lipshitz, an engineer who also worked evenings helping with the structural design. We became close friends and he later became my collaborator on various apartment building projects.

Friday was a special day of the week for everyone. Work stopped shortly after two o'clock, and there was a big rush to do last-minute shopping for the Sabbath celebration, Friday evening and Saturday. Candy shops and flower markets were the busiest. To have flowers for the Sabbath table was a tradition. I also took part in the festive activity, although on a limited scale. Often I would invite four or five friends over to visit on Friday nights, so I too shopped for candies, fruit, and flowers. Fresh orange and grapefruit juice were the favorite beverages. Frequently, however, I was the invited Friday-night guest at a friend's house for the Sabbath dinner.

The times I looked forward to most, however, were Friday afternoons and Saturdays when I went out with my sketch pad and watercolors. There was no shortage of subject matter—the old Arab quarter in Jaffa, the older unpaved streets of Tel Aviv with large trees still standing in the middle of the roadway, the seashore, the colorful neighboring Arab villages. This delightful activity culminated in a watercolor exhibit of my work in the Maskit Art Gallery in Tel Aviv in 1936. For the invitation to the opening I made a woodblock print showing the street scene with the trees. Because mail delivery was slow and unreliable, the gallery director suggested having the invitations hand delivered. The young man hired to do this delivered only a few of the two hundred invitations and threw away the rest, as we discovered later. Luckily, a newspaper announcement appeared several days before and about sixty people came to the opening reception. It was a happy occasion, but I was even happier later to receive a letter from the gallery director stating my "Boats on the Yarkon River" had been sold for three and one-half pounds (about eighteen dollars), considered a substantial price in the art market.

Meanwhile, my cousin Sonia had plans for me. Even before I arrived she was intent on making a match for her friend Hannah, an attractive woman in her late twenties. She was head nurse at a nearby hospital and commanded a good salary. Sonia lost no time in getting us together, and Hannah was a frequent visitor at Sonia's apartment those first evenings in Palestine when I stayed with her. She managed to leave us alone as often as she could, and it was easy and comfortable for me to be with Hannah. She was kind and freely expressed her attraction to me. When I moved to a rented room, she brought things to make it more liveable—a lamp, a small throw rug, some ceramic bowls and platters. In those early days, transplanted to new surroundings with an unknown future, I looked forward to being with her, but I wanted to avoid deep personal involvements. Somehow, deep in my heart I felt that my stay in Palestine was temporary and that I would eventually return to the United States to live. Still, I had no timetable set for my return. When I left Detroit two years earlier it was more or less understood that I would be away about three years. The main purpose in my mind was to continue working as an architect. Two of the three years had passed. Letters from Riva and Sol in Detroit kept reminding me of our plans to be reunited. When I explained to Hannah how torn I was between my conflicting feelings, she felt shocked and left abruptly for home. I was now more confused than ever about my feelings. Hannah came to my place several days later in a serious mood. She talked about her own feelings and said that she decided to continue our relationship anyway, even though it would be temporary. The next six months were happy ones for us. We were constantly together in our free time and enjoyed our intimacy. As time went on, however, I began to have feelings of guilt. I believed that by continuing our affair until the time of departure I was only compounding the difficulty for Hannah. Were she not involved with me, she would have a better opportunity to meet and marry a suitable man. It was most difficult and heart rending to tell her that I wanted to end our relationship. Deep in her heart she had hoped that I would stay in Palestine and marry her after all. The breakup was so distressing that she left Tel Aviv to work at a hospital in Haifa. My cousin Sonia was so upset that she came to lecture me about my irresponsible behavior and moral obligations to this fine woman. Fifteen years later in 1950 while on a visit to Israel, I saw Hannah with her husband on a busy street corner. Sonia had told me she had married within a year after the breakup. I wanted very much to stop and greet her; I even followed them a short distance before deciding that meeting her now might be painful.

I tried to divert my mind from this unhappy situation. Garfinkel, an engineer friend, wanted to have a land valuer's license. Land valuation appraisals was a lucrative profession. The examinations under the British mandated government were very difficult to pass. The applicant was required to be knowledgeable about the old Turkish as well as the British laws. These laws included the rules for the sale and transfer of properties, along with laws compensating the displaced native owners. Garfinkel had failed to pass this examination several times. When he complained to me about the complexity of the tests, I said, "Is it really that difficult?" He answered, "If you are so smart, why don't you try it?" It was the right time to take up this challenge. For the next six months I plunged into this new field of land law. I ordered several books from London and some from the Jerusalem bookstores for preparation. When the day of the exam arrived I thought I was reasonably ready. The exam was in two parts—one involved Turkish and English laws of the land, the other, actual cases for the land evaluator. It was this latter part that caused the most difficulty. One problem I recall was: "If an Arab sells his land of ten dunams (2½ acres) in addition to the sale price, what other compensation would he be entitled to?" The answer entailed the ability to meet the practical needs of the Arab farmer, such as number of cows, sheep, donkeys, seed, and a plow. I can't recall my exact answers, but they must have been acceptable since I passed the exams.

As happy as I was with the results of this hectic six months of study and keeping up with some architectural work, there had been no time for any recreation or even painting. I joined a group of young artists, part-time professionals who met weekly in the evening at a studio, to draw from a model. There were eight to ten men and women who were interested in doing charcoal life studies, sketches for future paintings. These sessions always ended up in a cafe or a bar in endless discussion and argument about various art theories and our preferences for abstract art over the realistic or humanistic approach. During the rest periods I had frequent chances to talk to Sally, our model, who said she liked my drawings. She was also an artist but had to work as a housekeeper during the day to support herself. She had come from Germany with her parents a few years before, an attractive, twenty-four year old, gentle, soft-spoken person with whom I was comfortable. One evening, a short time later, there was a knock on my door. There stood Sally smiling. "Surprised?" she asked. I certainly was! We spent a pleasant evening talking about ourselves and our hopes and dreams for the future. This was the beginning of our intimate friendship. Sally posed frequently for me. After several weeks, at the end of one of the drawing sessions, she said: "How about you posing for me?" I was taken aback at first. When I did agree, I posed with a towel around my waist. Sally was amazed at this display of modesty. By sheer coincidence, a few hours after seeing Hannah in Tel Aviv in 1950, while walking down Allenby Road with my sister Rosa and her husband, I saw another familiar female figure rushing by. It was Sally. I was so taken by surprise, that it took me a few minutes before I realized who she was and followed her. But alas, I was too slow! She had disappeared in the bustling crowd. It was like looking through a peephole watching part of my past life flash by.

Another aspect to the social life of Tel Aviv involved the famous Hebrew Habimah Theater, transplanted from Moscow, which gave excellent performances of new and old plays in its repertoire. A comedy theater and several dance groups offering classical and Yemenite dance programs were also favorites of everyone. But by far the most important cultural development was the creation of the Palestine Philharmonic Orchestra, now known as the Israel Philharmonic Orchestra, one of the most prestigious symphony orchestras in the world. In 1936, when Toscanini arrived in Tel Aviv from Italy as the first guest conductor, it had no auditorium or space with proper acoustics for rehearsals. Rehearsals took place in an empty concrete pavilion left over from the Levant Fair. Toscanini said that if the seats could be filled with people, the acoustical problem would be solved. The human body, he explained, serves as an acoustical absorption unit. The news of his request spread like wildfire and within two hours the rehearsal pavilion was filled to capacity, so great was the thirst for good music. The city put out its banners and flags, the bakery shops decorated cakes with frosting of musical notes, and the day of the concert was a truly festive holiday.

Side by side with the increasing tempo of cultural life in the Jewish homeland, there was a surfacing of Arab unrest instigated by the Mufti, the Muslim religious leader of Jerusalem who was supported and financed by the Nazi elements in Germany. The Mufti welcomed this help in preventing the establishment of a Jewish state. These Arab rumblings began to have an impact on the life of the country. Travel from place to place was in boarded-up buses as stone throwing from the Arab villages along the roads was a common occurrence. Work and traffic continued uninterrupted, as the Jewish population was determined not to give in to threats, but construction activity did slow down as a result.

The danger of another World War was already becoming increasingly apparent, and I began to think of returning to the United States. Letters from Sol and Riva in Detroit urged me to return to renew our family life and work together. Also, to retain my American citizenship I had to return within a five-year period. Yet another factor speeded up my decision. Regardless of the threats of war, the International World's Fair was being built in Paris, to be opened in August 1937. Palestine was participating with its Jewish Pavilion. The pavilion was being planned by the same firm that built the Levant Fair two years earlier. I was asked to join the architectural team responsible for the design and supervision of the construction of the pavilion. This offer coincided with my ultimate plan to return to the United States to establish my architectural practice. Architectural commissions were becoming more and more scarce in Palestine, and the importance of maintaining continuous involvement in my profession was always uppermost in my mind. I was to report to the job in Paris the first week in May. By leaving Palestine earlier, I would be able to visit my parents in Grodno and my brother in Warsaw for the Passover holiday. It had been eight years since my last visit. My parents were almost seventy years old and this visit could very well be my last. After a six-week stay I would proceed to Paris, arriving in May to work on the fair. Then in August, after the opening, I would leave for the States. I made arrangements with my friend Shimon Lipshitz to take over my jobs in the planning and construction stages. I had faith in his ability and integrity to complete the buildings. There was no problem in disposing of my few pieces of furniture—some I sold and some I gave away. I spent my last few days in Tel Aviv visiting and saying farewell to friends, colleagues, and co-workers. The ones most unhappy with my decision to leave were my longtime friend Yedidia Yanovsky and my sister Rosa and her family. They had always hoped I would stay permanently.

It was March when I left on the first leg of my journey home. The four-day boat trip from Haifa to Venice was relaxing and pleasant. It was a single-class tourist boat with many European travelers returning from their vacations. Some were Jewish officials and businessmen going on vacation with their families, along with a number of young people visiting their families in Austria and Poland. I did a number of watercolor sketches on the boat. As usual my sketching attracted many onlookers, some of whom became interesting companions. One successful sketch was the head of a young woman who was on her way to Argentina to marry her fiance. She was an art student and our common interests and discussions made the trip an enjoyable experience. In Venice I boarded the train for Vienna. As the train passed through the snow-covered Alps, I thought of traveling through those mountains seventeen years ago with a group of teenagers on the way to an unknown future in Palestine. How enriching and varied these years had been and how unexpected. There seemed to have been some continuity of purpose in my professional life, some pattern of progress, as though I had carefully planned it step by step. In reality, as I looked back it seemed as if an "unknown hand" had been guiding me in the right direction.

A shocking contrast awaited me in Vienna. It was a different city now from what I had known on my two previous visits. The atmosphere was already one of apprehension as Hitler and his party went from success to success. It could be seen in the grim faces of the people in the cafes reading war-threatening headlines in the newspapers and in the blank expressions of others on the streets going about their errands. I was glad to get away and board the train for Warsaw, but little did I know my experience there would be even more traumatic and threatening.

In my train compartment were several well-to-do Poles returning from an Italian holiday. They welcomed me into their group, and the conversation was lively, the atmosphere easy and cordial. This mood changed imperceptibly but gradually as we neared the Polish border. Right after the border crossing conversation stopped entirely and the same people now behaved like complete strangers to me. I was shocked at the sudden change. My own explanation for this was that outside their own country they behaved like cultured people. Once back in their land, they reverted to their deep-seated prejudices against Jews. Later, when I related the incident to my family, I was told about the intense anti-Semitism now publicly expressed and encouraged in Poland. My brother Wolf, his wife Pola, and sons Gabriel, age five, and Samuel, twelve, were at the station and a joyous reunion took place. Warsaw was as gay as ever, with expensive shops displaying the latest in European luxuries and fine restaurants filled to capacity. We spent several days shopping for Passover gifts for my parents and my sister Elsa in Grodno, and for my brother Yakov's family in Suwalki. The family was to be reunited, as on my last visit to Grodno on Passover. The year was 1937 and I had a premonition that this might be our last time together.

At the train station in Grodno we were met by my parents, Elsa, cousins, and friends. It was good to feel their closeness and love. They had arranged for horse-drawn carriages to carry the group through the main streets of Grodno to my parents' apartment. The apartment looked the same, spotlessly clean as usual, filled with the enticing smells of my mother's baking and cooking for the holiday. My parents showed very little change. They were excited over this long-awaited family Passover reunion, though it was evident they were worried about the Nazi repressions against Jews in Germany and feared an oncoming conflict in Poland. Elsa, now 24 years old and unmarried, looked as lovely as ever. Because of the Depression, there were few jobs available for young men and almost none for women. For Elsa to marry, she would need the traditional dowry of a substantial amount of money, several thousand dollars, a sum my parents did not have. She was in love with a young man who was unable to find employment. My parents, however, favored another suitor who was in a good financial situation and had persistently courted her for several years. (She eventually accepted him and they were married just before the German invasion in 1939.)

I wanted to look up old friends and classmates, but found that those remaining on my last visit were now gone. Elsa introduced me to a number of her young friends, all eager to come to the United States. As the Polish quota for immigration to America was limited, the girls were desperate to marry an American citizen and immigrate to the United States as his wife. Again I was the target of their attentions, especially two friends of my sister with whom I spent many enjoyable hours. If there were any temptations for me, they were quickly dispelled by the cold facts that I was far from being self-supporting and faced an uncertain future. My parents still operated their store, mostly for high-ranking Polish officers, but it had become a hand-to-mouth operation. My father did not have enough capital to keep it fully stocked with military goods. As usual, I was amazed to see how well my parents managed with their tiny income. What especially stands out in my memory are the appetizing dishes prepared by my mother and the frequent pauses for tea with her homemade cookies and cakes.

During my visit I decided to make a bust of my father. His curiosity was so aroused that he went to a brick factory and bought enough processed clay to make a full-sized portrait. He sat patiently for an hour every afternoon for about ten days. Occasionally he would drowse. He was very pleased with the likeness that I achieved; however, my mother disliked it—she thought it resembled a death mask. I also made a number of charcoal sketches of his head that they both liked. I felt I was able to capture the inner spirit of this quiet, sensitive, and wise human being. Upon returning to Detroit I sculpted another portrait of my father from memory. This portrait, which is now in my studio, brings constant memories, both happy and sad.

As the time of departure drew closer, the atmosphere in the house became gloomier. With the news of rising Nazi power in Germany, we concluded this visit might be my last. The situation in Germany threatened the lives of the Jewish population along with intellectuals of whatever nationality or religion who opposed the Nazis. The worst part was the utter helplessness of people like my family, with nowhere to turn awaiting an unknown fate, while life went on as usual on the surface. No human mind could yet foresee the Holocaust, which was to sweep across Poland in two or three years.

I had planned to stay in Poland for six weeks before reporting for work on the Jewish Pavilion at the Paris World's Fair in May 1937. Deep in my heart I felt an almost physical fear of being trapped in the ever-narrowing circle of hostilities. To leave my family and escape to a safer world made me feel even guiltier. When the departure date arrived, my father preferred to say goodbye at home without going through the emotional tension of parting at the railroad station. It was the last time I was to see him. The rest of the family, my friends and my sister's friends, were at the station gathered in small groups. Even after so many years it is painful to recollect my failure of not talking more with my grieving mother. I was nervous and impatient to get the uncomfortable moments of parting over. We tried to console each other as best we could. Deep in our hearts we felt the painful finality.

I stopped again for two days in Warsaw with my brother Wolf's family. Here the atmosphere was more forbidding than it had been when I arrived. The newspapers were full of war headlines, but life appeared to go on normally and with more than the usual hustle and bustle. Wolf, Pola, and their twelve-year-old Mulek, saw me off at the train station when I left for Paris. The younger son, Gabriel, was running a high temperature and had to remain at home. I did not say goodbye to him because the family did not want to distress him with the news of my leaving. He was a handsome bright youngster to whom I was much attached. This made my leave-taking even more sad. Here, too, was the same feeling of finality. The Paris-bound train made one stop in Berlin. The unprovoked attacks against Jews were already in full swing with the Nazi government's participation. Although I was an American citizen, I was fearful when the uniformed Nazi train guard checked my belongings, removed all my reading matter, and ordered me to follow him to his office. I saw teenagers in the railway station carrying signs with anti-Semitic slogans and shouting "Death to the Jews." After filling out several questionnaires I was allowed to return to my compartment. When the train finally crossed the border into France, I felt as if I were coming out of a dungeon into bright sunlight.

The exuberant spirit of Paris contrasted sharply with the depressed atmosphere of Grodno. Paris, the center of the arts and the mecca of tourists from around the world, was full of excitement and activity, for it was May and the World's Fair was to be completed and formally opened on 1 August 1937. It did not take me long to settle down in a small but adequate hotel near the exhibition grounds of the fair. I immediately reported to the management of the Palestine Pavilion and joined the group of architects with whom I had worked previously in Tel Aviv for the Levant Fair. Our staff of ten architects and engineers, under chief engineer-architect El-Hanani, was housed in temporary quarters near the site within the city. The design concept was contemporary, with only one element suggesting the mideastern character of Palestine—a large dome over the exhibit hall. I was assigned to the interior design section to develop spaces for the various exhibitors. Many of these represented newly established firms and businesses. Despite the slowness of our work routines and frequent coffee breaks, our pavilion was one of the few that was completed on time. Most other pavilions were unfinished and far behind schedule two weeks before the opening. The main concourse of the fair was still an immense excavation. In desperation the French government mobilized ten thousand men to work around the clock. They draped the unfinished buildings with flags and covered the rough grade of the concourse area with temporary sodding and trees. They even managed to put in and hook up a few fountains. Officially the Fair opened on time at 10 A.M. on 1 August 1937.

On that day I watched from the roof of our building the procession of dignitaries from all the participating countries, headed by the president of France. It was a sight to behold—a sea of top hats rolling across the grounds below! As the dignitaries took their places on the special platform, the bands played and the flags of all the exhibiting nations were unfolded. Several thousand people crowded into the temporary seating areas to listen to the optimistic speeches of the French and other world leaders. Twenty-four hours later all the temporary coverings were removed and the work to complete the pavilions began anew. In addition to our pavilion, only the Russian and the German pavilions were completed. If any building ever succeeded in expressing the inner character of the regime it represented, those did. The German Pavilion had a huge eagle mounted over a fortresslike building, its guards' uniforms emblazoned with swastikas, while the Russian Pavilion had an industrial character and featured huge figures of a man and a woman marching, holding between them in outstretched arms the flag of their revolution. These graphic symbols were a portent of the forthcoming Armageddon. Even as the exposition was being completed, the rumblings of war were felt in the seemingly gay and carefree atmosphere, and many Frenchmen were cynical about the propriety of holding the fair with a world catastrophe in sight.

Our spirits were boosted by an unexpected invitation from Baron Edmond Guy de Rothschild to an evening reception at his home in celebration of the success of the Palestine Pavilion. This event introduced us to a "fairy tale" world. Our group of ten met that evening at seven o'clock at the gate of the historic Rothschild palace. We were escorted by a guard through the landscaped gardens. The door was opened by a footman who directed us up the marble circular stairs to the second floor gallery-reception room. There we were received by the baron, an aristocratic looking man of about fifty. He immediately put us at ease, asking about our family backgrounds and the way we had reached our decision to help build Palestine into a Jewish State. The conversation was enhanced by the excellent Rothschild wines and the buffet of delicacies. Then he took us to see his collection of rare paintings and tapestries. It was like visiting a museum with an exceptionally knowledgeable and proud guide.

At the end of the evening the baron thanked us warmly for the successful completion of the pavilion that he had sponsored and told us of his lifelong commitment to the cause of Palestine as a Jewish homeland.

Now that our work was completed, most of us stayed on a while longer. By this time the remaining pavilions were completed, and we were interested in seeing the various approaches in building design and exhibits. I was intrigued by the colorful pavilions of Mexico, Argentina, and Brazil, as well as Japan and India. This was a time to revisit the museums of Paris—the famous Louvre, the Rodin, the Luxemburg. As I wandered through the century-old quarters of the city, I made numerous water-color sketches of the neighborhood buildings. Evenings were spent sitting at side-walk cafes with friends watching the crowds go by. But that carefree time was nearing its end. While in Tel Aviv I had already arranged my tourist-class passage on the Queen Elizabeth for my return "home." Now, as I was getting ready to leave, disquieting thoughts about the uncertainties of the future began to plague me. I had no idea what the prospects were in Detroit for getting work in an architectural firm. Uppermost in my mind was the hope that despite the depressed economy, I would be able to have my own office. My future seemed to hang in a precarious balance as my ship drew near the States once again. These thoughts persisted during my waking hours and even in my dreams. No fortune teller could possibly foresee the future that awaited me.

Self-portrait in stone, December, 1929.

Portrait of Clemence Van De Sande, 1930.

"Modern Living Quarters," Detroit, 1931, watercolor by author.

Three-story apartment/retail building (proposed), 1935.

M. Grosbard apartment building, Tel Aviv, 1935.

Apartment building, Tel Aviv, 1936.

8

DETROIT ARCHITECT
Early Years, 1937–1949

Returning to Detroit in August 1937, not surprisingly, it took several days to catch up on the many happenings each of us experienced over the past four years. Sol and Riva were sharing an apartment with friends, a doctor and his wife. There was also an extra room for me. Riva continued to teach French part-time in a private school and Sol was a manager in our cousin's luggage store. He worked long hours, six days a week, and hoped upon my return to help me set up an architectural office. The Depression was still a negative factor in the city and state economy. I spent the first week in Detroit renewing contacts with friends and making inquiries about employment prospects in architectural firms. I applied to a number of offices without success. The reply was always the same—"Come back in six months." Then and there I decided, with the encouragement of my family, to start my own office. My sister Riva was a "natural" to be the receptionist-typist-bookkeeper and caretaker of the housekeeping chores. From this small beginning she would become the chief accountant for a sixty-man office and remain for thirty years. Sol contacted architectural firms to get orders for printing and for perspective drawings. As he became more familiar with the building trades and the contracting business, he became the business manager.

Finding office space was no problem. We rented a small office in a building on Woodward Avenue, the main street, about a mile from the downtown business district. Our office was on the second floor over a store and was reached by a flight of steep stairs. The rent was only twenty-five dollars a month, and the space was divided into a small reception room and a drafting room large enough for two drafting tables. A door led from this room to a printing room. The idea of a printing room grew out of our strategic planning. I realized that it would take some time before architectural commissions would come our way. I thought I could meet expenses if I could provide special services for other architectural firms. This would include special printing of blue lines on white paper and making presentation drawings and perspectives seldom done in their own offices. The printing idea had its inspiration from my experience in Palestine. There, most of the architects did their own printing by putting the original tracing over sensitized photo paper and then exposing it to the sun for a few seconds. The paper would then be put into a cylinder filled with ammonia fumes for developing. I was planning to use this primitive method in my practice. My frustration knew no limits when I discovered the level of sun brightness was so low in Detroit that it would require ten times as much exposure as it did in Palestine. As a result of this miscalculation, I had to look for other means of making blue-line prints. I ended up buying a small printing machine on monthly payments. At that time most of the architectural offices were using white lines on standard blue print paper. Years later blue lines on white paper became the accepted practice. Soon we had a small but steady printing business for drawings. The printing pick-up and delivery was done by a young high school graduate who used a bicycle.

Within a short time our printing orders increased to such an extent that our small, slow machine could not produce fast enough. We soon considered buying a larger and faster machine. Little did we know that we were encroaching on a very tightly controlled field of blueprint operators. One day two men walked into the office requesting small printing orders. They also wanted to see our operation. We immediately suspected that this might be an investigative maneuver by the established printing firms. Our suspicions were confirmed when our order for a larger printing machine was "stalled" without valid reason by the suppliers. We decided to manage as we were for the time being.

The printing activities, as limited as they were, brought us unexpectedly to another field by a chance talk with Valter Poole, the assistant conductor of the Detroit Symphony and a friend. I suggested that the symphony librarian and composers could write the music on standard transparent sheets with musical graphs. We could then print these on our machine in the same manner as we reproduced architectural drawings. Our prices would be competitive with those of printing firms. The idea caught on and orders came in from several radio stations and professional bands. Our "office song" became "and the music goes round and round. . . ."

I kept up my work of making perspectives for other architects. This too was not without its troubles. The architects usually did not allow me enough time to finish their commissions. One unfortunate incident stands out in my memory. I had just finished two drawings and one needed to be trimmed off the edges to the right size. In my rush to finish the drawing on time, I did not notice that one was lying underneath the other. My hasty trimming resulted in the ruination of the perspective. I had to stay up all night to re-do it. As it turned out all these problems were a blessing in disguise. They compelled me to return to my main goal for which I was striving—to build up an architectural practice.

My work in Palestine influenced my designs to a great extent. My first large residence in Detroit was designed with concrete block walls and a plaster stucco finish. All buildings in Palestine were made with poured concrete walls and a variety of cement plaster finishes. The plaster was mixed with marble chips and the results varied with the color admixture of the marble chips. Structurally and in appearance the residence is still attractive after many years. Because it was difficult to find qualified craftsmen for the stucco finish, I decided to use the accepted technique of the brick-veneer construction—a combination of wooden studs covered with insulation boards and a four-inch brick wall attached to the studs. In my design, however, I kept the contemporary approach and before long our office was sought out to design buildings in the modern idiom. At that time the colonial and English styles were in vogue.

One incident stands out in the trials and tribulations of starting an architectural office that nearly put an early end to it all. The time was mid-1937. The project involved was to convert and remodel a one-story store building with basement into a small nightclub near the downtown area. The plans called for removing a number of columns in the basement and putting in longer span beams to support the first floor. Until these new beams arrived, it was planned that the floor would be temporarily underpinned (supported). The deadline for completion was the last week in December to ready the premises for a gala New Year's opening celebration. As the January first date grew closer, it was evident that only the first floor could be made usable for the party. Pressured by the owner, the contractor hurriedly prepared the premises, neglecting to provide the proper underpinning needed to support the floor to accommodate over a hundred celebrants. Imagine my shock when the following morning on New Year's day the big news on the radio was the collapse of the nightclub floor, causing one death and a number of injured celebrants. I was stunned. In a state of panic I expected at any minute a knock on the door by police or the building authorities. My first thought was that some of my plans were not followed explicitly by the contractor. We were not engaged to do the supervision so there was no way of checking the contractor's work. No matter where the blame would be placed, a tragedy of this magnitude would leave a scar and could reflect on the professional reliability of the office. It took several days for the Detroit Building Department to investigate the cause of the floor collapse. To my great relief, after anxiously awaiting the findings, it was concluded that the contractor was at fault in not following the plans indicating the use of temporary support for the floor. It was also fortunate that my name did not figure in the news reporting since the contractor had taken out the building permit in his own name. The last report I heard was that the police were looking for the contractor who had disappeared the same morning as the news came out. From this unfortunate incident our office has learned to insist on the inclusion of at least some basic structural supervision in our architectural services. In the years to follow many cities and states adopted mandatory requirements for inclusion of supervision in their architectural projects. Moreover, in the ensuing years liability and malpractice insurance became a costly but vital instrument for the protection of all involved—architect, owner, contractor, and the public.

Meanwhile a boost to my spirits came from another source. Watercolor painting, which was to play a significant role later in my professional practice, brought my name before the general public. Earlier, before leaving for Palestine, I had exhibited my paintings in my studio and at the Detroit Artists Market. The reports of my successful show in Tel Aviv were factors in arranging for a show at the J. L. Hudson Galleries entitled "Palestine Impressions." This exhibit attracted my first client for the design of a large modern-style house in the prestigious Palmer Park area of Detroit. Tom Borman, the client, was also the owner of two Tom's Food Markets. This contact led to our commission to remodel and update the stores—our first entry into the commercial field.

Another important commission followed the art exhibit. The Workmen's Circle Organization, a Jewish fraternal society, had acquired land on Linwood Avenue near

Detroit Central High School and asked me to design their new headquarters. My rendering of the proposed modern-style building was published in the *Detroit News* real estate section and caught the attention of a number of interested developers. It also caught the attention of Henry Abrams, an architectural engineer and a former classmate at the University of Michigan. He approached me with a proposal to form a partnership. I recognized that the firm needed greater expertise in engineering services and so we formed a partnership in 1938—Redstone and Abrams. This partnership lasted until the outbreak of World War II, when Abrams left to enter a war-industry firm.

One of the happy occasions of the summer of 1938 was the marriage of my brother Sol, following a brief courtship, to an attractive Detroit girl. At that time we all moved to an apartment building near the office. Riva had her own one-room apartment and I shared a large apartment with Sol and his wife Nellie. It was a natural sequence that Sol's marriage stirred my thoughts in that direction.

My social contacts at meetings of the local chapter of a Zionist group, the Histadrut, provided an opportunity to make friends with people interested in supporting the goal of a Jewish homeland in Palestine. At one of these meetings I decided to practice my amateur palm reading that I had recently learned from my sculptor-teacher Sam Cashwan. It didn't take long to spot an attractive young woman who was willing to have her palm read. She was Ruth Rosenbaum. Ruth was born in Ogdensburg, New York, the eldest of five children of Ely and Fannie Rosenbaum. Her father came to the United States as a young immigrant from Russia and after a brief stay in Syracuse, married and settled in Ogdensburg with relatives. Ruth was a Phi Beta Kappa graduate from Saint Lawrence University in Canton, New York. After teaching several years at Hemlock Union High School in the Rochester, New York area, she decided on a career in social work. Following two years of graduate study at the School for Jewish Social Work in New York City, she moved to Detroit in 1930 to work for the Jewish Social Service Bureau and later as a casework supervisor for the City of Detroit Welfare Department. We realized we were deeply attracted to each other and that we had similar interests and outlooks on life. Several months later in June 1939 Ruth and I were married in a private ceremony in Rabbi Abraham Herschman's home, with family and a few close friends in attendance. The following day a large garden reception for friends and family was held at the home of Mr. and Mrs. Karl Segall, whose daughter Ruth was a close friend.

We were on our delayed honeymoon trip in September visiting the 1939 World's Fair in New York when World War II "exploded." From the radio news announcements we learned the Germans had occupied, by arrangement with the Soviets, the western part of Poland including Warsaw, while the eastern part, including my hometown Grodno, was occupied by the Soviets. Upon returning to Detroit, we were able to communicate by mail with my family only in Russian-occupied Grodno. This contact ceased a year later when the Nazis declared war on the Russians. In Grodno the Nazis established a ghetto where my family and all other Jews were forced to live. We never heard from them again.

In Warsaw my brother and his wife's family were moved to the walled Warsaw ghetto together with the rest of the Jewish population. We had one communication from Warsaw in 1942 through the Red Cross. The message received was that they were "safe." However, none survived when the ghetto was totally liquidated after fierce resistance in 1944. In recent years some details of life in the Warsaw ghetto relating to my family came to my attention in a very unexpected way. One of the few survivors, Fania Reims, a close friend of the family, had immigrated to Buenos Aires, Argentina. Over the years she edited a Yiddish magazine *Echoes of Grodno*. In it were descriptions of her experiences in the Warsaw ghetto that shed light on the fate of my family.

My oldest brother Wolf and his wife's family were in the candy manufacturing business. Because the military wanted their luxuries, the family was allowed to continue their candy business. Despite the horrors happening around them—the daily deportation to the death camps—the family was lulled into false security that they would be spared the fate of the others. But their respite was short, lasting about six months. My brother was suddenly seized on the street and deported with others to the camps without any notification to his family. This shocking tragedy made everyone realize that it was merely a question of time before all would be taken away. The factory was left with a skeleton crew and continued the operations until the final destruction of the ghetto. At that time my sister-in-law had a chance to escape and be hidden by a Christian family. She refused to leave her sick elderly mother and her son Gabriel. They all perished in the 1944 ghetto uprising.

There were four weeks of fierce but futile resistance by the underground fighters, both men and women. They had few guns, limited ammunition, and, home-made hand grenades to defend themselves against the armored tanks and well-equipped SS guard units. In the final act of destruction, the Nazis put the torch to the buildings, bringing fiery death to nearly all. A handful of the last defenders were able to escape through the underground sewers, to be saved by a few friendly Poles on the other side of the ghetto walls. Only one member of my brother's family, his sixteen-year-old son Samuel survived. Samuel came to America after the war, studied architecture at the University of Michigan, and became a principal in our firm.

It took a number of years to comprehend the immensity of the tragedy that had happened to my family and the entire European Jewish community. Years later a number of events brought the implications of these tragic events to the surface from the depths of my psyche. One occurred on Yom Kippur. It was a beautiful autumn day and I was walking alone in the woods near the Lake Michigan dunes. Suddenly the images of my hometown flashed before my eyes and a deep flood of emotion swept over me. Hysterical, I burst into tears. Another occasion bringing a similar spontaneous reaction of hysterical grief was the viewing of a television documentary on the Holocaust showing the piling up of mounds of skeletons at a Nazi concentration camp. In a quite different setting I again experienced the immensity of this cruelty of man to man. I was in Ann Arbor at a football game, attended by over 100,000 people. As I looked over this colorful and happy crowd, young and older, talented, vital, with hope and promise for their future, it suddenly dawned on me that sixty times that number were forced to go to their death. It was a shocking visual revelation.

A revealing account of what happened to my hometown came unexpectedly one evening in April 1985. The phone rang. A man with a heavy accent asked for Louis Redstone, formerly Leon Routenstein from Grodno, Russia. My thoughts raced back over the eighty-two years. The caller introduced himself as Abraham Goldman, born in Grodno. He had come from France as a tourist and was traveling by bus through the United States with his eighteen-year-old son. They were on their way to Montreal to return to Caen, their home since World War II. He was a friend of my cousin, Israel Routenstein, who like himself had escaped the Holocaust. I knew that the survivors of the Grodno ghetto, some in South America, some in France and the United States, had kept in touch with one another in a loosely formed organization. He said he would be only a few hours at the bus station, had recently made a trip to Grodno, and wanted to share his experiences with me.

There in the large waiting room a sixty-year-old man of slight build, worn and weary, was sitting with his frail-looking son, waiting for us. The next two hours were spent in learning what happened to Grodno since 1945, the Allied victory year. He brought an elaborate brochure published by the Soviet government in 1984 describing life in Grodno. On the cover there were pictures of a robust healthy-looking young man and woman dressed in the traditional embroidered costume of the region. In the background were the high, newly built housing developments. Inside the brochure the pictures showed a prosperous and vital city. "And what about the Jewish community?" we asked.

He shook his head sadly. Only three elderly Jews remain—two women and one man. The Jewish cemetery presented a picture of total neglect; broken gravestones covered with weeds. As for the vestiges of the thirty-thousand-member vibrant Jewish community—the synagogues, the schools, the orphanage, the home for the aged—all no longer existed. Some buildings had been converted to government uses, others destroyed.

As much as I had already known from published reports from the news media, hearing the words from an actual witness sickened my heart. It was shocking to contemplate that the good life of the people of present-day Grodno was built on the ruins of the once-thriving predominantly Jewish community. All in the span of only forty years!

Almost as a therapy for my disturbed feelings and worries for my dear ones in Europe, I threw myself into my work. There were a number of innovative projects on hand that were successfully completed. The House of Chairs, a furniture store, attracted national attention. It featured a one-hundred-foot storefront displaying a number of complete room settings. Libby Owens Ford Glass Company described it as "the best visual storefront in the nation" in 1946.

In the housing field, especially in the design of small homes, we worked out an improved method of poured concrete basement wall construction with a contractor, Art Arrighini. The new feature was the use of modular reusable wooden forms. The ease of this kind of installation allowed a complete basement to be finished in a day, a significant saving in time and material. This method soon became standard building practice.

The projects continued to come in, both in variety and size. In the design of residential projects I introduced another innovative concept that would utilize the backyard garden area to the best advantage of the owners. The standard procedure for site layout of residences was to place the garage at the rear of the lot. This arrangement took up much of the garden space, especially with the necessary driveway. My idea was to plan three or four adjoining residences with attached garages at the front and to eliminate the dividing fences between the properties. This would allow a large combined garden area for the visual enjoyment of all the owners. It so happened that we had four clients who knew each other and were receptive to this idea. Among the four were two young teachers, one young attorney and wife, and one middle-aged symphony violinist and wife. The idea appealed to them, and they were willing to experiment in living without the dividing fences. The success of this arrangement in 1938 exceeded everyone's expectations.

I used this same concept the next year, in 1939, when planning the three residences for my brother, my partner, and myself. We bought four forty-by-ninety-foot lots in the newly developing northwest area. A brick fence enclosing the entire back yard was built of the same reclaimed common brick used for the houses. Integrated into the fence was an outdoor grill and seating ledges to be used by all the families. A number of small stone ledges were interspersed along the brick wall for placement of sculpture. Shortly thereafter Cashwan's lyrical carvings were placed on these ledges. At one far-end corner was a ceramic table with stone seating. A few years later a small concrete pool, ten feet by fourteen feet and twenty inches deep, was built in the center of the area. The water spouts on both ends came from two concrete snails designed in Cashwan's studio. Here again the concept worked out so well that it was publicized as the new "Backyard U.S.A." in the local papers. Several years later, when I was studying for a master's degree at Cranbrook Academy of Art in Bloomfield Hills, Michigan, under Eliel Saarinen, he lauded this small but initial step to improve the everyday living environment. Properly landscaped, this area has all the advantages of a small private park. With some playground equipment, it is the center of children's activities, in contrast to the unsupervised dangerous street play commonly seen. By installing permanent outdoor stone table and benches, the adults have the advantages of outdoor living. This landscaped area lends itself well for neighborhood meeting and group celebrations, such as Halloween parties for children. From a few committed neighbors on one block, to a larger neighborhood area of many blocks, there was a potential to reach out to the total urban community. Starting in the late sixties, when condominiums began to be in demand, environmental improvements in the site planning came to the fore with the inclusion of gardens and recreation areas shared by all the owners. Of the many projects that were planned in the office during the early years, the most satisfying were these environmentally oriented residential projects.

In the midst of the office activity, Ruth and I decided to take a week's vacation at Saugatuck, Michigan, a small resort village on the southeast shore of Lake Michigan. We had heard this area attracted many artists from Chicago and Milwaukee because of the wide variety of subject matter—lake, sand dunes, woods, river streams with boat houses, fishermen's nets, and century-old houses. There were also a large number of tourist houses as well as inns. It was the day before July Fourth when we drove the two hundred miles across Michigan to arrive in Saugatuck about midafternoon. We inquired about lodging at the houses where the vacancy signs were posted. At first we didn't pay too much attention when we were told there were no rooms available. After repeated refusals, it finally dawned on us that Jewish vacationers were not wanted. One lady advised us that a small hotel across the Kalamazoo River would welcome us. We felt like leaving this inhospitable place, but as it was getting late in the afternoon, we decided to stay one night. Thus we found the friendly Mr. Pfaender, the owner of the small hotel on the hill across the Kalama-zoo facing the road leading to the Lake Michigan beach. He also had several attrac-tive individual cottages in the wooded area of the property, which he offered us. Our spirits lifted and we decided to stay.

The next few days as we were exploring the sand dunes and nearby areas, we came upon a narrow dirt road marked "No Trespassing." Our curiosity got the better of us and we followed the winding road through the woods to the end. There it opened into a cleared area with a number of old wooden buildings facing an inland waterway. Here was the Oxbow School of Art, a summer project of the School of the Chicago Art Institute. It did not take us long to get acquainted with the small friendly group of instructors and students who were of all ages. I was invited to join the watercolor class and share in the week's activities—outdoor painting at different locales, working from models, evening discussions around the fireplace, and a Satur-day critique of the completed work. Right then and there I enrolled in the painting classes. How can I describe the "magic" of this isolated and peaceful place? I became completely engrossed in the painting so that every available moment of the day was jealously devoted to it. There was also the stimulation of talented peers and learning of new techniques.

As excited as I was about joining this creative group, the physical surroundings left a great deal to be desired. The complex consisted of an old dilapidated inn and a few lumbermen's wooden houses and one-room cabins. The inn was used for the cooking and dining and the large living room for social activities. The second-floor rooms were used for sleeping; most did not have doors and the rooms doubled as work places. The advantage of the one bathroom per floor was that people socialized while standing in the long waiting line. Rowboats along the river lagoon were few and only one had oars. One of the artists who shared the boat with me was Susan Keig, a young art director from Chicago.

And so it was that Oxbow School became my magnet for creative effort during the coming decade. I recall arriving one summer afternoon after the four-hour drive from Detroit; within one hour my bags were put in my room, my clothes were changed to shorts and sandals, large watercolor sheets were rapidly stretched on boards ready for the sketches, and I was ready for action. As I look back, it seems I was driven by a compulsion to work without letup. I especially recall one summer week when I returned home with enough paintings to cover our entire living room floor of fourteen feet by twenty feet.

Added to the joy I got from the creative work, was the warm camaraderie of the group members. Some were to become lifelong friends. One who was to play an indelible role in my professional life was Susan with whom I shared the rowboat. In the following years we kept in contact, visited, and shared our professional expe-riences. It was during one of these visits that she opened a new phase of my life. We were discussing my philosophy of the integration of art and architecture. I suggested that we might write a book on this subject together, since she was an experienced art director for a Chicago publishing firm. Susan responded with enthusiasm and within a few weeks, she produced two specially designed book jackets and suggested several sample page layouts. It was unbelievable how just the sight of the book jackets gave me the confidence to take the writing project seriously. Several weeks later she phoned that she would be unable to coauthor because of the pressure of her own work. I realized that it would be a much more difficult task for me to take on without her because of her long and successful background in the book publishing field.

At first I was stunned by this turn of events, but Susan reassured me that she would remain my critic and help in contacting possible publishing companies. The seed had been planted and with Ruth's encouragement, I decided to embark on this first-time venture. As it turned out *Art in Architecture* was the first of my five professional books, all published by McGraw-Hill Book Company over the period of the next eighteen years. But I am getting ahead of my story.

In 1942 with the outbreak of the war private construction virtually ceased because most of the essential building materials were earmarked for war projects. I went to work for the firm of Kahn and Stonorov who were designing housing for workers engaged in defense projects at the Ford factories at Willow Run. When this project was completed I worked on the design of tank factories in the architectural office of William Kapp. Both here and at the Stonorov's offices, each had a staff of fifty architects and engineers. The work schedule was often twelve hours per day. The work efficiency was generally low, a consequence of the Defense Department's indefinite instructions, resulting in continuous changes in drawings. These defense jobs were temporary in nature. The time between jobs was channeled into a creative experience that was to make a great impact on my future professional life.

Alongside the activities connected with the war effort, there was a rising awareness among architects of the need to improve the urban environment. To work towards this goal the local chapter of the American Institute of Architects formed the Civic Design Group, a voluntary group of thirty-seven architects. I was the vice-chairman. Our purpose was to prepare a master plan for the redevelopment of the city of Detroit, an ambitious and challenging project. What made it more exciting was our freedom to dream up any concept without the usual worries about city codes, budget limitations, or approvals by clients. We were both architects and clients. The project was compelling and evolved into a "work of love" when Eliel Saarinen, the president of the Cranbrook Academy of Art, agreed to serve as a consultant to the group. We were offered the use of its architectural ateliers for working and meetings. We worked evenings and Saturdays, and during the first several months under Saarinen's guidance the group developed their overall schematic plans. Once the scheme was agreed upon, the city areas were divided into segments and were assigned to smaller groups of three or four architects. We studied population trends, traffic and public transportation facilities, and the proper mix of residential and commercial areas, giving special attention to the revitalization of the central business district and the Detroit River waterfront. The entire group adopted the technique used at Cranbrook for its urban studies. These so-called "bubble diagrams" consisted of circular paper cutouts, each representing a certain size area (acreage). This was an efficient way to study various schemes by moving the circles on a city map to find the best solution within the general confines of the existing street patterns. The next step was to transform the circles into shapes of tentative building forms. At this stage the architects met again to review and make the necessary adjustment so that the overall plan would tie in with each of the individual segments. In the final stage, models were made to present our ideas in a realistic form. The models showed the main roads, secondary circulation arteries, landscaping and the proposed buildings, as well as the existing buildings that were to be preserved.

The final comprehensive report was made at a public meeting held in the main auditorium of the Detroit Public Library. About one hundred citizens attended, including officials from the planning department, the city council, and architects. Since Saarinen shied away from public appearances, the plan was presented by his spokesman from Cranbrook Academy. Unfortunately the reaction to the presentation was one of skepticism. People questioned the realism and practicality of the planning approach. The chairman explained that even though some parts of the master plan were projected for the distant future, the main purpose of the study was to stimulate people to improve the city. To our dismay, the meeting ended on a negative note. In spite of the letdown felt by Saarinen and the committee members, we each felt that as individuals we had gained an understanding and insight into the processes of city planning that were to influence our professional thinking for the rest of our careers. One should remember that this transpired in 1943. It seemed that few people, from the highest in power to the average citizen, were aware of the extent of the city's impending decline. It took almost forty years for Detroit to make "eleventh-hour" efforts to reverse the deterioration of the central business district. It was a deep satisfaction to me to see that many of the recommendations of our design group were finally being implemented. The riverfront development, especially, was long overdue until the Hart Plaza was built in the seventies, with its Noguchi fountain, and open air amphitheater for summer ethnic festivals and special programs. This was the beginning of the improvement planning for the entire riverfront on the Detroit River, extending east from Woodward, three miles to Belle Isle and west from Woodward, one mile to the Ambassador Bridge.

One factor that impeded the revival of the city core was the accepted thinking by most people that the spread and strengthening of suburbia was the wave of the future. My personal conviction has always been that the city should not become an empty shell with meager and minimal activity in its central business district. The city had a healthy base to build upon. It had a viable financial and administrative center in the central business district. Within a radius of two miles it had one of the largest medical centers in the country and the campus of Wayne State University, a large state university. In addition, it had a major art museum, historical museum, science museum, children's museum, a new Afro-American museum, the Center for Creative Studies (art and music schools), an outstanding main library, the International Institute (sponsor of ethnic cultures and Americanization), Your Heritage House celebrating black achievements, as well as other institutions. The salvaging of Orchestra Hall (built in the 1920s) by a handful of dedicated music lovers led by Paul Ganson just twenty-four hours from the wrecker's ball, deserves special attention. This music hall with its excellent acoustics is now restored and has become an important cultural "anchor" in the total complex. These anchors are the basis for a healthy and liveable city. Still missing are residential complexes to fill in what has become decayed and slum areas surrounding the anchors. As of this writing, 1988, a beginning has been made. A number of new apartments have been completed and others are in the planning stages, but the momentum has to be maintained.

The experience with Eliel Saarinen and the committee inspired my further exploration and study in the urban design field. Despite office pressures, I decided to enroll at the Cranbrook Academy to study for a master's degree in urban studies. To attend even the required minimum hours meant having a hurried dinner, then parting with family from six to midnight three times a week. It was not easy for me to be away from my two young sons, Daniel, five, and Eliel, three, but I felt that future benefits would offset the temporary sacrifice of family closeness.

It was almost twenty years after I had graduated from the University of Michigan with a bachelor of arts degree when I received my master of arts degree in Urban Design in 1948. My Cranbrook thesis stressed the point that improvements in urban environments do not have to wait for long-range government or corporate planning. It can start at the level of the homeowners. The planning for my own house illustrated this concept. The thesis stressed the necessity of innovative planning by private developers, corporations, and government agencies. The basic principles inherent in good urban planning are still applicable today. These include open landscaped areas, provisions for parking, proper circulation and traffic patterns, as well as integration of art forms to bring delight and pleasure to the people. The balanced mixture of the residential, commercial, and recreational areas is, of course, a must.

I enjoyed immensely my association with Eliel Saarinen. The students had complete freedom in their choice of types of urban areas to be developed. Saarinen, whose studio and residence was across the narrow landscaped walkway from the architectural drafting room, would visit during the day or evening (work never ceased there). The importance of his input was revealed in the philosophical and ideological discussions with the students and was always intermixed with humorous comments. At that time his book, *The City,* was just published and he was working on another book, *Search for Forms.* All of us hesitated to visit him at his studio, apprehensive that we might interfere with his work. One afternoon I took courage and knocked at his door. To my pleasant surprise he received me with open arms, served me a drink, and asked whether I was interested in hearing excerpts from the manuscript of his forthcoming book. Only then did I realize how pleased he was to have his students visit. Subsequently, we had frequent exchanges of ideas. One visit stands out in my mind. As I entered his studio he ran up to me and exclaimed: "Look what I just received, a telegram from Sibelius congratulating me on my seventy-fifth birthday!" For him it was a supremely happy moment and a beautiful birthday gift indeed. Many of his random remarks showed the modesty of this man who claimed that most "original" ideas have their roots in the minds of his many predecessors. One of his favorite pronouncements was: "It's the end results that count. We are all like relay race runners, carrying the torch and transferring it to the next one." This was his way of pointing out that we are the inheritors of all the creative ideas and talents of those who preceded us and that each one of us, in turn, adds his contribution. This thinking and his natural tact were also expressed in the considerate working relationship he developed with his clients. He used to say that he always prepared two schemes and invariably saw to it that the one he favored the client claimed as his own idea.

My association with Cranbrook helped intensify my lifelong interest in the promotion of art in architecture. I had always felt that art should become a part of our daily living instead of being set apart and confined to museums and exhibition halls. Throughout the years in almost every building I succeeded in allotting a small budget for art to be integrated as part of the overall concept. In the 1950s a big boost in the use of art was given by the development of regional suburban shopping centers being built throughout the country. One of the first of its kind, designed by Victor Gruen, was the Northland Center in Southfield, Michigan. Free standing sculptures, fountains, landscaping, street furniture, graphics, signing, and lighting were all part of the total design. This decade of open mall centers was followed in the 1960s by a succession of closed mall centers, which provided even greater opportunity for commissioning meaningful art work. The inner courts allowed for a larger variety of art work since the art was sheltered from the weather.

At that time our office was commissioned to plan a number of large shopping centers, three of which were designed in association with Victor Gruen Associates of Los Angeles for the J. L. Hudson Company—Westland and Southland in the Detroit area, and Genesee Valley in Flint, Michigan. Later, Crossroads Mall in Kalamazoo, Michigan, was designed by us for the J. L. Hudson Company. Other regional enclosed centers, Livonia Mall and Macomb Mall, were also designed by us for the prominent developers, Shenkman and Klein and Schostak Brothers. These projects provided opportunities for many artists, both local and nationally known, to create significant works, expressed in many forms. They varied from free-standing sculptures to complex fountains, colorful wall murals, play sculptures, mobiles, specially designed lighting fixtures, all in a setting of landscaped areas with trees, shrubs, and flower beds.

Art was just beginning to be recognized as an essential element in the total shopping center design. Artists of national and even international repute were commissioned. At the same time a considerable number of talented local artists were included in the total art program. Among the artists commissioned in both categories were: Harry Bertoia, Morris Brose, Irving Berg, Samuel Cashwan, Hubert Dalwood, Marshall Fredericks, Earl Krentzin, Louise Nevelson, Narendra Patel, George Rickey, Jan Peter Stern, Hannah Stiebel, Alden Smith. Eventually these experiences of commissioning art for shopping centers would be included in my first two books: Art in Architecture (1968) and New Dimensions in Shopping Centers and Stores (1973) published by McGraw-Hill Book Company. The favorable reaction to these books, especially from young architects entering the profession and the architectural educators in the colleges and universities, gave me an added incentive to continue to share my knowledge and experiences in other books. The books have a wide readership in foreign countries. In 1985 one of Japan's large architectural firms, Takenaka Komute and Company Limited, sent one of its young architects, Hidetoshi Dote, with his wife and two children, to serve a year's internship in our office.

Tom Borman residence, Detroit, Michigan, 1939.

Backyard of our three-house complex showing the
ornamental wading pool, 1939. (Photo by Elmer L.
Astleford)

Wilshire Motor Sales Building (with added airbrush
signage to photo), 1951.

333 West Fort Street Building, a model of the parking
garage, Detroit, Michigan, completed 1971. (Photo by
Lens-Art)

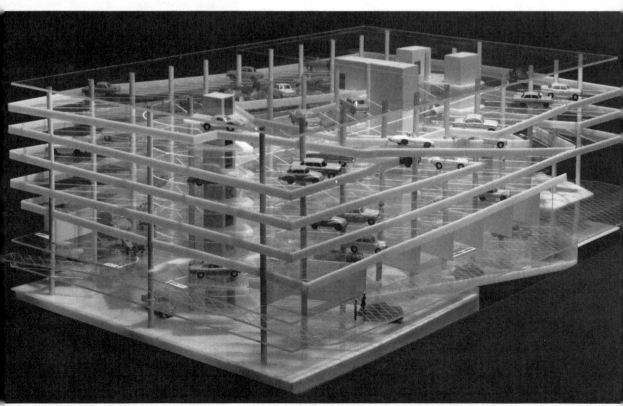

Residence for William Sucher, 1951, Palmer Park,
Michigan. (Photo by Elmer L. Astleford)

Prototype for Speedway 79 Gas Station. (Photo by Elmer
L. Astleford)

The House of Modern Chairs, Detroit, Michigan, 1946.

Camp Tamarack Amphitheater, Holly, Michigan, 1959.

Krolik Elementary School, Detroit, Michigan, 1963.
(Photo by Lens-Art)

Manufacturers National Bank, Birmingham, Michigan,
1965, Honor Award, Detroit Chapter AIA. (Photo by
Balthazar Korab)

Southland Center, Taylor, Michigan, in association with
Gruen Associates, Inc., Louise Nevelson, artist, 1966.
(Photo by Balthazar Korab)

Manufacturers National Bank Operations Center, Detroit,
Michigan, 1971, Robert Youngman, artist. (Photo by
Balthazar Korab)

Manufacturers National Bank Operations Center, Detroit,
Michigan, 1971, Robert Youngman, artist. (Photo by
Balthazar Korab)

Manufacturers National Bank Operations Center, Detroit,
Michigan, lower lobby, Samuel Cashwan, artist, 1971.
(Photo by Balthazar Korab)

(*Left to right*) Collaboration between owner, bank Vice-Chairman Kenneth Aird, sculptor Robert Youngman, and author. Manufacturers National Bank Operations Center. (Photo by J & L)

333 West Fort Street Building, Detroit, Michigan, 1971.
(Photo by Balthazar Korab)

Congregation Beth Achim Synagogue, Southfield,
Michigan, 1973. Poplack garden court and sculpture,
"Vision of Peace," by Roda Reilinger. (Photo by Balthazar
Korab)

Michael Berry International Terminal, Detroit Metropolitan
Airport, 1974, Robert Youngman, artist. Engineering
Society of Detroit Award. (Photo by Balthazar Korab)

Louis G. Redstone Associates, Louis Redstone's office,
Livonia, Michigan, 1976. (Photo by Balthazar Korab)

Louis G. Redstone Associates office entrance, Livonia, Michigan, 1976. Bas-relief mural by author. (Photo by Balthazar Korab)

Louis G. Redstone Associates office, 1976. Note use of
gate from former office that serves as part of the entrance
sign. (Photo by Balthazar Korab)

Jewish Community Center, West Bloomfield, Michigan,
1976. Brick mural by author. (Photo by Balthazar Korab,
Ltd.)

Underground library, landscaped area, daylighted by
areaways. Wayne H. Buell School of Management,
Lawrence Institute of Technology, Southfield, Michigan,
1982. (Photo by Walter G. Bizon)

Grand Traverse Tower, Grand Traverse Resort Village, near
Traverse City, Michigan, 1986. (Photo by Balthazar Korab,
Ltd.)

Manufacturers National Corporation Operations Center,
Livonia, Michigan, 1988. (Photo by Beth Singer, Inc.)

LOUIS G. REDSTONE ASSOCIATES, INC.

RIVER PLACE PLAZA

Stroh River Place Plaza, a historic conversion from
warehouse to apartments, Detroit, Michigan. Estimated
completion, 1990. Owners: the Stroh family; Arnold
Cohen, Stanley Berger, and Walther Cohen.

9

ARCHITECTURAL
PRACTICE
AND TRAVELS
1949–1989

Active interest in the workings of the American Institute of Architects (AIA) began in 1949. Until then, I was unable to take time to attend the national AIA conventions, but I couldn't resist the appeal of the upcoming convention in Houston, Texas. In addition to the scheduled workshops, the program highlighted a major address by Frank Lloyd Wright, as well as a postconvention tour to Mexico, hosted by the Mexican architects.

Frank Lloyd Wright was to be the recipient of the Gold Medal, the highest award of the institute. I had always believed that for Wright it was a long overdue recognition by his fellow architects. Other countries around the world had recognized his genius, but American architects for various reasons generally resisted the philosophical approach inherent in the development of organic architecture. In his acceptance speech, copies of which were distributed to convention members, a dramatic looking Frank Lloyd Wright, white haired and wearing a flowing cape, took the large audience of four thousand architects to task, appealing to their consciences and urging them to work to create the best of human habitats. Some of the highlights of his acceptance speech revealing the inner feelings of this great architect follow:

> . . . now what must an architect be if he is going to be really one worthwhile, if he is really going to be true to his profession? He must be a creator. He must perceive beyond the present. He must stay pretty far ahead. . . .
>
> But he must see into the life of things if he is going to build anything worth building in this day and generation. . . .
>
> And do you know we ought to be the greatest builders the world has ever seen. We have the riches, we have the materials, we have the greatest release ever found by man in steel and in glass. We have everything. We have a freedom that never existed before. . . .
>
> We have got the kind of buildings we deserve. We have got the kind of cities that are coming to us. This city of which Houston is an example, we did it. It came to us because we are what we are, and don't forget it. If we are going to get anything better, if we are going to come by a more honorable expression of a civilization such as the world is entitled to from us—we put ourselves on a hill here, in a highlight, we talk about the highest standard of living the world has ever seen, we profess all these things and we don't deliver. . . .

146

I think if we were to wake up and take a good look at ourselves as ourselves, without trying to blame other people for what really are our own shortcomings and our own lack of character, we would be an example to the world that the world needs now. We wouldn't be pursuing a Cold War. We would be pursuing a great endeavor to plant, rear and nurture a civilization, and we would have a culture that would convince the whole world.

The impact of his philosophy and organic approach to architecture—the "marriage of the building to the natural surroundings," was even greater thirty-five years later when I visited Fallingwater, the Kaufman house at Bear Run near Pittsburgh, Pennsylvania. Designed in 1936, the focal point is the high setting over a waterfall. Large cantilevered concrete sections give the dramatic image of suspension in midair.

Edgar Kaufman, Jr., lived in the house until 1963 when he gave it to the Western Pennsylvania Conservancy as a memorial to his parents. This is an excerpt of his talk at the presentation ceremony, 29 October 1963, published as a brochure that year by the Western Pennsylvania Conservancy:

> Designed for this setting, the house was hardly up before its fame circled the earth; it was recognized as one of the clearest successes of the American genius, Frank Lloyd Wright. The house is usually perceived through a swarm of fables; it seems to breed them spontaneously. What is the house really? After more than a quarter century of knowing it, living in it, caring for it, I should be able to reply. It is one of the most beautiful works made by man for man. It takes but an instant to see the character of the house; yet, after all these years, there are details and relationship in it which I've discovered only recently. Its beauty remains fresh like that of the nature into which it fits. It has served well as a home, yet has always been more than that; a work of art, beyond any ordinary measures of excellence. Itself an ever-flowing source of exhilaration, it is set on the waterfall of Bear Run, spouting nature's endless energy and grace. House and site together form the very image of man's desire to be at one with nature, equal and wedded to nature. . . .
>
> Such a place cannot be possessed. It is work by man for man, not by a man for a man. Over the years since it was built, Fallingwater has grown ever more famous and admired, a textbook example of modern architecture at its best. By its very intensity it is a public resource, not a private indulgence.

The postconvention trip to Mexico City was to be the first of my many trips to Central and South American countries. Nearly two hundred and fifty American architects availed themselves of this opportunity. The warm and festive hospitality accorded us made our experience memorable. During our five-day visit the local architects provided tours to the historic Pre-Columbian ruins and pyramids, as well as to the new modern buildings that were beginning to rise throughout the city. The now sprawling and handsome University of Mexico was in the beginning stage of its construction. The existing field of large lava stones was being utilized in the construction of some of the university buildings as well as the residences of the new nearby exclusive suburb of Pedrigal.

It was exciting to witness the total integration of the mosaic murals that covered every inch of all four exterior walls of the university library. The murals, designed by the well-known architect-artist Juan O'Gorman, depicted the history of Mexico. In the years following, nearly every building on campus had either free-standing sculpture elements or deep concrete bas-reliefs painted in bright colors. Since 1949 I have followed the careers of talented Mexican sculptors and painters, some of whom are commissioned for projects in other countries. In the process of selecting examples of art in architecture for my books, I came to personally know and enjoy the friendship of a number of talented sculptors. Among them are Mathias Goeritz, Helen Escabedo, Sebastian, and Juan O'Gorman. As I look back, the Mexican experience was an important stepping stone to my own approach of using art in my buildings.

Back to our 1949 Mexican celebration. The first three evenings were hosted by Mexico City's mayor, the president of Mexico, and the president of the Society of Mexican Architects—all testifying to the importance and esteem felt for the profession by the government. The friendships we made with a number of architects were to last far into the future. By the time we reached Acapulco our group had dwindled to about twenty. This smaller number was conducive to even closer relationships. I noticed one of the ladies was carrying a watercolor pad and paint box. As usual, I had my watercolors with me to sketch the exciting mountain scenery. The strong colors in the intense sunlight—the yellows, the blue of the sky and water, the white of the villas—presented a challenge of how to express these impressions on paper. The lady, Rosa Ferreyra de Roca, an accomplished watercolor artist from Cordoba, Argentina, was the wife of Jaime Roca, a well-known architect and a University of Michigan graduate. Our interest in watercolor painting led to a friendship with the family over the next forty years.

As we were parting the Rocas said, "You must come to visit us someday soon." At the time I thought this merely a polite gesture. In my wildest imagination, I never dreamed that I would be able to visit that faraway country and their home in Cordoba, six hundred miles west of Buenos Aires. Unexpected surprises in life, for better or for worse, are many. Five years later in 1954, when I joined the first group of American architects to visit South American countries, I notified the Rocas of my coming. I hardly expected that we could meet again because of the long trip from Cordoba. My excitement knew no bounds when I was paged in my Buenos Aires hotel. It was Jaime Roca and his teenage son Miguel, an architectural student, who drove from Cordoba to be personal hosts for three days for me and a young Chicago architect Jerry Shea, one of our group. (As for Jerry Shea, who could ever imagine that a few years later he would join my staff and eventually become the president of the Redstone firm?)

In the years ahead, in 1960 and 1969, during the international architectural conferences in Argentina, my wife and I were happy to visit the Roca family again. In the intervening periods Jaime, Rosita, Miguel (now an outstanding architect and teacher), and their daughters made several visits to Detroit. Each time their visit resembled a joyful family reunion. The most satisfying news capping the longtime friendship came in a long-distance phone call from Miguel in Cordoba. He was indeed excited, reporting that my nomination of him for a 1985 Honorary Fellowship in the American Institute of Architects had been approved. It was exhilarating also for me that we would be celebrating this great honor together at the 1985 national convention in San Francisco. None of my travels to conferences and international meetings would have been possible without the encouragement of my wife, my associates, and my brother Sol at the office who took care of the management details.

Synagogue design played an important role in the postwar years of the firm. Featured under the title of contemporary religious buildings in the *Detroit News* Pictorial Magazine of 2 July 1950 were Temple Beth El in Flint, Michigan, and an orthodox synagogue, Beth Shmuel on Dexter Boulevard in Detroit. To follow later was a conservative synagogue, Beth Aaron on Wyoming Avenue in Detroit. With the population flight to the suburbs in the sixties, the congregations of Beth Aaron and Ahavas Achim joined together to form the new Beth Achim in 1968 in Southfield, Michigan, and we were commissioned to design the building. Presently we are on the consultant list for the Union of American Hebrew Congregations.

In the following years the office was busy with a number of large strip centers. One inquiry that at first seemed to be of minor interest turned out to be an important corporate commission, keeping part of the staff busy over a period of several years. The problem was to design an innovative yet typical gas station for a large local oil company whose main requirement was to achieve maximum visibility. Our staff designed a compact triangular station. Connected with it was a fifty-foot exposed steel base that supported a revolving sign consisting of only two numerals, "79," the logo of the corporation. The design was received with enthusiasm and our office proceeded to adopt the model for a large number of different sites. Unexpectedly this became the starting point of a long and productive association with the Manufacturers National Bank (at that time known as the Industrial Bank), one of the major national banks. The president of the oil company served on the board of this bank and recommended our firm.

Our first commission was to design a drive-in branch on Vernor Highway in the southwest part of the city. The concept of drive-in banks was new to Detroit and this branch bank was one of the first. Consequently the bank management was cautious and commissioned the structure with only two drive-up windows and without complete branch facilities. The successful operations of this drive-up soon became evident and the bank ordered the completion of the main branch facility. Since 1952, drive-in banks became standard design throughout the country. Our office proceeded to design over fifty branches for this client. We took great pride when we were commissioned in 1970 to design their eleven-story main operation center of five hundred thousand square feet in the downtown Detroit financial district. In the late 1980s another large computer center of two hundred thousand square feet was designed for this bank in the nearby city of Livonia. Our successful experiences in bank planning brought us in contact with the First Federal of Michigan, another large banking establishment. Here too, we designed a large number of branch banks and an operations center.

I had little appreciation in 1950, thirteen years after I left Palestine, of how much my inner being had been molded by my early experiences as a pioneer and later as a professional. Being a part of the initial stages of rebuilding a homeland for the Jewish people left an indelible imprint on my philosophical, political, and world outlook. Probably one of the most important factors shaping my personality was in the basic values developed during that early period. The unselfish ideal that brought the pioneering group together to work "by the sweat of the brow" for the common good instilled a feeling of accomplishment and self-esteem. Monetary values, only to the extent of meeting minimum basic needs of food, clothing, and shelter, did not affect the happy human relationships we experienced. These values served me well in the years ahead. During the Depression of the early 1930s, when jobs were scarce and money in even shorter supply, there was rarely a letdown in spirit or feeling of real deprivation.

I had a great longing to visit my sister in Israel and to see firsthand what transpired there after the declaration of the state of Israel in May 1948. In my mind's eye I tried to reconstruct the scenes I had left nearly thirteen years earlier: my friends in Tel Aviv, the small restaurants I patronized, the bathing in the Mediterranean, the kibbutz life, and the many familiar faces and places. Before leaving I wrote about my arrival plans to both my sister Rosa who lived in the Kibbutz Ein Shemer, and my former partner Shimon Lipshitz in Tel Aviv. When I arrived at the Lod Airport in Israel at midnight Shimon was there and, together, we waited for my sister Rosa to arrive to meet me. After about a half-hour, we decided to put my luggage in Shimon's car and go to his home for the night. As we were about to leave Rosa and her husband Benyu arrived to take me to the kibbutz, an hour and a half distance away. I found myself in a very distressing situation: to disappoint my friend after all his efforts to meet me and take me to his home, or to disappoint my family by not going back with them that night. We finally made a compromise solution: I would stay overnight with Shimon and I would go to the kibbutz the next morning. Even with this, I felt guilty as I sensed their sadness and letdown feelings. It seemed that I was punished for my decision. Shimon's apartment windows opened on to the City Zoo! All that night (what was left of it) I heard the roar of the lions, and the howling of other animals! In the morning, completely dazed from lack of sleep, we made our way to Kibbutz Ein Shemer.

It was an emotional and joyful meeting with my nephews thirteen-year-old Amnon and ten-year-old Gabriel who had been up most of the night waiting to meet their "uncle from America." We would be meeting for the first time. They knew I was bringing gifts and they were excited with anticipation. Although the kibbutz provided the essentials of food and clothing, there was no allowance for items that could be considered dispensable. The boys' faces lit up at the sight of the Boy Scout wristwatches, the fountain pens, the sleeping bags for camping, the weatherproof jackets, and the sweaters. When they learned that we would all go to Tel Aviv to buy a bicycle, their joy knew no bounds.

There was also a sad side to this otherwise happy reunion. My sister's youngest child, an eight-month-old girl Dorit had been delivered at birth with the tightened umbilical cord around her neck. This left her impaired mentally and physically. At that time, there were only a few indications of this handicap and my sister hoped that with proper care, patience, and therapy she might outgrow it, or at least be nearly normal. Rosa could not forgive herself for having the baby delivered at a small infirmary at the kibbutz rather than the nearby hospital. With proper medical attention the cord could have been loosened, and the child could have grown healthy and beautiful. As it turned out, Dorit's care became a lifetime worry for all the family, and a continuous obligation of the kibbutz to pay for institutional care. The social structure of the kibbutz, with its deep concern for the welfare of its members, helped mitigate the family's heavy burden. During the early years the kibbutz assigned a nurse's aid to be with her throughout the day in the nursery quarters. Years later, as a young adult, she was sent to a special school for the handicapped in a nearby town.

Unfortunately, this was not the only tragedy the Harudi family was to experience. In the continuous struggle for survival since the establishment of the State in 1948, Israel has relied on all its citizens from eighteen to fifty-five to train and serve in the reserve army. It was during the Six-Day War in April of 1967 that Amnon, a twenty-six-year-old paratrooper and father of two sons and an unborn daughter, was killed when his battalion entered the Old City of Jerusalem. In his last letters to his wife Edna and to his parents, he speaks of this fervent hope for peace.

On the eve of war 4/6/1967

My dear Edna,

I write this letter with a deep sense of foreboding. I know that when it reaches you, this will be during fateful hours for us all. A thousand and one thoughts filter through my mind. One thing has served to encourage me: my furlough. It was short, but wonderful to see both you and the children.

I think only of you and the children, during this miserable War of Nerves. One of the factors that keeps me going is the knowledge that others feel worse than I do. This is small comfort for me, as at a time like this my emotions are much stronger, and particularly I want to see you!

Perhaps our only choice is to do the unbelievable—for the State cannot exist as at the moment. Perhaps we won't go very far (as far as territorial conquest is concerned) because that is not what matters. One thing is clear—we must break the blockade, even if it means many losses and wounded. I hope and trust that will come right. At any rate, I don't know when I'll see you again.

While at home things seemed to be all right—just don't make light of the little things and all will end in peace. Today, more than ever before, I dream of this wonderful word. Peace: a word which symbolizes all the good and the beauty of our world. If only my wishes could reach the hearts of those who decide the fate of the world!

In general our morale is high, in spite of occasional tension. At the moment, for instance, I'm miserable. Let's hope my mood will improve. Where we are, we can see fields of unharvested wheat and other grain, and hay still spread over the ground—it simply hurts to see such a situation.

I send you lots of love—kiss the children for me, and look after them well. Keep up your spirits—as you know how in difficult times.

Love, from Amnon
See you soon.

Letter from the War

My dear parents!

It is a fateful hour for all our people today. You are not used to hearing such words from me! But I feel good, everything is O.K. and our victory is not in doubt. We cannot be beaten. And our morale is high.

I have always wanted peace. But if we are forced into it, we shall go to war. And we shall win. There will be losses, but that is the sacrifice to be made for peace, for Israel and the Jewish people. There is no doubt about the final result. We cannot allow any other result.

I am confident that you will manage in the trying conditions of the coming period. I feel good and we are all well. I think of you all the time and hope to see you again soon. Keep well.

Yours,
Amnon

For a small country like Israel, with its constant concern for security and survival, the loss of even one person is taken as a personal tragedy by all. The most touching aspect to me was the large memorial sculpture erected for Amnon and Hanan, his friend, which is placed in the central landscaped area of the kibbutz.

Physical comforts in the kibbutz had improved considerably during my thirteen-year absence. The original wooden barracks were replaced with small two-room cottages. The toilet and shower accommodations still were communal and located centrally. Food was adequate, mostly fresh vegetables, soups, cheese, and occasionally meat once or twice a week. Generally the food situation in the kibbutz was much better than in the cities.

The country, still suffering from the effects of the 1948 War of Liberation, was short of all basic food supplies. The Jewish population had nearly tripled in the past two years, growing from 600,000 to over 1.5 million. Immigrants were arriving daily by ship and plane from many corners of the world, mostly from the Arab countries of Iraq, Egypt, Yemen, Morocco, and Algeria. The immigrants were temporarily housed in tents or in abandoned military barracks. One of these compounds was near the kibbutz. I was invited by Rena Harudi, Benyu's sixteen-year-old niece who was assigned there as a nurse's aide, to see firsthand how the new arrivals lived. There were about 350 families in the compound. Only the simplest accommodations existed. Most of the men were artisans, craftsmen, tailors, and bakers. As yet there was no organized employment agency for them. During the interim period while they waited to leave the compound, they bartered their belongings and exchanged their services among themselves. In some cases the more aggressive were able to set up minibusinesses. These families were the most difficult to relocate since they were fearful of the unknown. The majority of the families had to wait several years before housing could be built and employment opportunities created. Before coming to Israel, I couldn't imagine how a million people could be "squeezed" into this tiny country in such a short time. I thought it would be "standing room only." To my amazement, I discovered that the country was greatly underpopulated and there was room for many more. This proved true three decades later, when the population, both Jewish and non-Jewish, reached nearly 4.5 million.

My visit to Tel Aviv shattered my nostalgic dreams. The little restaurant on a side street where I usually lunched with my friends was gone. Bathing in the ocean, which for me was the big Tel Aviv attraction, was temporarily forbidden because of the polluted water. Shortage of food kept most of the restaurants closed and the ones that were open served mainly eggs with pitas. Even here I learned that I had to be an "early comer" to get some food. What helped sustain many families was the food assistance program of the Care organization, which provided food packages that could be sent by relatives and friends from the United States. In Israel a system of distribution of food coupons for the population and for the tourists was strictly enforced. I did not know that as a tourist I could buy additional Care packages. The few that I had turned out to be the best present I could bring my friends. As I had promised my nephews, we arranged to go shopping for a bicycle in Tel Aviv. Because of the poor economic situation, most of the nonessential imports had been curtailed. We inquired unsuccessfully at a number of stores until we finally found one for sale in an out-of-the-way store. The boys were jubilant.

After a week I started to look up my friends from the construction group of the early pioneering days. I was anxious to meet my close friend Yedidia Yanovsky, who lived in a small apartment with his wife Rachel in Jerusalem. I asked him to invite other friends who lived nearby. I still recall the nostalgia of that evening—long hours of reminiscing and being brought up to date on their personal lives. Generally each held important leadership positions in the construction industry such as foreman or superintendent for large buildings. Others remained kibbutz leaders, pursuing their ideals of communal living that brought them to Israel in the first place. I kept my promise to Shimon Lipshitz to return to Tel Aviv to spend time with him and we planned a trip to the northern part of Israel. He had an old Ford that was still serviceable. Benyu, who was familiar with all the roads and areas, joined us and was our guide. We drove to the northern part of Israel, the Galilee, the ancient city of Safed, and the most northern village of Metullah. This trip evoked nostalgic memories of a similar journey made by foot almost thirty years earlier by our group members. At that time they were celebrating the commemoration of the Trumpeldor heroic resistance against an Arab attack at Tel Hai. The four-day trip was an exciting and joyful experience, except for the food problem. We made good use of the Care food packages I had brought along. Even so, we had to do some careful rationing of the canned meat, which was the main staple.

The several British fortified concrete garrison buildings along the way were a tragic reminder of the bitter struggle for the Jewish homeland. These had been turned over to the Arabs in 1948 by the British when they accepted the United Nations Resolution for an independent Israeli state. The Arabs did not recognize the resolution for the partition of the land into Jewish and Arab states and fought bitterly against it. These fortresses, located in strategic spots, controlled main highways. As we looked at the concrete walls, scarred with large holes and cracks caused by dynamite and shelling, we were reminded of the heroic tales of the ingenuity and bravery of the Jewish fighters who suffered many casualties and overcame great odds in storming these fortresses.

The joy of my visit was clouded by news of the outbreak of hostilities in Korea and the United Nations' police action, which was to be directed and fought primarily by United States forces. The American consulate advised American visitors to return home. This general atmosphere of apprehension was reflected in the growing lines of Americans at the consulate office requesting more specific information. Many people did leave the country posthaste. As for me, I kept my original summer departure date.

On the way home I stopped in Brussels for a short visit with my cousin Shefka. Twenty years earlier in 1930 she had married a Soviet sympathizer, a journalist, who went from Poland to Russia with the idea of settling there. During the Stalin purge of the Jewish intelligentsia—writers, doctors, lawyers, and others—he was arrested and executed. Shefka was allowed to return with her eight-year-old son to Brussels where she had friends. During our visit as we talked about these tragic events in her life she showed me a recent letter from the Russian authorities stating that her husband had been mistakenly accused and that his name was now cleared. The letter only intensified her bitterness and grief at the useless sacrifice of her husband's life.

I was glad to return home, realizing anew how much I missed the love and warmth of homelife. I found the office work increasing and decided to add another architect to the staff. My brother and I began to consider building our own office away from the downtown area. We chose a site in the northwest section about six miles away. The building was designed for a capacity of eight draftsmen and the space seemed large enough for future expansion. The entrance lobby and my private office overlooked a small landscaped court, enclosed by a brick wall with a sculptured gate. The court featured a small ceramic fountain designed by my friend, Sam Cashwan. The bronzed copper gate was the work of Julius Schmidt, the director of the sculpture department at Cranbrook Academy of Art. We had become friends while I was studying at Cranbrook and I admired his new techniques in casting metal sculpture. The interior of the brick wall was highlighted by inlaid ceramic bas-reliefs designed by Walter Speck. His bright colored enamel glazes gave a special lustre to the wall. Several projecting stone brackets were designed to hold a small sculpture. What a satisfying experience it was to be able in my own office building to put into practice my ideas of integrating art with architecture. It became the trademark of our office.

We moved to this building in 1952. It was destined to serve us for twenty-five years until our next move in 1976. The building, however, underwent constant changes and additions. The office continued to expand to occupy adjacent medical and dentist office space. As the need for more space increased, we built a second floor over the parking area. Finally, our expanded needs, lack of parking, and growing security problems in a changing neighborhood prompted us to move again.

The move in 1952 to our new office building was a satisfying and happy event, but it also had its heartbreaks. This was the period when Senator Joe McCarthy's "witch hunt" for "fellow travelers" based on irresponsible, unsubstantiated, and erroneous charges was in full swing. My sister Riva belonged to a liberal group that was on his black list, her name appeared in the local newspaper, and she began to receive harassing telephone calls. She knew she was unfairly accused and feared that the negative publicity would reflect on us and harm business relationships. In reaction to this kind of aggravation she decided to move to Los Angeles. Although we expected her move to be temporary, it was a sad parting. Riva was one of the cornerstones of our organization from its very inception when she served as receptionist, typist, and accountant. After several years we persuaded her to return to Detroit and assume her former duties as comptroller-accountant in the office.

The McCarthy period was also stressful for me because of the occurrence of some tense incidents connected with Riva's publicity. At that time our office was involved in several important bank-building projects and we were in the process of designing several school projects for the city. We also had a large food warehouse building under construction, and an incident occurred on the premises of this construction project. Although I was advised by friends to avoid too much visibility, I had decided to continue my work and my visits to the projects as part of my normal routine. I visited the warehouse site with some trepidation, anticipating possible unpleasant confrontations. No sooner did I start my inspection tour than I was surrounded by a group of workers who bombarded me with belligerent questions. Did I have any connection with my sister's group? Did I support my sister in her activities? I replied in as calm a tone as I could muster that my sister's political views were her own, and rightly so, just as the political views of their sons and daughters might differ from their own. My open and straightforward answers disarmed them and one by one they went back to their chores. There was only one other unpleasant moment that could have had serious consequences. As I was passing close under a masonry scaffolding, a concrete block seemed as though by accident to fall off the scaffold within inches of my head. At that time protective safety helmets were not required. Even though momentarily shaken, I considered the incident the act of a belligerent, misguided person. Within a few weeks the situation on the job site returned to normal.

One positive development emerged from that tragic period. My faith in the fairness of the American people was reaffirmed. On one of my school building projects, one board member questioned my retention as the architect, even though the contract was already signed. A majority of the board members rejected the implication of my being guilty by association. My clients in the private sector were also loyal in their confidence and no contract was cancelled.

As the commissions increased in size and complexity of functional and aesthetic requirements, I felt the need for a responsible associate. There were the time consuming conferences with the owners; the preparation of preliminary design sketches; the checking of the working drawings—architectural, structural, mechanical, and electrical; and finally, the supervision of the actual construction. The pressure to take care of all these details became overwhelming. Yet I realized that choosing a compatible associate who could eventually become a full partner was a vital move. I let my intentions be known through the professional "grapevine," which resulted in a number of applicants. As desperate as I was, none of these turned out to have the combined professional and personal qualifications I was seeking. However, a recommendation by a mutual friend brought Allan Agree to my attention. I had known Allan from the early 1940s when we worked together on a large tank-arsenal project. He was a capable, experienced architect who could be responsible for the production of the architectural drawings. It turned out to be a good choice and he remained for ten years, when he left to start his own practice. This association was important not only in sharing the major office responsibilities, but also in allowing me to explore new architectural trends in a number of South American countries, especially Brazil.

As fate would have it, the American Institute of Architects was organizing an educational tour of South American countries in 1954. When I look back now, I really do not know how I had the audacity to consider a six-week trip, but it turned out to have had a great impact on my future. Our departure point was Miami, and on the first evening the entire group met to get acquainted. Most of the architects (some with their wives) were middle-aged or older. It seemed to me that architects who could afford a long trip were already well established or near retirement. An exception was a young architect in his late twenties. Leo (Jerry) Shea had just returned from the Korean War and service in the Marine Corps. He had decided to spend his savings on this trip before he "settled down" to start his career. Though decades apart in age, Jerry and I hit it off immediately and became good friends from the first evening. Both of us were eager to absorb the new knowledge and experiences.

The first stop was Panama. We were met at the airport by the dean of the School of Architecture and a group of students. We visited their newly built architectural school; this modern concrete building was designed for the tropical climate, with grilled openings for cross ventilation. The highlight of our visit was the tour of the Panama Canal locks. What made our visit even more memorable were the warm hospitality and friendly receptions.

Before leaving Detroit, an art gallery director gave me the names and addresses of two Peruvian painters, Senora Galvez Wolff and Alberto Davila. One free morning in Lima, Peru, Jerry and I asked the taxi driver to take us to Senora Wolff's home. I had imagined her to be a struggling artist, living in moderate circumstances. To my surprise, the driver took us to a commercial center of the city where she had a studio apartment in a high-rise building. We went up to the tenth floor and rang the bell. A small middle-aged woman with distinct Indian features greeted us. She had heard from the gallery owner that we were coming and had been expecting us. Naturally, she was eager to show us her studio and her acrylic paintings. Most of her subject matter involved the native folklore of the Peruvian Indian. She insisted we stay for lunch so she could tell us more about the local art scene. Although she personally had a number of commissions and seemed prosperous, she told us that most of the artists were struggling to make ends meet. While dining, we were amazed to see on top of a cabinet an actual mummy she had dug up on one of her archaeological trips. This was a well-preserved figure in fetal position. Needless to say, it wasn't very appetizing to look at it while lunching, yet it did not diminish our pleasure in her gracious hospitality.

It took us a few days before we successfully contacted Davila. He spoke no English so that it was difficult to communicate, and his time was divided between his studio and teaching art classes. Davila's paintings were abstract, in earthy brown, black, and yellow colors, reflecting the grim and harsh nature of his Indian background. His work attracted international attention and he regularly represented his country in the São Paulo Biennale International Art Exposition. He was married to a former art student who had come to Lima from England; she acted as our interpreter. I was impressed with the quality of his work and promised to help arrange a show in Detroit. Upon my return home, I was happy that the Donald Morris Gallery agreed to have a one-man show for him. Thus began a friendship that lasted over the years.

Lima was an interesting place to shop. A chance browsing in one of the many antique shops made me stop and admire an unusually well-preserved Inca vessel. I knew very little about Inca history and culture, but I was always attracted to ceramic crafts and did not concern myself with such matters as authenticity. Because of the moderate prices, both Jerry and I bought several pieces. I did not know then that this was to be the beginning of a life-long hobby of collecting Pre-Columbian art.

The highlight of our visit was the trip to Cuzco and Machu Picchu. Cuzco, the ancient capital of the Incas, is situated in the Andes, twelve thousand feet above sea level. The plane we took, primitive by today's standards, was not pressurized and the passengers were given oxygen masks to use throughout the flight. On landing in Cuzco we were told to lie flat on our back for several hours so that our body would adapt itself to the high altitude. Most people followed this suggestion. As for me, I could not wait to run out with my sketchbook to take in the special character and beauty of this ancient city. The main architectural features were the red tiled roofs and the plastered walls that gave a unified aspect to the entire city, the winding stone-paved streets, and the city plazas dominated by churches. Of special interest to the group were the Inca fortification walls. We looked with disbelief at the huge masonry walls and speculated about the technical skill, craftsmanship, and the mechanical contrivances necessary to accomplish this feat. The walls were built of huge-sized stones, some as large as three by five feet, cut to such perfection that they fit without mortar. The saying was that "one couldn't squeeze a dime in the joints." The visit to Cuzco was only the "appetizer" for what was coming next—our trip to Machu Picchu, the last known holdout of the Incas against the Spanish conquerors. It was built high in the Andes, but at an altitude two thousand feet lower than Cuzco. Within the mountain peaks were the remains of what once was the last center of the Inca religion and culture, nestled into its natural surroundings, making an integrated design. It is probably one of the best examples of the integration of architecture with its surrounding environment. The day passed by climbing around the ruins of individual buildings, mostly temples, water reservoirs, grain bins, sundials, sacrificial altars, and residences of the priests. The construction was similar to the stone fortification we saw in Cuzco. But here, on the sloping areas, it was even harder to understand how the huge boulders were brought, cut to size, and put in place. Here too, even on a much larger scale than in Cuzco, the stones were cut to fit with such precision that no mortar was required for the joints. This excellent stone work was especially interesting to me since it recalled my experiences as a stonecutter and stonemason in my early pioneering days in Palestine.

I looked forward eagerly to our next stop, Buenos Aires. In the late 1930s my maternal aunt with her three daughters and son immigrated from Bialystok to Argentina just before the outbreak of World War II. There had been no contact with the family for over fifteen years, but reports about their living in Buenos Aires came through other members of the family who had settled in Israel. The women had married but I did not know their married names. The phone book listed the son's name, but to my dismay I learned from the caretaker that he would be out of the country for a prolonged period. I explained my predicament to our guide who also served as driver and interpreter. He was a Jewish immigrant who had come to Argentina about the same time and from the same city as my relatives. He said he knew this family and offered the same evening to drive me to find them. The way he went about finding them made me suspect that he actually did not know my family but was pretending in order to have more hours of taxi service. He drove me to the Jewish district and made frequent stops to ask people the whereabouts of my three (Grudsky) cousins. After a long and fruitless evening, he confessed that he did not know the family but would try again the next evening to locate them by inquiring at the main Jewish family restaurants in the neighborhood. And so it was that the next evening we started out again. We went from restaurant to restaurant, talking to the proprietors and asking their assistance. Finally we found a restaurant owner who had come from Bialystok and knew the family. From him we learned the married name and the address. It was near midnight when we walked up a steep flight of stairs in an old wooden building and knocked on the door. Imagine the shock and surprise of my two cousins when I introduced myself. Sophie and Rachel were women in their fifties. Rachel was married and had a teenage daughter. I had remembered them as attractive young women in 1920 on my visit to Bialystok from the United States.

After a lapse of thirty-five years it was hard for me to recognize them. We were all eager to reminisce, but because of the late hour they invited me to come back for dinner the next day.

The apartment was set up with the same pieces of traditional furniture they had brought with them from Poland. The heavy dark lacquered wood was highly polished and looked like new. The dining room table was set with their best linens, dishes, silver, and glassware. Most of all, from the kitchen came the fragrance of foods so familiar in my childhood home. Everything was prepared with special care. To me, it was like reliving a day with my family in Russia. We spent the time reminiscing and being brought up to date on the members of the family who had come to Buenos Aires and Montevideo where another cousin Luba lived with her husband and two sons. I took her address and promised to look her up. I never dreamt that I would be visiting them again six years later in 1960 and again in 1969.

As I described earlier, another heartwarming surprise awaited me in Buenos Aires. Architect Jaime Roca and his son Miguelangelo had traveled most of the night from Cordoba to Buenos Aires to meet me. Such was South American hospitality. At this time the Rocas joined the festivities the local architectural society had arranged.

One of the innovative features of downtown Buenos Aires was Florida Street. It was probably one of the first attempts to eliminate traffic in a very popular shopping district. During business hours a number of blocks were open to pedestrians only. The result was astonishing. The sidewalks and roadways were filled with shoppers, creating a festive and enjoyable mood. The pleasant quietness of the shopping street contrasted with the tensions created by extremely noisy, continuous horn-blowing drivers, notorious for their speeding habits and disregard for traffic lights and signs. In the following years many large cities around the world adopted this traffic-control feature.

Following the hospitable home receptions were the farewell festivities at city hall hosted by the mayor, himself an architect. Each of us received a certificate making us honorary citizens of the city. This honor had some dubious connotations in light of the fearful political atmosphere permeating the capitol. Nineteen fifty-four was the last year of General Peron's dictatorship. Eva Peron's name and picture were plastered on walls and buildings everywhere. People were afraid to freely express their opinions since criticism was severely punished.

A flight of only thirty minutes brought us to Montevideo, Uruguay, and the effect on us was like a breath of fresh air. Our first introduction to this democratic (at that time) country was on the chartered bus taking us from the airport to the hotel. An attractive guide welcomed us with these words: "You are now in a free country. You can think and say what you want." The most enjoyable and meaningful experience was the warm hospitality we enjoyed in fellow architects' homes. These contacts led to lifelong friendships, several return visits, and subsequent reunions at the Pan American Congresses of Architects. The Delfinos were one family that became especially close to us and we kept an uninterrupted contact for over thirty years. One of the Delfino family, Elena, with her husband, later emigrated to Africa. In Zaire (formerly the Belgium Congo) they helped to establish a local architectural school and Elena taught English. Through her letters we followed the progress of this newly established independent country.

The head of the Delfino family, Humberto, and his wife became our close friends and treated us as part of their family. Delfino especially wanted us to see how the School of Architecture operated. There we saw first-year students making models, which at that time was an innovative approach. Its advantage was to explore the latent design abilities of the students to assist them in deciding their career.

I excused myself from the hectic group schedule and set about to look up my family. They knew I was coming because they had been notified by my Argentinean cousins. Our reunion was a tremendously exciting event for all of us. Luba and her husband were in their fifties and their two sons were teenagers. The family lived in a poorer section of the city and occupied a small one-story wooden house with the front room arranged as a general store, serving farmers on credit. They also used an old Ford auto to peddle wares in the villages. In back of the store area was a dining room and two small bedrooms. Much to my amazement they had in their possession many photos of my parents, even their wedding photos, and there were photos of me as a child I had not seen before. One rare document was the marriage license of my parents dated 1884. Here too, as in the apartment of my Buenos Aires relatives, the furniture had been brought from Europe and the dining "commode" or cabinet was the same kind we had in our home in Grodno. That visit was the beginning of a family correspondence and several subsequent visits.

On to Brazil. Our first impression of São Paulo was overwhelming. High-rise office buildings under construction stared at us from every direction. It was said that a new high-rise was started every four hours. That seemed believable, judging from the endless movement of trucks with building materials and modern heavy equipment. Huge cranes dotted the landscape. The building activity attracted hundreds of European engineers—German, French, and Italian—and many entrepreneurs. Side by side with the enormous physical growth, São Paulo's art museums were an additional source of pride. The International Biannual Exhibitions attracted the best talent, not only from South America, but from around the world. Our architect hosts were eager to show us the University City, an enclave of modern designed university buildings.

We found a more relaxed atmosphere at our next stop in Rio de Janeiro. Here we were impressed with the masterful and successful adaptation of buildings to the mountainous and hilly topography. Many of the new multistory apartments and buildings were virtually wrapped around the sharply sloped sites. The architects applied inventive ideas to the functional requirements. For example, the access to the different floors was one of the most difficult problems as no elevators were used. They solved this problem by providing one entry at the midpoint of the higher elevation, approximately in the middle of the building. From this midway level one could easily walk to upper or lower levels. The main entry was at the first floor level. One floor in the middle of the building was reserved for a day-care nursery, kindergarten, laundry room, community hall, and some recreational facilities.

The architecture of Rio, at that time the capital of Brazil, was influenced by the influx of European architects. Oscar Niemeyer spearheaded the modern style. Burle Marx, internationally known landscape architect and artist, worked closely with Niemeyer and others to integrate his garden designs with the character of the buildings. His main forte was to create, with plants and flowers, colorful forms and designs. I visited one villa on the outskirts of Rio where Burle Marx designed mosaic murals for the exterior of the building. He also designed gardens for public parks and large community buildings. Although the colonial influence on Brazil was Portuguese, there was little evidence of this remaining except for the spoken language of the country and the famous pavements. The best known of these pavements is the wide and seemingly endless sidewalks at the Copacabana beach. The intricate designs made of black and white ceramic tile are similar to those seen in the public squares in Lisbon and in other Portuguese cities.

Since this was our last stop, we wanted to take advantage of the chance to rest and find an excuse for our final celebration. Someone suggested that I put up an art exhibition of the travel sketches that I had made throughout the trip. This show was to be combined with our farewell party. I was happy to oblige, but the problem was where to hang the thirty watercolors. The hotel management did not allow tapes, tacks, or other temporary attachments on their expensive wallpaper, and for this reason the large white-tiled bathroom was chosen as the "exhibition-party" place. Jerry Shea helped me tape the sketches to the walls; as we did so, we relived our trip and reminded ourselves of the shared experiences: the imposing locks of the Panama Canal; the awe-inspiring views of Machu Picchu; the ancient streets of Cuzco; the beautiful resort scenes of Chile's Vino del Mar; city scenes of Buenos Aires, Montevideo, and Rio de Janeiro. The "catering" was spontaneous. Glasses, drinks, snacks, fruit appeared as if by magic. The warm camaraderie nurtured throughout the trip climaxed at this farewell party in a most unusual setting.

Together with the joyful experiences, we also had a frightening one that happened on one of the narrow, winding, mountain roads. Our Brazilian driver was true to form in the prevailing South American style of driving fast, blowing the horn continuously, and taking chances maneuvering the many dangerous curves. On one of these precarious turns, the oncoming driver had the same idea. He was driving a large gasoline truck and when our bus driver saw him coming it was too late to avoid a head-on collision. His only alternative was to swerve off the road into a deep embankment and pray for the best. As the front wheels of the bus went over the precipice, we feared this was the end. By some miracle the rear wheels had been caught in a sewer manhole, leaving the bus suspended in mid-air over the precipice. We crawled slowly to the rear door of the bus, grateful in our hearts that we were alive!

Six weeks does not really seem to be a long enough period in which much could happen. However, on my return to Detroit, I learned that my associate in charge had suffered a severe heart attack two weeks after my departure. A letter with the upsetting news was put in the mail for me, but my brother and his associates immediately regretted their decision to notify me and with much effort and luck were able to retrieve the letter from the post office. Even though I found my associate recuperating fairly well, taking over additional duties created a hardship for me. Another setback, a financial one, concerned a two-million-dollar building project for the state of Michigan. The bids from contractors came in 25 percent below our estimates on which our fee was based. The low bids were due mainly to the highly competitive construction market and the depressed economic conditions in Michigan. This meant that our fee was also 25 percent less—much under our actual expenses. I was reminded of a Russian general who, after one costly victory over the Germans in World War I, sent a telegram to the Czar: "One more victory like this and we will lose the war. . . ." However, our "war" was not completely lost. One positive result was that the project received a design award from the Detroit Chapter of the

American Institute of Architects.

Going through this experience made me think of the many uncertainties and unforeseen surprises inherent in the practice of architecture. Once an architect establishes a medium-size office (fifteen to twenty-five employees), he anticipates new commissions to keep the staff busy. Architecture is historically one of the first professions to feel the economic downturns and the last to recover. During these slow periods every attempt was made to keep the staff intact, up to a point of severe financial loss to the office. Since it was my routine to be in contact with each person daily, my relationship with the staff members was that of a friend. Naturally, it was very painful for me to lay off staff unless I could find temporary employment for them in other offices.

Our work expanded into larger commercial centers. We were commissioned to design our first regional open mall shopping center, Wonderland, in Livonia, Michigan. The center included a number of major works of art commissioned from both local and nationally known artists. The featured symbol of the center was a 60-foot-high obelisk of light structural steel sections interlaced with colorful baked enamel panels, created by Samuel Cashwan. We chose a wide variety in art forms. One of the outstanding innovative works was a colorful fountain by the late talented and inventive Richard Jennings. The various moving parts were activated by powered water jets, which in turn were synchronized to go through openings in other moving parts. Appealing especially to children were the delicate metal "bug family," designed by Betty Conn, and the Rooster made of baked enamel sections by Donald Buby. Nathan Kaz's "Whirling Dervish" rotated on an electrically powered base. Another form of art integrated with the building was a glazed brick mural, 80 feet by 10 feet, depicting in color the four seasons, also by Jennings. A precast concrete mural wall, 120 feet by 11 feet, incorporating abstract shapes in earth colors was designed by Marjorie Kreilick. This art provided a festive, colorful environment and created a marketplace that made shopping a pleasurable and interesting experience.

With the steadily increasing work load and accompanying increase in staff, five years passed before I could take off enough time in 1955 to visit my sister in Israel. My brother Sol joined me on this trip; it was over thirty-five years since he had last seen her in Poland, and it was his first trip to Israel. We wanted a firsthand view of recent developments and progress in the country. It was a heartwarming reunion, not only with Rosa, her husband, and children, but with my many friends there. Improvements in the living standards for kibbutz families, now three hundred members, were evident everywhere. There was an on-going program to provide small but comfortable living units built of concrete blocks, each with its own kitchen and bathroom. Those who had been living in the wooden barracks were given first choice. The children's living quarters were expanded and improved. The kibbutz carpenters used their ingenuity to build play equipment from castoffs such as parts of bicycles, buggies, wooden planks. The children played happily on their homemade swings, seesaws, and carts.

I was eager to see the progress being made in the expansion of the Technion, the Institute of Technology in Haifa. I recalled working on the original Technion building in 1922 in my pioneer days as a stonecutter as it was being prepared to house the first Department of Architecture. Construction had been stopped during

World War I and it stood unfinished until 1922. Now a new campus was being built on the slopes of Mount Carmel overlooking the city and the harbor. I was particularly interested since I was one of the founders of the Detroit Chapter of the American Technion Society and served as its president in 1948, providing a continuing link to my stonecutting days. The American Technion Society counted among its members leaders and professionals in the fields of architecture and city planning, engineering, technical research, physics, agriculture, and chemistry, and they contributed generously to the new campus building. In 1986 Ruth and I established a Research Fund in Architecture and were named Patrons of the Technion. The School of Architecture practiced a functional approach in student training. The second-year class was given a design problem that was to be followed through from preliminary sketch stages to final working drawings and construction details. This system trained the student to think not only in terms of pure design but also of structural application.

It was hard to recognize the Tel Aviv I had known from the early 1920s and even as recent as five years ago in 1950. So much construction was going on—apartment buildings, commercial buildings, hotels, and government buildings—that the city was truly a haven for architects. They continued to come mainly from England, Belgium, France, and Italy; there were only a few from the United States. Most buildings were designed in the modern style, were built of reinforced concrete, and were finished in pastel colors. One feature that unified the appearance and character of the residential areas was the use of the ground floor as an open area to capture the morning sea breezes. This design provided a garden area with colonnades supporting the upper structure. I was particularly anxious to learn how the apartment buildings I designed in the midthirties had withstood the test of time. It was gratifying to see how well they related to the contemporary style of the newer buildings. The person who kept me abreast of the latest architectural developments in Israel was the kibbutz architect, Kuba Geber. On each of my visits over the years he was my special guide, traveling the length and breadth of the country to show me new buildings—industrial complexes, apartments, museums, and other cultural institutions. What he was most proud of were the new concrete main kibbutzim two-story buildings that combined recreation, dining, and administration facilities for as many as eight hundred to nine hundred people.

In Milan we contacted the editor of the architectural magazine *Domus,* a well-known international publication. To my amazement one young woman was the whole operation—editor, layout, and advertising person. Enrichetta Ritter was interested in seeing my work, but the only photos I had with me were of my own recently completed office building in Detroit. The garden patio with the sculptured metal gate by Julius Schmidt attracted her attention and it was published in a subsequent issue of *Domus.* She arranged for architect Piero Bottoni to take us to see the postwar reconstruction of bombed-out areas. Bottoni explained that because of the industrial character of Milan, architects were not bound as closely to tradition as in the other Italian cities. However, housing was laid out in suburban districts in accordance with the best principles of city planning—safe walking to schools for the children and ample recreational and park areas. An unusual feature in the newly remodeled shopping district of Milan was the design of individual door handles for each shop. Created by sculptors, the handles were made of cast bronze, aluminum, or enameled copper. The subjects of the handles varied from historical themes to appealing female figures. People would remember the stores as much by these handles as by the shop name. The attention to detail and variety in each building was remarkable.

On my return to Detroit, I was called upon to lecture on my favorite subject—the role of art in the environment. There were also a number of local television interviews. In one of these talks, I spoke about my architectural trips to South America and to Israel. When the interviewer asked if I had seen Japanese architecture, I replied "not yet." At that time the seed was planted; the next trip would be to Japan.

It so happened that the 1956 national AIA convention was to be held in Los Angeles in June and a postconvention architectural tour to Japan was being planned to sponsor better relations between the architects of both nations. Kenneth Nishimoto, an American-born architect from Los Angeles, conducted the tour of sixteen architects and their wives. Our first stop was Hawaii where we were hosted by the local architects' chapter of the AIA, complete with hula dancers and the traditional roast pig barbecue. As usual, I was eager to get out my sketchbook and watercolors, and it was my good fortune to have a pretty volunteer show me the unusual sights around the islands.

On our first evening in Tokyo a festive reception was arranged for us by the Japanese Society of Architects at International House. After the excellent hors d'oeuvres and hot sake, we were each given interesting gifts. Mine, which I still cherish, was a carpenter chalk line wound around a small wheel—designed as an intricately carved sculptural piece. How surprised I was that evening to find Sam Washizuka from our Class of 1929 at the University of Michigan among the Japanese architects. We spent most of the evening reminiscing about our college days; he offered to be my personal guide in Tokyo. We met again the next day for lunch. He told me about his World War II experiences and his miraculous survival. At the outbreak of the war he was commissioned an officer in the Japanese army and sent to the Philippines. At the war's end his contingent, disbelieving that Japan had lost the war, retreated deep into the jungle. There was little food left and all were suffering from malaria and malnutrition. Seeing the hopelessness of the situation, he persuaded his contingent to surrender to the Americans. His troubles, however, did not end there. His knowledge of English aroused the suspicion of his American captors that he was a Japanese spy. Only when the American command verified his records with the University of Michigan was he released and given special care to recuperate and regain his health. Since then his fortunes had taken a spectacular turn. Utilizing his knowledge of Japanese and English and his background as an architect, the American government put him in charge of appraising the Japanese bomb damage of Manila and other cities in the Philippines. With a large staff at his disposal, he prepared a list of reparations the Japanese government was to pay to the Americans. At the time of our meeting, he was semiretired and had ample time to be with us. (A year later we met again at our twenty-fifth class reunion in Ann Arbor, Michigan.)

In Tokyo we were taken first to the residential areas, rebuilt in the ten years since the end of the war. It was a panorama of traditionally styled, neutral-colored wooden buildings with monochromatic gardens. Because land was expensive the one-story houses were small and the garden area as tiny as six feet by twelve feet.

Every garden had wood or bamboo fences. The skillful use of shrubs, dwarf trees, volcanic rocks, water, and moss ground covering, made the space seem much larger. In design, the modular concept continued to dominate the character of houses as it had for centuries. The basic unit is the *tatami* or the floor mat that is three feet by six feet, and all of the prefabricated elements are of the same size. The main features of the basementless Japanese house are: extensive roof overhangs for weather protection, sliding doors and windows on the outside, and sliding wood and paper panels and thin plaster walls on the inside. The entire basic structure is of untreated wood; the excellent finishes on the inside are achieved by expert hand planing. Some of the finest detailed work is done by elderly craftsmen, many over sixty years of age, who use magnifying glasses to obtain maximum perfection.

But the traditional skills and beauty of the wooden architecture were difficult for the Japanese architect to adapt to the design of the new large commercial buildings of concrete and glass, created in the modern idiom. What primarily influenced the extensive use of concrete was the Japanese experience with severe earthquakes in the 1920s. While much of the city was left in ruins, the Imperial Hotel, a concrete structure designed by Frank Lloyd Wright, remained undamaged.

Our stay at the Imperial Hotel gave us first-hand knowledge of this building, considered one of Wright's masterpieces. All the dimensions of the rooms were geared to the short-statured Japanese. The room height was lower, the door sizes smaller, the toilet stalls narrower, and the furniture was designed in similar proportions. Wright did not foresee that in the coming decades the Japanese would become taller and heavier, requiring the established American standards. Thus despite its historical importance, the hotel was demolished in the seventies, to be replaced by another building.

In the commercial district where traffic was becoming increasingly congested, the plan of closing streets for pedestrian use only was initiated. These areas were popular with the shoppers. For American visitors some signs in English brought smiles to our faces, such as "For Street Walkers Only." Two important historical Japanese cities that escaped wartime destruction were Nara with its magnificent temples, and Kyoto with its temples and theaters. My viewing of the temples of Nara turned out to be an uplifting experience. To walk through the narrow pathways lined with enormously tall trees, some more than fifty feet high, made one feel humble. The temples seemed new and in perfect condition. We were told that after a number of years, when the wooden temple structure deteriorates, another temple is built next to the one existing site and copied exactly in all details. The old temple is then dismantled.

Our last evening was a symposium arranged by the Japanese architects and the Society for East-West Relations. We were asked to discuss different aspects of the practice of architecture in the United States. A large audience was attracted to this meeting in which the topics ranged from emerging new design approaches to practical aspects of new construction systems. My topic was "Art in Architecture," for which I had prepared a paper. This talk was reprinted in full in the next day's English-Japanese newspaper, *Asahi*.

Coming home from my Far East cultural experience was not only a matter of coping with jet lag, but also with the mental and emotional readjustments. How did the family fare in my absence? What took place in the office? Most of my apprehensions disappeared at the airport when I saw the happy faces of my wife and sons, now fourteen-year-old Dan and twelve-year-old Eliel. Both boys seemed to have grown inches in the six weeks I was away. Joining us was my brother Sol, his wife Nellie, and my sister Riva. On the way home, with all of us crowded into one car, the animated questions and answers seemed unlimited. The boys were eager to tell me about their plans to return to summer camp Arowhan in the Canadian Algonquin Park. At home, not a minute was lost before we opened the suitcases and found their gifts.

In the office the projects were proceeding on schedule. I was elated to learn that during my absence our firm was commissioned to design the new Berry elementary school for the Detroit Board of Education. For a number of years we were unsuccessful in obtaining architectural work from the board. Ugly rumors prevailed that anti-Semitic prejudices influenced the selection of architects. Jewish architects had not been selected in the past. This was not the only negative aspect of the administration's performance. There was public criticism, expressed in letters to the newspapers and in the editorials, on the poor design quality of the schools. The change occurred with the appointment of a new building superintendent. He was a forthright person, and he proceeded to set up new standards for selection of architects that were based on competency and quality of work.

The office enthusiastically took on this challenge to design a first-rate school. The Detroit Board of Education initiated a new experimental approach in planning school buildings that was to begin around a conference table where the architects would meet with a Citizens Advisory Committee consisting of representatives of the parents, Berry staff, Board of Education, City Plan Commission, and the Department of Parks and Boulevards. The eight weekly meetings proved fruitful. Following these conferences, plans were drawn for a structure that would not only serve as a school but could also be used for many community activities. The building was composed of three wings, one of which was two stories in height, with the upper grades on the second floor. The completed building had fifteen classrooms, including two kindergartens and a library. In addition, there was an assembly room, kitchen, principal's office, general office, waiting room, clinic, teachers' lounge, and a storage area. The school's total capacity was 512 students, and its general design aimed to achieve an inviting and warm setting that would help bridge the gap between home and school environments. Our experience with commercial buildings with strict budgetary requirements served us well in our cost projections for this school building. Our reputation for design and reliable cost estimating was established with this school. Other school commissions followed for the next decade.

One of the elements that distinguished our schools from others was the use of art. The Berry school had a colorfully designed floor-to-ceiling glazed brick wall mural in the entry corridor designed by Richard Jennings. The interest the children showed in the mural was heartwarming. The story is told that one ten-year-old girl was found standing in front of it as though mesmerized. When asked what she was thinking, she replied: "I just look and look and can't take my eyes off of it." In the Glazer school, where the classrooms were clustered around two interior courts, a glazed brick mural of abstract design by Narendra Patel was the feature of one wall. At the Krolik school a stylized group sculpture, done in concrete by Arthur

Schneider, was placed outside near the main entry. The theme was a teacher surrounded by four children. The youngsters utilized the sculpture as a play element for climbing. In some instances, it served as an outlet for expressing frustrations with the teacher. (A small boy was seen hitting the teacher figure with his baseball bat!) In the Alexander Graham Bell school, a free-standing alabaster sculpture by George Rogers, symbolizing sound waves, was placed in the center of the main intersecting corridors. While the brick murals in the other schools were accepted as an integral part of the building, the free-standing art was a different story. The maquette and the cost had been approved by the Detroit Board of Education. This did not prevent the newspapers from publishing letters to the editor on the "wasting of tax payer's money on art." Because of this publicity, the board retracted the expenditure for the sculpture. I was shocked at this turn of events and realized the heartbreak of the sculptor who was abruptly stopped from installing his first public commission. I was determined not to let this happen and persuaded several friends interested in promoting art to join together with me in assuming the cost. And that is how the sculpture was installed at the Alexander Graham Bell school.

Because of my interest in the international scene of architecture and my knowledge of Russian and several European languages, I was asked to serve on the International Relations Committee of the American Institute of Architects. This committee worked closely with the International Union of Architects (UIA), with headquarters in Paris. My first activity was to attend as a delegate the Fifth Congress of the UIA, which took place in Moscow. This time, happily, Ruth was able to join me, as the boys were at Camp Arowhon. On 20 July 1958 our plans were to fly to Moscow from Vienna on a Russian plane, but that month the Americans invaded Lebanon. An official of the American Embassy in Vienna advised us to cancel the trip because of Russian opposition to this American action. After talking to several tourists just returned from Russia, we learned that there was no outward hostility toward Americans so we decided to proceed with our plans. Our scheduled flight was on a Saturday, but because a large Hungarian delegation had the priority, we were assigned to a flight the following day. This delay turned out to be a "blessing in disguise." Our group of five were the only passengers on the plane. The stewardess was attractive, young, and very hospitable. Before I left on this trip I had been advised not to let people in Russia know that I spoke Russian. In my desire to talk with her, to be briefed, and to discuss Russian life, I decided to use my Russian. This four-hour flight to Moscow, with a short stopover in Kiev, turned out to be one of the high points in my Russian trip. We discussed politics—the positives and negatives of our two political systems. She told about the terrible human losses and sacrifices endured by the Russian people during the war and the enormous task of rebuilding. By the time I left the plane I felt I was leaving a friend. She presented me with a small Russian-English dictionary and I gave her a fountain pen, at that time one of the most cherished items in Russia.

Fifteen hundred architects came from fifty countries to participate in a week-long seminar and discussion on the theme "Construction and Reconstruction of Towns, 1947–1957." That the Soviet government attached great importance to the architects' congress could be assumed from the opening fanfare in the Hall of the Soviets in the Kremlin at which Khrushchev himself spent almost two hours with the

Executive Committee of the Architects Congress. According to Henry S. Churchill, FAIA, member of the Executive Committee of the AIA: "Mr. Khrushchev talked architecture and city planning with the Executive Committee for an hour and three-quarters. He was interested, interesting, and well informed. He did not make a speech and he used no notes, and he also listened." The congress ended with a gala garden party at the Kremlin for all the delegates and their wives. Although the American delegation of twelve was one of the smallest of the participating countries, its contribution to the congress was strengthened by the outstanding panel exhibit of American buildings put together by Peter Blake and Julian Neski.

Moscow itself in its physical appearance made a striking impression. The Kremlin, the historic seat of the early czars and now the seat of the Soviet government, formed the backdrop for the entire city. Architecturally, with its walled enclosure, ancient churches, and palace wings, it is interesting and significant as an honest expression of the turbulent Russian past.

The architectural style used by the Russians for the previous thirty years had been along monotonous neoclassic lines. After a flurry of modernism in the late twenties, in which French and American architects took part, the Russians settled down to a neoclassical style. I heard many explanations for that choice, but most agreed that it was Stalin's choice and speculated that he assumed the classical style would produce buildings that would immortalize him better than the cold, ornament-free modernism of the thirties. So Moscow architects went all out for ornaments, columns, and statues, and as Moscow went, so went the country because any sizeable project had to be approved by the Chief Architect's Office in Moscow. Some people theorized that the ornamental buildings gave the average Russian a certain pride of achievement that in some way compensated for the harsh and drab surroundings of his daily environment. This might have accounted for why the subway was a palatial labyrinth of marble, sculpture, painting, and fancy ornamentation.

I noted the biggest progress in the fields of city planning and housing development. Housing development and the rebuilding of Moscow was a great accomplishment. If we consider that Moscow started not so long ago with predominantly wooden structures and looked at the present multistory concrete buildings and wide boulevards, we could evaluate the tempo of their construction more accurately. The year before, eighteen million square feet of apartment construction and twenty-six schools were built; the following year the program called for twenty-two million square feet for apartments and thirty schools. Row upon row of new apartment buildings were going up as far as we could see. The apartments were compact one- and two-bedroom types, and there was a long waiting list of tenants ready to move in. Most of the tenants came from the area of Moscow condemned for street widening; others came from the movement of the farm population to the city (43 percent of the population was urban). The rent was low in relation to the individual earnings. In visiting the architectural department of Moscow University we learned that the students' reaction against the prevalent style expressed itself in designing their projects in the contemporary European genre. This was happening in spite of the knowledge that there was hardly a chance of influencing the official government hierarchy.

Our daily schedules were planned to enable us to see the highlights of Moscow and the surrounding countryside. What stands out in our memory are a rewarding evening at the Bolshoi Ballet, attending an extraordinary puppet performance (representing a sixty-piece symphony orchestra), a room-by-room tour through the historic Kremlin, the visit to Lenin's Tomb, and a trip to the permanent agricultural exhibition featuring the products of each region of the USSR. Our group was invited to a reception at the American Embassy as guests of the ambassador. The reception was also attended by the American track team competing with the Russian team that week. It goes without saying they were the center of attraction. During this week there had been demonstrations against the American Embassy, in which many of the window panes were broken and ink was splashed over the building. Headlines and posters carried anti-American warnings to "get out of Lebanon." To our surprise we found friendly reception and hospitality everywhere—on the streets, in buses, from officials, and especially among our Russian architects-hosts.

At the end of the convention, AIA members separated from the group. Our plans called for a visit to the World's Fair in Brussels, with stopovers in Stockholm, Copenhagen, Rotterdam, and Amsterdam. Arriving in Stockholm from Moscow was an experience in cultural shock. We felt the weight of the heavy-handed bureaucracy in every phase of our stay in Moscow: in the hotel where all floor activity was monitored by a lady attendant whose desk faced the elevator, in the Gum Department Store where it took endless time and a number of checkpoints to make a single purchase, in the time-consuming effort to find a phone directory and a public phone, in our experience at the Central Synagogue of being followed and watched by a Russian undercover agent who tried to overhear our conversation with the elder congregation members. These bureaucratic frustrations reached a climax on the day of our departure. At the hotel it took nearly a half day to get our passports returned and then submitted to various departments for careful perusal before being approved and stamped. When we arrived in Stockholm the speedy, efficient procedure of entering the country was like a "breath of fresh air." Added to this, the pleasantness of the Swedish people and the relaxed prevailing atmosphere raised our spirit.

I was familiar with the Swedish experiment in planning new satellite towns on the periphery of the large cities. One of the successfully completed satellites was Vallingby, a twenty-five minute ride by subway from Stockholm. The town of twenty-seven thousand was laid out around a small central business area. The public square was paved with ceramic tiles in the form of large circular designs in blue and light grey colors. The designs were made to continue over the curb and become a part of the sidewalk pattern. Each shop had its own specially designed wrought iron emblems or "signatures." This was a pleasant contrast to the accepted painted metal and neon-lighted lettering used in most urban settings. The delivery of goods to these shops was by an underground service road. The residential areas surrounding the center contained one-, two-, and four-story brick apartment buildings. Several high-rise apartment buildings in strategic locations served as an accent in the total design. Secondary and main streets were designed for easy access to the center.

Back in Detroit it was a real satisfaction to see the office practice grow and be recognized as one of the prestigious firms in Michigan. My view of the role of the architect implied more than designing individual projects. My studies with Eliel Saarinen a decade earlier reinforced my thinking that urban planning should be the concern of all architects. With the support of Charles Blessing, director of city planning of the city of Detroit, I undertook to recruit architects from the various offices to form a study and work group. I was encouraged that thirty-five responded. At the first meeting the name Urban Design Collaborative was selected and I was asked to serve as chairman. The area chosen to be studied was the eight-hundred-acre downtown area comprising the central business district (CBD) of Detroit. There were several phases to this project. The first part entailed a review of the master plan and the existing data on the CBD, which was provided by the City Plan Commission. The next step was to divide the CBD into seven areas, each to be studied by teams of five architects. These studies were to be periodically reviewed by the entire group for discussion and coordination. Never did we dream as volunteers in afterwork hours that it would take four years to study and arrive at what seemed to be a satisfactory solution. We met regularly in the evenings on the fourth floor of the old city hall building. Most of us felt as if we were back at school as we climbed the steep stairs to reach the top floor. This building, erected in the late nineteenth century, had twenty-foot-high ceilings, which made the four-story climb equivalent to present day six or seven stories. Along with the hours of concentrated work, we enjoyed the warm camaraderie, the time for coffee and doughnuts, and the heated discussions.

In March 1959 the final scheme, complete with drawings and models, was presented at a luncheon meeting of the CBD membership and other community leaders. The project was reported with enthusiasm in the press, but the political and financial support of the city leaders were lacking. As I look back twenty-five years later, I see that many of the ideas are still valid today and some are being implemented. Some of these are:

> To create an environment conducive to pleasant and relaxed shopping, recreation, personal and government transactions (created by large open plazas free of traffic hazards).
>
> To preserve and renovate existing historical buildings and to replace obsolete buildings with new structures designed for contemporary needs.
>
> To provide proper and efficient facilities for bringing in and accommodating large numbers of vehicles. (To solve this problem alone would require a new radical and imaginative approach in transportation techniques.)

For a time it seemed to me that some of the urban planning ideas might materialize. In 1962 a corporation was formed by Walter C. Shamie to develop an International Village complex. The area of twenty-three acres, bounded by Michigan Avenue, Abbott, and First Streets was known as skid row—a collection of bars and flop houses until the city of Detroit and the federal government bought the properties and razed the buildings. Plans for the first ten-million dollar stage included a 2200-seat performing arts theater, thirty restaurants, a 250-room motor hotel, three 12-story office buildings, and a number of international courtyards, each with shops and decor appropriate to a particular part of the world. Three Detroit architectural firms combined their talents on this project. They were Gunnar Birkerts and Associates, Incorporated, Louis G. Redstone Associates, Incorporated, and Frederick Stickel Associates. The interior design was to be handled by Ford and Earl Design Associates. Financing from city and federal agencies was almost complete, the funding lacking only a seventy-five thousand dollar pledge from the private business sector. When this minimal support was not forthcoming, those of us who worked on this exciting project for nearly three years were shocked and deeply disappointed. Another rare opportunity to revitalize the "heart" of Detroit was missed. Two years later in 1967 the community was shocked and totally unprepared for the violent racial riots that erupted. It is hard to pinpoint the causes, but the failure to implement good urban planning could have been a contributing factor.

Because of my continued interest in urban design, I chaired a two-day workshop in May 1961 on this subject. Experts in their fields discussed these topics: problems of the large cities and the middle-size cities development and renewal, new conceptions in housing design and open spaces, problems of working with the government. Keen interest was shown by the attendance of three hundred architects, planners, and students. It was decided to have a seminar on these problems the following year, 1962, at the Michigan State Architects' Convention in Detroit. Again, the attendance of six hundred architects from the entire state was beyond expectation. This subject was also being given one of the top priorities by the national leadership of the AIA.

These one-time projects did not divert me from my major interest in the integration of the arts in architecture. The local chapter was supportive of the idea. The official response was: "O.K., you be the chairman." Thus the Allied Arts Committee was started with twelve enthusiastic architects. It was to last nearly a decade. Our goal was to bring together architects, artists, and owners to get acquainted and to achieve some understanding and appreciation of each other's perspectives. The culmination was a major annual festive event. One year internationally known sculptor Richard Lippold was invited to talk, another year, the well-known architectural critic, Sibyl Moholy-Nagy spoke; another event presented a colloquium of architects, artists, and owners. Roger L. Stevens, Chairman of the National Council of the Arts, was the speaker in 1968. Paul Damaz, an author and writer on the arts and Peter Blake, architect, author, and managing editor of the monthly *Architectural Forum*, were featured at the yearly meetings. Meetings were held in the attractive settings of Cranbrook Academy of Art, Detroit Art Institute, J. L. Hudson Fine Arts Galleries, and the McGregor Memorial Building of Wayne State University. Connected with most of the meetings was a walking tour of nearby galleries.

The attendance for these events of two to three hundred persons expressed the vital interest in the arts by both professionals and the general public. Preparing for these events was a "work of love" for the committee. The planning sessions were generally held at my home in the evening, in an atmosphere of cooperation and friendship. However, the political events of the last years of the sixties—the growing involvement of the United States in the Viet Nam War and the racial riots in Detroit in 1967 changed the priorities of the chapter program. That summer also had sad memories for my family. My sister Riva, after two years of chemotherapy treatments for diagnosed lung cancer, died. Throughout her illness she was remarkably self-composed, never complaining or making demands. I came to realize more than ever how important a supportive role she played in my life, not only during my early youth, but also throughout the thirty years of being with us in the firm. Somehow we took for granted Riva's role of complete devotion to all the Redstone families—my brother Solomon, my nephew Samuel, and my own. Her love and interest were manifest in every phase of our family life: birthdays, holidays, celebrations, graduations, weddings, and frequent get-togethers. She played a major part from the very beginning in 1937 in the office development. From the three-person office in which she did the secretarial, bookkeeping, and other office chores, she became the executive secretary and chief accountant for our sixty-man office. Her presence added an important element of stability and cohesion in the office atmosphere.

As our professional reputation grew for reliability, performance, and good design, we were called upon by the Detroit Library Commission to plan a new library, the Cheney Branch on Grand River at Six Mile Road. Our goal was to provide an intimate and warm atmosphere for reading, both for adults and children. A community room for exhibits, meetings, and programs was planned with a separate entrance for evening and after-hours events.

The success of this building led to additional library projects, The Laura Wilder Branch in northeast Detroit was located on a busy traffic artery. Because of this factor the building was set back from the sidewalk line about eight feet. The space was used for a canopied patio as a screen from the street traffic. The rooms were planned around an open inner landscaped court. Three of the walls were glass. On the fourth wall, which was brick, a mural composed of four copper sculptural shapes, depicting scenes from the Laura Wilder children's stories, was placed. The artist was Narendra Patel.

We also designed the libraries for the nearby smaller cities of Lake Orion and Berkley. As we gained more experience with library buildings and their use, we became increasingly convinced of the importance of art, not only for the adults, but especially for the children. Because the Berkley library was the main branch, we insisted on including a budget item for art. This resulted in seven small bas-relief ceramic panels on the front exterior wall by the Cranbrook artist Svea Klein.[1]

Side by side with our growing professional recognition were the sustaining and heartwarming pleasures of our family life. Watching our sons Daniel and Eliel along with Paul and Miriam, Sol and Nellie's children of similar ages, develop strong and close relationships through shared activities was a constant source of satisfaction. The open arrangement of the garden backyard area was ideal for developing togetherness. In their early years the swings, slide, sandbox, and wading pool were the main attractions. Here the birthday parties and other celebrations were held with their neighborhood friends. In the winter the yard was transformed into a miniature rink for ice skating and hockey. While this was the highlight of the winter for most of the players, for Eliel it became his favorite sport, which he continued for many years as an adult. This positive experience created lifelong friendships even though as adults they live in different parts of the country. The yard served as a garden setting for family celebrations—weddings, special anniversaries, and open house receptions. Who would have imagined that in the years to come, Daniel's children, Adam and Carly, would also be playing in the same pool and running around the same yard? When Eliel's family visits from San Francisco, his son Ariel joins in.

Not all was pure joy and without problems. The boys were allergic to pollens and molds, resulting in asthma. This prompted us to look for a summer camp in a pollen-free area. Camp Arowhon, situated in the beautiful Algonquin Park of northern Canada, four hundred miles northeast of Detroit, turned out to be the solution.

---

[1]Walter Midener, at that time president of the Center for Creative Studies in Detroit, carved wooden figures for one of the interior walls.

The boys, together with their cousins, stayed for ten summers, first as campers, then as counselors and staff instructors. The allotted one-time visit for the parents to the camp was the highlight of our summer during those years. One of the many personal enrichment experiences of camp life was the friendships that developed with campers from Canada as well as from states other than Michigan. These friendships were so meaningful to the boys that all the Redstones came to the twenty-fifth camp celebration in Toronto in 1984 from distances as far as San Francisco, Denver, and Detroit.

In 1989 we are still in the same house built nearly fifty years ago. Although there were some families moving to the suburbs as far back as the late 1950s, our neighborhood had remained relatively stable. The 1967 riots marked the turning point in the composition from predominantly white to almost exclusively black. To us the panicky exodus seemed tragic and we were hurt to see our neighbors and friends leave. Our families, my brother's and mine, remained with a few others. Primarily, back of the decision to stay was the reluctance to follow the panicky crowd, leaving a well-kept neighborhood. As for our own daily routines, the house with a skylight studio conducive to creative work of painting and writing, has made our stay here satisfying. An added factor is the friendship with our immediate neighbors who share concerns for each other. Over the years our home was a welcoming stopover for visitors from many countries—architects, artists, and educators whom I had met on my travels and with whom I had become friendly. Among them were the Roca family of architects from Cordoba, Argentina; Vaquero Turcios, sculptor from Madrid, Spain; Pierre Szekely, sculptor from Paris, France; Joop Beljon, director of the Royal Academy of Art, The Hague, Holland; Erwin Rehmann, sculptor, Switzerland; Sculptor Sebastian and Mathias Goeritz, architect-sculptor from Mexico City; Moishe Castel, painter from Israel; Kosso Eloul, an Israeli sculptor from Toronto, Canada; and Shigeo and Tetsuo Hirata, father and son architects from Japan.

On several occasions we have opened our home to foreign professionals as part of the hospitality program arranged by the Detroit International Institute at the request of the United States State Department. Among these visitors were Daiso Imai from Japan, an executive of Nippon Steel Company who came with his interpreter; a group of four Bulgarian architects; an architect and his wife from Spain; and an architectural engineer, Oreste Depetris from Santiago, Chile.

What stands out in my memory is the visit of sculptor Jacques Lipchitz and his wife Yulla. My friendship with him began with a chain of unusual events. As I wrote earlier, his brother Paul, my high school classmate in Grodno, asked me to look up Jacques, a struggling artist in Paris when I visited there in 1929. It wasn't until 1966 when I came upon the graduation photo of our class, which I mailed to him at his home at Hastings-on-Hudson near New York, that I first got in touch with him. His response was immediate. He was eager to meet me and talk about his brother who had perished in the Holocaust. Thus began my close, warm friendship with him. I visited him with Ruth, Eliel, and niece, Miriam. He received us with open arms and we spent hours over lunch at the corner eatery. We were enthralled by the account of his early struggles as a sculptor in Paris, his escape from Occupied France during World War II, the tragic fire that burned down his studio in Manhattan, and his happy relocation in Hastings-on-Hudson. After lunch we went to his studio, which was filled with numerous full-size plaster casts ready to be cast in bronze, many small bronze castings, and a number of small maquettes—preliminary studies for commissioned works. It was inevitable that our conversation would lead to the role of art in architecture. When I told him that my book on that subject was to be ready for publication soon, he questioned the wording "Art *in* Architecture." To him art should become an integral part of the architectural entity. He agreed to write the Introduction to the book to explain his philosophy.

We visited him shortly after the publication of the book. He looked the book over carefully, page by page, and commented, "I think it should go a long way to encourage the marriage of art and architecture." It took three years of continuous investigation through personal contacts and through intensive research and analysis to complete the manuscript. This task of getting the material together—photos, permissions to publish, descriptions and statements from artists—required uninterrupted hours, evenings, weekends, and even vacations. Sharing in these tasks was my wife, Ruth, whose research and editing made a profound contribution to the book's success. I was very pleased with the special interest the design staff of the Professional Books Division of the McGraw-Hill Book Company displayed. *Art in Architecture* was both a challenge and a change from their usual method of publication of professional books. Their special effort, even working overtime on their own, paid off well, with the sale over the years of approximately ten thousand copies—a record for this type of book.

Heartened by the public acceptance, I began to consider writing professional resource books on subjects in which I was fully involved. McGraw-Hill Book encouraged me to do this and so it was that four more books were published in three to four year intervals. These were: *New Dimensions in Shopping Centers and Stores* (1973); *The New Downtowns: Rebuilding Business Districts* (1976); *Public Art, New Directions* (1980); *Masonry in Architecture* (1984). I also edited *Hospitals and Health Care Facilities* (1978) and *Institutional Buildings* (1980).

My main purpose in writing these books was to advance my belief in the importance of humanizing and improving our living environment. Through my research and writing, I gained valuable insight into ways of achieving these goals. I believed these publications would stimulate improved communications between all parties concerned—architects, artists, city planners, city officials, and developers. I wanted to share my views and practical advice based on my own experience. Included in the books are analytical descriptions of the sequence of planning; designing and building shopping centers; the process of downtown revitalization; and the methods of introducing public art. These books also contained legal contract forms for commissions, safeguarding the interests of both artist and owner. Generally, the books were reprinted a number of times and were well received, both by the profession and the public at large. The most gratifying experience was the welcoming reception by the participating professionals whom we met on our travels, whether in Europe, the Middle East, or Far East. These face-to-face contacts reinforced the friendships that grew out of the continuous correspondence about the books that still continue with letters and visits.

These visits were pleasurable and informative, keeping us in contact with current happenings in the architectural and art world. Our sons benefitted as well by these friendly cultural contacts, which may have been a factor in their choice of studies at the University of Michigan School of Architecture. Who could have predicted that in 1969 our younger son Eliel would be a Peace Corps architect in Salvador, Brazil, where he would join us at the International Conference on Housing in Buenos Aires. His assignment was to design and supervise the building of small housing units for slum families being moved from the nearby beaches to more remote areas. Currently he has his own office in San Francisco. And who would ever have predicted that our older son Daniel would become president of the Redstone architectural firm in 1985?

Other challenging projects followed in the seventies. Among these were the design and construction of two high-rise office buildings in the Detroit downtown business district. The 333 West Fort Street building was commissioned by Earl Heenan, president of Detroit Mortgage Company and longtime business client and friend. This building is noted for its integrated nine floors of parking area (three underground) and its popular gourmet restaurant, the Money Tree, at ground level. The marble walls of the main lobby of the building are enhanced by two large colorful tapestries woven in Mexico based on my watercolor paintings. The other project, one block away, is the Manufacturers National Bank Operation Center. This commission followed the successful completion of nearly fifty branch bank buildings over the years. The Manufacturers National Bank building also has several floors of inner parking. The two floors aboveground level are faced with twenty-six large bas-relief concrete panels, twenty feet by twenty feet, created by sculptor Robert Youngman, which depict symbols of industrial Detroit. Each of these major downtown buildings occupies a full block; they have become landmarks on the downtown map of Detroit.

Another highlight of this period was the designing of the Michael Berry International Terminal building for the Wayne County Airport Authority. Our goal was to create an aesthetically pleasing building in which foreign visitors would form their first impressions of Detroit. This was accomplished by integrating art as part of the structure. The front portico is supported by twenty-four concrete columns, each with different designs by Robert Youngman. The same theme is carried into the central supporting concrete columns near the escalator. The other design challenge was to create a circulation pattern for both incoming and departing passengers. In this airport passengers check in at the ticket counter on the main floor and take the escalator to the waiting area two floors above, ready for security check and departure at the nearby gates. The same simplicity was achieved for the arriving passengers. The area for the immigration check was planned to minimize the clearing time for passengers. An element worth mentioning is the hospitable atmosphere of the departure lounge. This was achieved by bright colors in the carpeting and the seating upholstery. A central feature of the lounge are the panels of hammered copper murals depicting major countries. These were created to set the mood of the departing passenger for his anticipated trip. The panels were designed by Narendra Patel. This building received the Engineering Society of Detroit Award of Excellence in Design.

Among other award-winning buildings is the School of Management and Student Activities Building for the Lawrence Institute of Technology in Southfield, Michigan. Centrally located in relation to other campus buildings, each of the three levels of this 115,000 square foot structure is accessible directly to the surrounding ground level, which is sculpturally shaped to meet the exit elevations. The library is located twenty-five feet underground, but the effect of the large clear story windows provides ample daylight. The building received the Walter Taylor Award for Excellence in School Architecture from the American Association of School Administrators, 1983, and the Honor Award of the Engineering Society of Detroit.

A different task was to design the new multipurpose community center for the expanding Jewish population in nearby West Bloomfield Township. The three-level, 200,000 square foot facility was planned to accommodate all age groups, from infants and children as well as young adults to senior citizens. The exterior design features large, unbroken brick wall areas. To add visual interest and meaningful expression, I designed a large brick mural showing a broken Menorah, the eight-branch candelabra symbolizing the Holocaust, and several sprouting wheat stalks indicating renewed hope.

An opportunity to "practice what we preach" came in 1976 when we built our new office in Livonia, adjacent to the northwest Detroit area. The wooded five-acre site bordered on the west by the Rouge River and state-owned land and on the east by a ravine, provided an ideal location where building, parking, landscaping, and art became integrated as a whole. The sculptured gate designed by Julius Schmidt from the garden entrance of the former building became the new outdoor sign. Thus it served as a symbol of continuity in the life of our office. Included in the plan was the future installation of a large outdoor sculpture. The installation of the sculpture by Sam Cashwan took place in May 1987 during the fiftieth anniversary celebration of the office.

Throughout the years my continuous participation in the professional activities on the local, state, and national levels of the American Institute of Architects brought me pleasant surprises. In 1964 I was elected a Fellow of the AIA, and in 1965, president of the Detroit chapter of the AIA. In 1969 I was the Gold Medal winner of the Detroit chapter, and in 1978 the Gold Medal winner of the Michigan Society of the AIA (state). In 1983 I received the Robert F. Hastings Award for contributing to the betterment of the quality of the urban environment. I was also elected fellow of the Engineering Society of Detroit. Also, in 1984 I was honorary awardee of the National Society of Interior Designers, and in the same year became an honorary life member of the Masonry Institute. The Masonry Award was in the form of a silver Honorary Life Membership Card in the International Union of Bricklayers and the Allied Crafts-men. I was told that there were only three or four of these cards issued in the United States. Interspersed with the professional recognitions, were the added rewards of friendships often connected with creative community projects.

I deeply feel that all of this recognition is in good measure due to the similar interests that Ruth and I have had throughout the years. My work as an architect and planner and Ruth's background as a family social worker inspired us to devote our time and resources to civic and community betterment. Ruth was active in a number of women's groups, serving as president of the Women's Division of the Greater Detroit Interfaith Round Table (National Conference of Christians and Jews), president of the Detroit Women's Division of the American Jewish Congress, and president of the League of Jewish Women's Organizations of Metropolitan Detroit. A charter member of the Women's Architectural League and the Jewish Parents Insti-tute, she has continued her membership and serves as a board member of many civic and cultural groups. In 1974 she was a recipient of the Heart of Gold Award from the United Foundation for her volunteer civic efforts. For her active role in the research preparation of the five published books and the shared authorship of "Public Art—New Directions" (1981), she was honored by the Detroit Chapter of the American Institute of Architects in 1988 with an honorary membership.

In the late sixties I met Kiichi Usui, director of the Meadowbrook Art Gallery of Oakland University, Rochester, Michigan. He claimed my book *Art in Architecture* (1968) inspired him to put on a gallery show and slide lectures on this subject. This was followed by a permanent outdoor sculpture exhibit by six Michigan sculptors on the grounds of Oakland University. Our friendship and interest in promoting public art continues in our work together to promote public art through the Business Consortium for the Arts in Southfield, Michigan, as well as in other nearby communities (Livonia and Pontiac). Usui also arranged an excellent Pre-Columbian Exhibition at the Meadowbrook Art Gallery in the spring of 1987, which featured a number of our pieces.

Another memorable occasion involved the planning with sculptor and teacher Michael Curtis for the sixtieth anniversary of Samuel Cashwan's appointment in 1927 as first head of the sculpture department for the Detroit School of Arts and Crafts (now known as the Center for Creative Studies). It also marked the beginning of our lifelong friendship. The exhibition took place 27 May 1987 at the Sarkis Gallery, Center for Creative Studies in Detroit.

I also recall with pleasure the exciting yearly summer vacation visit to the National Music Camp at Interlochen in Northern Michigan. Traditionally, the highlight of the summer program is the Van Cliburn Benefit Concert featuring winners of the Cliburn Competition. The World Youth Symphony Orchestra of 140 of the world's most accomplished high-school-age musicians accompanied the piano soloist. Our visits served as a reunion with many of the faculty and staff with whom we have similar interests in the arts. The warm hospitality extended us by President Roger Jacobi and Mrs. Jacobi will always be remembered.

What remains unforgettable in my mind was the unusual happening in 1979 in The Hague, Holland, at the three-hundred-year-old prestigious Royal Academy of Fine Arts. I was invited by Joop Beljon, the director, to receive an honorary fellowship from the Academy in recognition of my "life-long efforts to promote the integration of the arts in architecture through the publication of books and watercolor painting." Ruth and I were given the "royal treatment." We were lodged in a historic hotel, assigned a special guide-driver, Onno Van Kuuyck, a graduate student at the academy. There was a tour of the city highlighting the historic Parliament buildings and a visit to the University of Utrecht campus where we saw Beljon's handsome concrete geometric shapes amid a man-made fountain pool. All of this was integrated with the surrounding rolling landscape. That evening a festive banquet preceded the awarding ceremonies. The Academy Hall was filled with two hundred invited guests, faculty, and students. After the president's official presentation of the fellowship certificate, I gave an hour-long illustrated lecture on "Public Art—New Directions." Up to this time there had been only twenty internationally known artists, sculptors, architects, and engineers chosen to be so honored.[2] I had mixed feelings of

[2]Herbert Bayer, Alexander Calder, Marc Chagall, Kosso Eloul, Richard Buckminister Fuller, Mathias Goeritz, Constantino Nivola, Jose Louis Sert, Pierre Szekely, Sebastian.

elation and at the same time unworthiness over my inclusion in this roster. In 1980 the Spanish Royal Academy followed suit and I was elected an honorary corresponding member.

France, Spain, and Portugal were still in our travel plans. In Paris we met Pierre Szekely, whose design for the Church of Carmel de Valenciennes, St. Saulde (Nord), France, was on the jacket cover for my first book *Art in Architecture*. He greeted us with flowers at the Paris train station, setting the tone for our three-day visit. Szekely and his friend Dominique Lassale were great hosts. We visited his studio in the newly developed La Defense section of Paris. His commissions were large scale, many done in granite with the rough textures achieved by torch. At that time he was completing a commission dedicated to world peace for the government of Hungary.

In Madrid we visited Vaquero Turcios, a brilliant sculptor we had met previously in Detroit and whose work in collaboration with his father Joaquin Vaquero also appeared in my first book. We arrived in Madrid several hours late on the afternoon of 30 September. It was just before the eve of Yom Kippur, the holiest day in the Jewish calendar. Vaquero and his wife, Mercedes, met us at the airport and because they were concerned that we might be late for the services, they rushed us to the Jewish Community Center. Here in a small chapel the services were to be held. We were surprised at the tight security at the entrance. To verify my being Jewish, I was asked to recite several Hebrew blessings. Both Vaquero and I were checked for weapons. The women's purses were also checked. We learned that these extraordinary precautions were taken because of the visit to Madrid on the same day of the PLO leader Yassir Arafat. The Jewish community was concerned about possible disturbances in the wake of his visit.

Our three-day visit with the Turcios family in their new modern villa outside of Madrid was an ongoing celebration of events. We felt like we were a part of this hospitable and talented family and their young children made us feel very much at home. Vaquero devoted most of his time to being our guide. We were especially interested in seeing his latest public sculpture—the *Monument to the Discovery of America*. The size of this sculptural concrete monument is enormous—270 feet long, 30 feet high and 36 feet wide. It is located on Columbus Plaza on one of the main axes of Madrid. Carved into the concrete surfaces is the story of Columbus's struggle to obtain royal approval and financing for his voyage. For the first time, names that had been omitted in the past for political reasons were now openly listed on this monument. One was Luis de Santangel, who was of Jewish origin and was finance minister to Queen Isabella.

I was especially interested to see the downtown sculpture walk in the Paseo de la Castillan where the public may view many large works by important European artists. Presently, I am chairing a similar project for my own area. Before departing for Portugal, we traveled to the historic and fabled places of Cordoba, Seville, and Granada in the south of Spain.

Our two-day stay in Lisbon was short, but packed with delightful surprises. We were to meet Eduardo Nery, an architect/artist who was known for his outdoor murals and designs for new public buildings, as well as the design for mosaic paving patterns for public plazas. (These mosaic paving designs were traditionally popular in Portugal and influenced the Brazilian paving designers.) Nery and his two associates, Helen and Christina Leiria, invited us to drive with them to a fishing village on the ocean. Over an excellent fish dinner, we learned the Socialist government was increasingly interested in supporting the arts and of Nery and his associates' personal hopes for getting new commissions. On the way back we stopped in Lisbon at the famous Gulbenkian Museum. Limitations of time did not allow us to fully absorb the excellent, rich, and varied modern art collection, both indoors and in the surrounding art park. That evening in a small neighborhood bistro we experienced a "taste" of real Portuguese folklore. Eduardo wanted us to hear, accompanied by a guitar, the special singers of the sad Fado melodies and songs.

Our last evening was spent at dinner with Maria Manuela Madureira, a talented ceramist, whose large-scale public commissions and murals are well known in Portugal. Her two teenage daughters who had studied English and French, accompanied her and served as interpreters. Maria was anxious to show us her studio and the large ceramic mural sections she was preparing for installation the following month. At the studio we were overwhelmed by the sight of over twenty large (eighteen by eighteen inches) colorful ceramic blocks laid out on the floor for final assembly. She welcomed our visit to her studio with expressions of delight. "If I could give you a part of my heart, I would gladly do so!" We thought this to be an expression of hospitality as we said our farewell. To our great surprise the next morning as we were about to leave the hotel for the airport, Maria and her daughters appeared in the lobby carrying one of the ceramic mural sections, lightly wrapped. She insisted that we take it as a token of her friendship. Our first reaction was shock and disbelief that she would part with such an important piece of the mural. When we pointed out to her that this twenty-five to thirty pound block would be difficult for us to carry, her reply was: "If you refuse to take it, I will break it up." We carried it, somehow. Today it continues to occupy a prominent place in the lobby of my office, and most important, a warm spot in our hearts.

Upon my return from this exhilarating trip, I found the office was still busy completing a number of projects. However, rumors abounded of an approaching depression for 1980–1981. As is usually the case, architectural and construction projects are the first to be affected. There were some cancellations, as well as postponements of projects. This meant that within several months of hoped-for improvements that did not materialize, the staff had to be reduced. This was a difficult and painful task. It takes years and much effort to build a staff of sixty-five architects, engineers, and supporting staff to create a smooth-running organization. Even reducing the staff to forty-five members did not create a viable operation. It is always a calculated risk to keep an experienced core of professionals on the payroll even though all are not gainfully occupied.

Michigan, with its auto-dependent industry, was one of the hardest hit states in the early 1980s. These were difficult years for most architectural offices. Yet our office made a comeback through the continued loyalty of our early clients. It was reassuring to be commissioned to design a new large office building in Livonia for the Manufacturer's National Bank, one of our earliest clients. Earl Heenan, president of Detroit Mortgage and Realty Company, for whom we had designed the ten-story 333 West Fort office building, recommended us as architects for the renovation of the Grosse Pointe Cottage Hospital and its new five-hundred-car garage. I am not sure whether the downtown one-hundred-year-old Globe Building restoration was the forerunner of another branch of activity for our office. It is more likely the consequence of the last decade's trend to preserve, restore, and reuse structurally sound buildings. Presently we are busy with several challenging projects involving restoration and preservation.

We were happy to be a part of a team in the Stroh's revitalization project for the Detroit riverfront called River Place. It was an adaptive reuse design to convert two former Parke-Davis warehouse and laboratory brick buildings into one- and two-bedroom apartments. The complex, originally constructed in the early 1900s, is part of the Stroh's River Place commercial, retail, office, hotel, and residential rehabilitation project. It has a total of three hundred units, including two floors on the roof of a newly built parking structure. The apartments vary in size from six hundred to seventeen hundred square feet. All exterior restoration work has been accomplished within the guidelines established by the U.S. Department of the Interior for the rehabilitation of historic buildings.

The trend for renovation and conversion is enthusiastically welcomed by the universities and colleges for reasons of economy and historic preservation. One such project, now in the implementation stage, is the renovation of Welch Hall at Eastern Michigan University, Ypsilanti, Michigan. Originally constructed in 1896, the forty-four thousand square foot Welch Hall now stands as the oldest building on the campus. It is being replanned and renovated to satisfy the University's programmatic demands by providing functional offices and conference rooms and bringing the building, facilities, and systems into current code compliance using up-to-date materials and equipment. The building will house the Office of the President, the Board of Regents' facilities, and other offices. Special attention will be given to the exterior to preserve its historic authenticity along with the reconstruction of the Renaissance balustrade and other lost building details.

Another challenging project in the planning stages is the adaptation and renovation of East Engineering Building of the University of Michigan. Originally constructed in 1923, this historically significant building on the campus in Ann Arbor was designed to house such facilities as machine shops, a foundry, and a large piece of engineering testing equipment. This 302,000 square foot building will be redesigned to house the Department of Psychology and Department of Mathematics. Among the facilities to be included will be faculty offices, general purpose seminar rooms, lecture halls, lounges, a mathematics library, teaching laboratories, bioresearch space including small animal research facilities, and computer facilities.

Two projects showing variety in the scope of our work are worth mentioning. One is the 192-unit, 16-story Condominium (Hotel) Tower and Conference Center of the Grand Traverse Resort Village near Traverse City, Michigan. The facility includes condominium guest rooms, dining facilities, ballroom spaces, specialty shops, and convention and conference meeting rooms. The Top of the Tower, the Trillium Restaurant, is designed to offer guests a breathtaking view of the bay. The building received the 1987 Engineering Society of Detroit's Building Recognition Award for outstanding building construction, and in 1986 the National Glass Association's honorable mention for excellence in the use of glass in design. Also, in Traverse City, a large addition to Munson Medical Center was completed in 1988, another project in our longtime experience with medical facilities.

In 1986 my son Daniel became president of the Redstone firm, succeeding Leo (Jerry) Shea, FAIA, who retired from the firm after twenty-five years of service. Dan graduated from the University of Michigan with a Bachelor of Architecture degree in

1965 and a Master of Business Administration in 1967. In 1985 he was elected president of the eight-hundred-member Detroit Chapter, American Institute of Architects. From 1981 to 1987 he was a board member of the Livonia Chamber of Commerce and is an active member of the United Foundation (local arm of the Michigan United Way). In his work he stresses the significance of the recent technological advances in computer-aided design and drafting (CADD) capabilities and is ably assisted by Alfred Gittleman, senior vice-president of operations.

The Fiftieth Anniversary Celebration on 29 May 1987 marked a milestone in the history of the firm. Over seven hundred friends, associates, and clients gathered for the evening's festivities honoring the firm's achievements. Held on site, the firm dedicated a hammered copper sculpture designed by Samuel Cashwan titled "Noah and the Bird."[3] Cashwan describes the symbolic intention of this sculpture: "Noah sending out the bird as a reconnaissance was a symbol of man's inner spirit which seeks to release to move into the hearts and minds of mankind around him." Added to the joy and excitement of the festivities was a surprise announcement by University of Michigan Dean Marjory Levy of the creation of two scholarships in my name. One scholarship would be awarded to a student in the College of Architecture and the other to a student in the School of Art. As a remembrance of the occasion, each guest was presented with a signed and numbered lithograph of my watercolor painting of Pont Neuf that I had done fifty years before in Paris.

I never thought that the Pont Neuf painting would serve as an "anchor" for my Retrospective Watercolor Exhibition a year later (April–May 1988). It had been ten years since the last show at the former Arwin Gallery in downtown Detroit. At the urging of my friends, nationally known artist Carol Wald, filmmaker Hermann Tauchert, and Cade Gallery director Joe Fugate, I agreed that my paintings would benefit from being presented in proper surroundings, with good lighting and adequate spacing — quite a contrast to the crowded condition of the home studio.

I was elated with the response of the over five hundred guests at the opening reception and the continued interest of the visitors during the four-week showing. What was equally encouraging were the favorable reviews by art critics. Joy Hakanson Colby of the *Detroit News* on 15 April 1988 observed:

> He uses his watercolors as a change of pace from the slower process of designing and erecting buildings. "Watercolor fits my nature," he explains. "Why? Because it's a fast medium, and I like doing some things immediately."
>
> His current exhibit begins in 1937 with Pont Neuf, a literal rendering of a Paris landmark. It ends with this year's abstract landscapes done in brilliant, melting colors. In all, there are sixty paintings that fall into two distinct groups — travel sketches made on site and the abstract works done at home in his studio.
>
> With the travel pieces, Redstone packs a lot of landscape into a small format. He works with an easy shorthand he has developed, omitting fussy details for broad effects. The little paintings emphasize space and the quality of light.
>
> Redstone lets go in the larger pieces he does in his studio. He allows his washes to flow freely, exploiting the watercolor medium for its spontaneity and glow. Although the pieces are abstract, they obviously are rooted in nature.

[3]The 7-foot sculpture was fabricated from the artist's 12-inch maquette by Michael Vizzini, former head of the metalsmithing department of the Center for Creative Studies in Detroit.

Unlike many painters, Redstone doesn't sketch with a camera. "I've never even tried to get information from photographs," he says. "That's too mechanical for me. If I squeeze and force an idea, it won't translate freely into watercolor."

For the last four decades, his watercolors have adorned the 1,000 holiday cards sent out by his firm, Louis G. Redstone Associates. But having his work reproduced on cards is different from showing in a gallery, Redstone notes. "I feel naked when I exhibit in a gallery," he confesses. "So I never push for shows."

Brian Lysaght, staff writer for the Livonia *Eccentric,* commented on 21 April 1988:

There is a room with a skylight in Louis Redstone's home and it is in that room that he paints.

The natural light that shines in his studio shows off colors in the best way possible and is important to his painting, he says. Colors fascinate Redstone, and this becomes clear in his paintings.

Colors, he says, give joy and make one feel good, even on the grayest of days. He paints for another reason—because it gives joy to others. . . .

The paintings, most of which date from about 1960 to 1988, show Redstone's preference for color over form. This de-emphasis on form is even more interesting considering Redstone's occupation. . . .

He began his training as a painter when he was studying architecture at the University of Michigan . . . where a course in art was part of his architecture studies.

He remembers vividly the brilliant colors he put on paper one day when his instructor, Jean Paul Slusser, led a painting class outdoors on a sunny spring day. He says colors sometimes lead him in his painting, which is much inspired by nature. "There isn't any abstraction that you don't find in nature," he said.

Redstone, who is 86, says his painting is a complement to his architectural drawings. "This is not an escape but a complete freedom of action," he said.

Thus, the celebration of the fiftieth anniversary of the firm and the Retrospective Exhibition seem to reassure me in my continuing quest for self-expression through architecture and art.

What moved me to write my memoirs one day was the view of the snow-covered garden from my studio window. The garden appeared as a large white screen on which my life images emerged. It is summer now. The trees and shrubs planted nearly fifty years ago are tall and flourishing. The yard shared all these years with my brother's family, Solomon and Nellie and their children Paul and Miriam, was the center of constant activities with our sons Daniel and Eliel and their friends.

The continuous outdoor celebrations, birthdays, bar mitzvahs and graduation parties, wedding and anniversary receptions and family reunions, strengthened our spirits and our faith in the future.

Now our young grandchildren fill the garden with playful sounds in the fountain pool. A new generation is beginning its own cycle.

New "images on the screen" will emerge.

AFTERWORD

by Susan Jackson Keig, FSTA

From a chance encounter in the late 1940s with Louis Redstone at the Oxbow School of Art at Saugatuck, Michigan, followed by an invitation to visit the Redstone home in the early 1950s with my travel companion, an Australian doctor, Detroit became for me a city "where the sun was always shining," as seen through the eyes of the Redstones, Louis and Ruth.

The minute one walks through their door a certain electricity is felt in the air: Louis is eager to show you his latest watercolors, Ruth has a list of new things to see in the city, and both wait enthusiastically to exchange news.

There is a feeling of energy in everything that goes on in the home and in the conversations. There is an eagerness to find out more, to question, to plan a trip, or to prod a reluctant participant. There never seems any doubt that something can be accomplished—"one should start out and things will fall into place" is the prevading philosophy.

Their home is now a collection of prized art, some pieces are those having been exchanged with friends. Hardly anyone who visits the Redstones leaves without a gift—one of Ruth's culinary delights or one of Louis's sketches from a recent trip.

The Redstones thrive on the interchange of ideas with friends, artists, and business associates. Each event is a melding of achievement and sharing, as are the autographing parties and art exhibits where clients become fast friends of the Redstones.

The roster of friends grows as the Redstones are recognized in the city for their generosity and personal warmth and talent. Newspaper articles by critics are frequent and reflect the impact of the architecture generated by the Redstone firm on the city. Then there are book reviews and art shows that keep coming.

From time to time Louis has requested that I design an announcement for a show, do the firm's first logo, write an article for an architectural journal, or design the firm's brochures. I have asked him to lecture at conferences and judge graphic competitions—and so the exchange of ideas continues between the worlds of design and architecture.

How does one value such friendship, such generosity, stimulation, and encouragement? These are intangible "gifts" that do not come often in one's lifetime.

Standing at the entrance to our first office at 3513
Woodward Avenue in Detroit, 1938. (*Left to right*) Brother
Solomon Redstone, his wife Nellie, author, and sister
Riva.

Ruth and Louis Redstone on their wedding day, 25 June
1939.

LEFT, the plan for Stevenage, England; right, for Chicago. Center (from the left), Eliel Sarrinen, Louis G. Redstone, Buford Pickens and Suren Pilafian look with the trained eyes of architects at a model for a portion of Detroit as it may appear in 1990.

BUT WE'D MOVE SLOW—FINISH JOB IN 1990

Detroit to Be Split into 22 Areas

BY KENNETH THOMPSON
Free Press Staff Writer

DECENTRALIZATION OF Metropolitan Detroit's industry and 2,000,000 population into 22 self-sufficient communities is the vision of 30 Detroit architects. The tentative date for completion of the plan is 1990.

The new city is to be quartered by fast expressways. Each of the communities will be dotted with open spaces. Neighborhoods will be built in small "U" groups so children will have no need to cross hazardous arteries. Greenbelts will screen relocated industry and major traffic boundaries.

Yet there will be no violent upsets in the lives of Detroiters as the plan is put into effect. The new city is to take form by gradual, natural processes. That's why that far-off date of 1990 was set by the Architects Civic Design Group, whose work has been pushed quietly for two years.

●

ELIEL SAARINEN, of the Cranbrook Academy of Arts, consultant and co-ordinator for the Group, explains that "we are merely studying the application of the principles of organic decentralization to the Detroit area over a period of 50 years."

Within 50 years most existing buildings and homes will have become ready for replacement, Saarinen believes. So, he and other Group members hope to be able to convince Detroiters that replacements should be built to fit into the plan that will make Detroit a much more pleasant place in which to live and work.

And they want planning to grow with the city.

"At the end of 10 years we can scrap the master plan we have now, draw up a new one for another 50 years and move ahead accordingly in the next decade," Suren Pilafian, another of the Group, says. "Re-analyzing Detroit's needs must be carried on continuously."

●

THE ARCHITECTS OF THE Design Group work Saturdays under Saarinen at Cranbrook and meet monthly for group discussion of their progress. Their time in the research is taken from their regular business. They receive no pay.

Each member has undertaken study of an assigned area shown on a "key" map. The map details tentative locations of major expressways and community groups according to population densities. It is based on studies made by Saarinen with the help of J. Davidson Stephen.

Area studies start with individual dwellings.

These form "neighborhoods" of approximately 200 families, or 1,200 persons. They are served by an elementary school group, and small commercial and recreational centers.

Several neighborhoods are served by a junior high school and commercial and recreational group.

A large number of neighborhoods, forming a "community" of about 40,000 persons, will have a high school and centers for

News clipping, 1946, from the *Detroit Free Press*. (*Left to right*) Eliel Saarinen, Louis Redstone, Buford Pickens, and Suren Pilafian work on a model for a portion of Detroit as it may appear in 1990.

"Old Shore Line, Mackinaw City, Michigan," watercolor by author, 1948.

Exterior of the three houses surrounding our "Backyard U.S.A." (From *left,* our house, my brother Sol's house, and our neighbors)

Author at home in Detroit, 1947.

Street scene, Paris, France, 1950, by author.

Machu Picchu, ancient city of Incas, Peru, by author.

Takasegawa River, Kyoto, Japan, 1956, by author.

Landscape, Northern Michigan, 1963, by author.

Rio Corcovado Statue, Brazil, 1969, by author.

"Anne Frank House," watercolor by author.

Memorial to author's nephew Amnon Harudi and his
friend Hanan, killed in the 1967 Six-Day War. Sculptor,
Roda Reilinger.

Palace at Udaipur, India, 1972, by author.

Author's son Daniel and family. (*Left to right,* Daniel, wife
Barbara, grandson Adam, and granddaughter Carly.

Author's younger son Eliel and family. (*Left to right,* Ariel,
Eliel, Linda)

Son Eliel, Jacques Lipchitz, and author.

Author addressing the six-hundred or more audience on the celebration of Louis G. Redstone Associates, Incorporated, fiftieth anniversary, 29 May 1987.